PRAISE FOR
AWAKE IN THE DAWN

Not always are musicians also composers. Craig Smith is both. Not always are composers of music also lyricists. Again, Craig is both. And rarely are composers also authors of books. Once again, Craig is both. Add to all of these the seasoned musings of a veteran pastor, a man who has walked with Jesus day-by-day for decades. These components coalesce in *Awake in the Dawn,* providing an incisive devotional that will enrich your year and point each day toward eternal verities. I'm so glad Craig has opened his heart to share his daily journey with us. This is one book you'll return to year after year.

—David Shibley, Founder of Global Advance

I just finished reading Craig Smith's new book *Awake in the Dawn* nearly from cover to cover. *Wow*...it is to the point, loaded with encouragement, and a perfect length to help you get started on the right foot every morning. I've known Craig for forty years, and I can personally testify that he is a source of powerful spiritual insights for your mind and spirit. When you get your copy of *Awake in the Dawn,* please don't let it be one of those books that just lies around the house. Be sure to read it for it may be the very tool you've been searching for to make a *big* difference in your spiritual life.

—Rick Renner, Pastor, teacher, author, broadcaster

I have known Craig Smith for over twenty years and after reading this book, I can tell you it is the perfect reflection of his heart and ministry. Craig's spirit and life mirror a devotion and heart for God like few people I have ever met. I need this daily guidance, this daily moment, this daily remembrance of the heart of God for me, and I encourage you to get this book and use it as intended...to bring you into the presence of a God and immerse your life in Him daily.

—Chris Thomason, President & CEO of in:ciite media

I am so excited to have a daily tool to fix my eyes back on truth. A good day starts with a good morning, and this devotional lays out the blueprints for everything you need to be spiritually focused and ready for the struggles of each day. Craig is full of so much wisdom, and I know he lives by every principle laid out in this book.

—Shay Mooney, multi-music and Grammy Award-winning singer and songwriter

I have known Craig Smith since I first heard his marvelous recording *Hymns*. Later he graced my Songs for Worship Volume II by singing in the choir where his golden tenor voice is clearly heard. It has been a joy to watch his journey into the pastorate and as he tirelessly helps orphans in Africa. He has blessed them, and me. This devotional springs from Craig's prayerful heart. It is not another theological treatment of the Our Father, of which Church Fathers and great theologians have already written masterfully. It is a simple and beautifully written prayer. I pray it brings the reader back to the heart of God the Father through Christ the Son in the anointing of the Holy Spirit. In Jesus,

—John Michael Talbot, Founder, Spiritual Father, and General Minister
of The Brothers and Sisters of Charity Little Portion Hermitage

I highly recommend *Awake in the Dawn* because I can highly recommend the author, my dear friend Craig Smith. Someone has said that true devotion is proven not by years, but by decades. I have known Craig for fifty years, and I can say I deeply admire his honest and true devotion to Jesus. He does not find his identity in what he has accomplished, or is doing, but rather in being a worshipper and a son of the Living God. Out of that root of integrity comes the fruit of this anointed book—a call back to the simplicity of devotion to Christ, and an evergreen first love. It brings us back to the sure foundation of the Lord's prayer, both for our lives and our prayers. May the Lord use this in your life to bring forth more of the image of Jesus in your life and the power of Jesus in your prayers.

—Rick Ridings, Founder Succat Hallel 24/7 House of Prayer overlooking the
Temple Mount in Jerusalem, international speaker, and author of
Shifting Nations Through Houses of Prayer

Awake in the Dawn is wonderful offering and tool for encouraging much-needed and consistent devotional quiet times.

—Jaci Velasquez, platinum-selling celebrity, award-winning recording artist,
author, radio/TV host, and speaker

I have known Craig Smith for over forty years, and we have worked on many projects together. None is more timely than his latest, *Awake in the Dawn*, a book of daily meditative devotionals based on the Lord's Prayer, the first prayer Jesus taught us to pray. I have seen Craig's walk with God throughout our friendship, his dedication above all to the Lord's will, and the sacrifices he's made to bring others to Christ, feed the hungry, give homes to the homeless—even literally risk his life to protect members of his flock. And yet, even with all those amazing experiences, what we have in *Awake in the Dawn* is Craig sitting on his back porch sharing in his simple, soft-spoken style, essential precepts, and teachings that will change our lives...if we'll pay attention! I highly recommend you start all your days with this wonderful book.

—Paul Mills, composer/mix engineer of *War Room, Woodlawn, Overcomer,* producer/mixer *I Can Only Imagine, I Still Believe,* artists Heather Headley, Twila Paris, Don Moen, Robin Mark, and Phillips, Craig and Dean

Jesus offered us his best template for prayer in what we call the Lord's Prayer. *Awake in the Dawn* uses this template to guide its readers along a year-long spiritual journey in solid biblical prayer path whether someone is just beginning to learn how to pray or already well established in their devotional time.

—Mark Schultz, platinum-selling, Dove Award-winning recording artist and author

In a world that has become challenged by disruptions, aggressions, uncertainties, and insecurities, *Awake in the Dawn* leads us on a daily path to hope and stability from the ancient, but proven keys within the Lord's Prayer.

—Rudy Pérez, 5-time Grammy Award-winning songwriter, producer, artist, and author

Singer, songwriter, and author Craig Smith has penned another masterpiece. *Awake in the Dawn* is a beautifully written daily devotional with 365 thought-provoking reminders about what is true in our lives and how knowing that truth changes us. Spend a few minutes here every day and find peace, safety, and direction.

—Dennis Welch, Author, songwriter, encourager, President and CEO of Articulāte, former senior staff writer at Gallup

Awake

IN THE DAWN

A 365-Day Devotional

Awake
IN THE DAWN

Living the Lord's Prayer

CRAIG SMITH

Published by Forefront Books.
Cover Design by Jenn David
Interior Design by Linda Bourdeaux, thedesigndesk.com

Library of Congress Control Number: 2022910582

ISBN: 978-1-63763-103-4 print
ISBN: 978-1-63763-104-1 eBook

INTRODUCTION

*Morning by morning He wakens me and
opens my understanding to His will.*

Isaiah 50:4

On the morning just before I began writing this introduction, I looked through the front window of my home. There was just enough light to see a mist hovering over the field between the house and the wooded hillside, and I could see deer foraging gracefully in the green grass.

I quietly opened the door, stepped out onto the porch, and immediately heard the soothing lull of the whip-poor-will, the tree frogs croaking, and the chirp of crickets. After a few moments of standing in the gentle sounds of predawn, I retreated indoors to one of my favorite spots to read, pray, and quietly contemplate.

I love early mornings, and for a very long time now they have been most precious, almost sacred, to me. Early mornings are usually quiet, still, uncluttered, and they make for a good time to spiritually prepare for the day. I started this practice years ago when our children were small. Often, the beginning hours of the morning—those hours before the daylight readies itself to appear on the horizon—were the only quiet moments in those early years of our family.

However, it seems I'm not the only one who enjoys early mornings for spiritual preparation. The prophet Isaiah appears to have preferred them (Isaiah 50:4), and the psalmist David favored them writing, "Wake up, my heart! Wake up, O lyre and harp! I will wake the dawn with my song" (Ps. 57:8). More importantly, Jesus Christ, the one whom we're to pattern our life after, also treasured the early morning hours, "Before daybreak the next morning, Jesus got up and went out to an isolated place to pray" (Mark 1:35).

Whether you're a 4 a.m. or 9 a.m. person, *Awake in the Dawn* is a simple and brief daily offering of encouragement from a fellow pilgrim and brother in Christ, and it is designed to give you a time of spiritual reflection, helping you start your day in a prayerful stance. As you read these offerings, my hope is you will daily fall a bit deeper in love with Christ, the lover of our souls.

Each day's writings follow one of the main themes of the Lord's Prayer. In a year, you will have had the opportunity to pray and apply the pattern of the Lord's Prayer *fifty-two* times. My hope is that, by diving into the major themes of the Lord's Prayer throughout the year, your relationship with the Lord will grow and be strengthened. Every daily devotional in *Awake in the Dawn* provides a scripture, a written thought concerning the passage, and a suggested concluding prayer, but please feel free to make your sacred prayer time your own.

Blessings,
Craig

HOW TO USE THIS DEVOTIONAL

Awake in the Dawn includes 365 individual devotionals, one for each day of the year, that each follows one of the seven main themes of the Lord's Prayer. Let's start by examining the Lord's Prayer together. Jesus instructs us to pray this way in Matthew 6:9–13:

> *Our Father in heaven,*
> *may your name be kept holy.*
> *May your Kingdom come soon.*
> *May your will be done on earth,*
> *as it is in heaven.*
> *Give us today the food we need,*
> *and forgive us our sins,*
> *as we have forgiven those who sin against us.*
> *And don't let us yield to temptation,*
> *but rescue us from the evil one.*

Looking closely, we can see there are six main themes found in the above prayer, and when we incorporate what's commonly referred to the "Lord's Prayer doxology," we find seven:

- A moment of praise and worship: *Our Father in heaven, may your name be kept holy.*

- A plea for God to reign and accomplish his will in the earth: *May your kingdom come soon. May your will be done on earth, as it is in heaven.*

- A request for provision: *Give us today the food we need.*

- A request for redemption for ourselves and others: *Forgive us our sins, as we have forgiven those who sin against us.*

- A request for holy conviction and protection: *Don't let us yield to temptation.*

- A request for redemption from and protection against the enemy: *But rescue us from the evil one.*

- A concluding moment of praise and worship within the Lord's Prayer doxology: *For yours is the kingdom and the power and the glory forever. Amen.*

Every week, the devotions will center on those themes and in that order. For each day, there are three individual sections: *Word*, a scripture included for meditation;

Thought, a provided reflection on the scripture or day's theme; and *Prayer*, a written prayer offered to jump-start your prayer time.

Feel free to think of this devotional as a tool to encourage your morning time of reflection with the Lord, allowing you to dive deeper into scripture and personal connection with Jesus. I hope *Awake in the Dawn* provides a genuine source to strengthen your prayer life, and helps you grow in your love for and understanding of the Lord as you accompany him in his wonderful and unparalleled spiritual adventure for you.

January 1

CREATED FOR WORSHIP

WORD

*Next the devil took him to the peak of a very high mountain and
showed him all the kingdoms of the world and their glory.
"I will give it all to you," he said, "if you will kneel down and worship me."*

*"Get out of here, Satan," Jesus told him. "For the Scriptures say,
'You must worship the Lord your God and serve only him.'"*

Matthew 4:8–10

THOUGHT

Near the conclusion of his forty-day desert experience, Jesus revealed the divine design for all humanity: *You must worship the Lord your God and serve only him.*

This response followed an offer from the evil one to lure Jesus from the will of God to a destructive path for him and would ultimately lead to hopelessness for all humanity, but Jesus would have no part of it. With a quick reply, the Son of God responded and brought purpose and privilege to all of humanity. He included no theological defense for God's existence, his superiority, or the fact that he's the Ruler over all things. Jesus only gave the clear purpose and justification for humanity's existence: there is no higher call, duty, or honor than the worship of God.

In a modern culture laden with materialism and self-gratification, the thought of all humanity existing for the sole purpose of worshiping God may not seem logical or appealing. However, generations upon generations testify otherwise. Genuine, abundant, and eternal life is experienced through Jesus Christ, in worship and service to God the Father.

PRAYER

*You alone are Jehovah God, the Father of all life, and you alone are worthy of worship.
I praise your name; there is no one else like you, Lord. You are exalted above all things,
and all things exist for your glory. Amen.*

Our Father in heaven, may your name be kept holy.

MADE FOR GOD'S WILL

WORD

May your Kingdom come soon.
May your will be done on earth, as it is in heaven.

Matthew 6:10

THOUGHT

When the disciples asked Jesus to teach them to pray, Jesus responded by praying. In his prayer, the first thing he did was acknowledge God as our Father in heaven, whose name is holy. The Father is to be honored first and foremost, and Jesus's next words revealed that God's kingdom and will are life's highest priority and our purpose here on this earth.

God created humanity, and when humans foolishly strayed into disobedience and suffered the consequences that came with it, God provided redemption. Our sin alienates us from God. Because he is holy our sin prevented us from relationship with him. However, through the provision of Christ who paid for our sin, and by the power of the Holy Spirit working in us, we become free from the blemish of sin, redeemed, and a part of God's family. In turn, we have the joy and privilege of becoming part of the unfolding success plan of the Father's kingdom and will: to bring heaven to earth and restore things to his original intent.

He paid our impossible and incalculable debt of sin. He gives us abundant life and invites us to honor him with the privilege of serving his glorious, unfailing plan for creation.

For the believer in Christ, loving God and doing his will is life's highest call and greatest honor.

PRAYER

You have given me life. You have filled my heart with joy and purpose. Continue to show me the way of your kingdom, that I might pray daily with wisdom and insight. Reveal to me the details of your unfolding will today as well as in the days that follow. To your name be glory. Amen.

May your kingdom come soon. May your will be done on earth, as it is in heaven.

NO DEEPER LOVE

WORD

For this is how God loved the world: He gave his one and only Son, so that everyone who believes in him will not perish but have eternal life.

John 3:16

THOUGHT

Blaise Pascal was born in Clermont-Ferrand, France, in June 1623. He was blessed with a remarkable mind. He was an inventor, mathematician, physicist, and theological writer. His mother died while he was a toddler, and he was raised by his father until his father was seriously injured in an accident that limited his abilities to care for his family. The accident resulted in the family being led to Christ by a group of Jansenists (a sect of Catholics who believed in predestination and divine grace) who were helping the family while the father was sick. This conversion influenced Blaise Pascal to become a devoutly religious person.[1]

Though Pascal is most remembered for his contributions to mathematics, a science grounded in logic and reason, one quote from his writings lends insight to the inexplicable depth of God's love for humanity, a love that defies the confines of reason and led Jesus Christ to the most extravagant act of sacrifice, selflessness, and provision for the human soul: "Love has reasons which reason cannot understand." As impossible as it is to comprehend God, it is equally impossible to understand the unlimited dimensions of his love. Truly God is the best example of love, but that is still a deficient statement. He is not only the essence of love, but love in purest form as he is love's sole source, for *God is love* (1 John 4:8). His every act is motivated by love because he is love. He does not separate, set aside, or diminish the quality and quantity of his love at any time or in any of his decisions or acts. God and genuine love are one and the same. God is love and love is God.

PRAYER

Father, I do not understand the depth of your love and certainly do not deserve it. I can only be a humble and grateful recipient of this unfathomable provision. Thank you, Lord, for loving me and saving me, and may I wisely seek the paths of your kingdom this day and each of the remaining days of my life. Amen.

Give us today the food we need.

TRUE FREEDOM

WORD

He gave his life to purchase freedom for everyone.

1 Timothy 2:6

THOUGHT

The end of the United States War of Independence from the British Empire was marked by the signing of the Treaty of Paris (1783). The document was a declaration containing the promise of peace, hope, and the path for continued freedom. The treaty between the two former enemies contained the commitment to "forget all past misunderstandings and differences that have unhappily interrupted the good correspondence and friendship which they mutually wish to restore."[2]

Lives were sacrificed to purchase the liberty that Americans now enjoy. However, an earlier battle in history contained an even greater sacrifice for an even greater liberty. The battle was waged for the souls of humanity, fought between the darkness of evil and the light of Christ. Jesus willingly sacrificed his life to create a way to liberate humanity from the captivity of sin. His strategy and ultimate victory brought freedom and redemption to God's original plan, which was to experience the apex of relationships. God and humanity were restored, and with even more power, depth, and permanency than the reconciliation of earthly kingdoms, our sins are forgiven and forgotten—*forever.*

PRAYER

Lord, thank you for forgiving and forgetting the sin that held me prisoner and separated me from you. Thank you for restoration. Thank you for the depth of your mercy and the freedom of your grace. Amen.

Forgive us our sins, as we have forgiven those who sin against us.

January 5

PEACE

WORD

But all who listen to me will live in peace, untroubled by fear of harm.

Proverbs 1:33

THOUGHT

The goal of Proverbs is revealed in the first few verses: "Their purpose is to teach people to live disciplined and successful lives, to help them do what is right, just, and fair" (Prov. 1:3). Then Proverbs 1:33 unveils the promise that comes with following the book's wisdom and guidance, which is to "live in peace."

Oh, what it would be like to be a people living in true peace! Jesus said his peace was not like the anemic, temporal versions from worldly sources[3]: the empty promises of politicians, the half-hearted truces amongst feuding families, the fleeting peace found in financial gain. His peace is supported by the promises of his Father's kingdom; it is a *grounded* peace—one that cannot be stolen, one we can rest in.

While we do have trustworthy peace from God, it does not eliminate harm in this earth-life. However, the peace we receive from being in Christ does allow us to live free from the fear of harm. What else but the divine peace of God could cause Paul to write, "O death where is your victory? O death where is your sting?" (1 Cor. 15:55). God's peace is beyond our ability to comprehend, yet we are invited to abide in him and live within it. In Christ, not even death can be victorious over us—a truth that frees us to live an abundant, radical life of obedience to God's call and kingdom work.

PRAYER

Lord Jesus, without you, all resemblance of peace is a mere shadow. But I can rest knowing you will always provide the level of peace equal to the task that you lead me into. Guide me into your will, and give me the faith to live a life of devout obedience to what you would ask of me. Amen.

Don't let us yield to temptation.

January 6

SECURITY

WORD

You are my rock and my fortress.
For the honor of your name, lead me out of this danger.
Pull me from the trap my enemies set for me,
for I find protection in you alone
I entrust my spirit into your hand.
Rescue me, LORD, for you are a faithful God.

Psalm 31:3–5

THOUGHT

Challenges will certainly come as we make it our lives' goal to love and serve Christ with a whole heart. However, in the end, we will have the privilege of knowing how God used us in the midst of challenges—how he guided us, protected us, and produced fruit for his kingdom through our lives.

Written by Martin Luther between 1527 and 1529, the hymn "A Mighty Fortress Is Our God" has served as a testament and reminder of God's protective love. This song has been treasured for generations as a proclamation of God's power and shelter.

Whatever challenges you will face in this life, know the Lord is your faithful fortress. May the words of Luther's powerful hymn encourage you this morning:

A mighty fortress is our God, a bulwark never failing;
our helper he, amid the flood of mortal ills prevailing:
For still our ancient foe does seek to work us woe;
his craft and power are great, and armed with cruel hate,
on earth is not his equal.
And though this world, with devils filled, should threaten to undo us,
we will not fear, for God hath willed his truth to triumph through us.
The prince of darkness grim, we tremble not for him;
his rage we can endure, for lo! his doom is sure;
one little word shall fell him.[4]

PRAYER

You are my fortress, my Lord, my God. Amen!

But rescue us from the evil one.

PRAISE THE LORD

WORD

Praise the LORD!

Psalm 149:1

THOUGHT

To make an emphatic declaration or command, an exclamation point is used at the end of a sentence or phrase.

The opening sentence of Psalm 149 concludes with such a mark. Humanity was created by God and exists for his purposes and desires. Praising him is our highest call. Honoring him is our greatest goal. Certainly, worshiping him is a privilege—but additionally a command we must observe. A command, however, which brings light, life, and liberation, not an unreasonable legalism.

Sing to the Lord a new song. Sing his praises in the assembly of the faithful.[5] Verse 1 reveals the psalmist's overwhelming love and admiration for God. Although simple, this opening line of Psalm 149 is filled with deep emotions of conviction, joy, passion, and internal fulfillment. This is no quiet introduction easing into an eventual crescendo. No, this song immediately bursts open with power and energy to declare God's praise—and this should be our own hearts' responses to the goodness of God as well.

PRAYER

Lord, you are the center of all things and the center of my life.
You have designed me to find my identity, purpose, value, and worth in you.
My heart finds deep solace knowing I am created for you. I am set apart to praise you in all things.
You are the source of life, so my heart bursts forth this morning in praise to you! Amen.

For yours is the kingdom and the power and the glory forever.

GOD OF WONDER

WORD

He counts the stars and calls them all by name.

Psalm 147:4

THOUGHT

One morning, I stepped outside the door of our home and into the dark stillness of predawn. My eyes were quickly drawn upward to a stunning array of stars; the sky was unusually clear, and the view was astonishing.

Surely psalmist David recalled early morning experiences like this one while watching sheep. He could close his eyes, imagining the stillness and the first hint of morning's light in the pastures and hillsides where he once tended his flocks. He knew what it was like to look into the sky and be dazzled by God's starry heavens. God had spoken them into existence, knew their number, and gave each a name. He could remember the sounds of birds in morning's first light, signaling the birth of a new day. David knew God's mornings, God's wonders—and in turn, he lifted praise to God.

All creation is a wonder, a display of God's magnificent and absolute creative power. Though we cannot fully comprehend the vastness of God, we can take pleasure and find peace in him. And just like he knows the name of each star, he knows our names and cares about the details of our lives.

PRAYER

I am humbled in your presence this morning my Lord, King, and Savior. Who is like you?
No one! You are magnificent and all you have made is a wonder. You are exalted and
worthy of all praise. Thank you for your love, your mercy, your grace,
and opportunity to worship and enjoy you forever. Amen.

Our Father in heaven, may your name be kept holy.

JOY, THE WILL OF THE LORD

WORD

Always be joyful. Never stop praying. Be thankful in all circumstances,
for this is God's will for you who belong to Christ Jesus.

1 Thessalonians 5:16–18

THOUGHT

Am I to be a teacher, pastor, or missionary in some faraway place? Which profession or career should I devote myself to? Should I work among the poor or help those suffering from injustice? We often ask ourselves these questions concerning God's will, but he will place us where he chooses and where we are best suited.

We are often anxious about positions, titles, and tasks—where we should be and what we should be doing to stay in the Lord's will. However, whatever our current position, title, or task, as Christians, there are internal qualities and attitudes that we are expected to manifest no matter our circumstances. These qualities reflect Christ and set us apart from the ordinary attitude of the world.

Always be joyful. Does that mean we demonstrate a shallow, carefree happiness and smile to conceal grief? No. The Scriptures here refer to displaying the deep-seated joy drawn from our trust and obedience in God and his Word, a joy given and maintained in us by Christ. This is the joy that comes from knowing that, in every circumstance, God is holding us, leading us, and even using difficulties for our good.

And as Paul reminds us in 1 Thessalonians 5:16–18, never cease praying. Prayer is the vehicle to hear and speak with the Father who loves us. Paul had learned to be content and joyful in whatever situation he was in—in the good times and even while imprisoned for his faith. Like Paul, we should also be grateful and content in all of our circumstances, no matter the position, title, or task we've been given.

PRAYER

Father, I'm able to commune with you through prayer because of your grace and power in my life.
I ask that the Holy Spirit would guide me to live and display your character
through all my circumstances, for this is your will. Amen.

May your kingdom come soon. May your will be done on earth, as it is in heaven.

THE LORD HAS SHOWN US WHAT IS GOOD

WORD

What can we bring to the LORD?
Should we bring him burnt offerings?
Should we bow before God Most High
with offerings of yearling calves?
Should we offer him thousands of rams
and ten thousand rivers of olive oil?
Should we sacrifice our firstborn children to pay for our sins?

No, O people, the LORD has told you what is good,
and this is what he requires of you:
to do what is right, to love mercy,
and to walk humbly with your God.

Micah 6:6–8

THOUGHT

More than lavish, showy, or dramatic sacrifices, God desires his children to do what is right throughout the day—living in accordance with the principles, standards, and the liberating life revealed in God's Word. He desires us to love mercy and to see the world and those within it as the he does. Above all, he desires us to live a life of humility before the Father as Jesus Christ did.

The Lord has clearly shown us what is good. At times, living out his commands can seem like too great a task to complete on our own, but he has provided us with his Holy Spirit to guide us along the way.

PRAYER

Father, it is my desire to worship you throughout this day. Your Word has given detail about what honors you. Guide me to the right decision for each choice facing me. May I embrace your heart of mercy in all that I do today, and may I be found walking in genuine humility as defined by you. Amen.

Give us today the food we need.

THE GIFT OF PEACE

WORD

I am leaving you with a gift—peace of mind and heart.
And the peace I give is a gift the world cannot give. So don't be troubled or afraid.

John 14:27

THOUGHT

One evening I arrived home from a challenging day at work. Walking toward the house, I noticed an unexpected package sitting at the door. I took it inside, opened it, and discovered apples from a well-known orchard sent to us as a gift from some very thoughtful friends. Strange as it may sound, their gift changed the tone of the day—it went from a tone of unrest to one of peace.

Thoughtful gifts, words of encouragement, and affirmation from friends are always welcomed for they can powerfully change the attitudes and direction of our days. However truly wonderful and appreciated gifts from friends are, the life-altering gifts from Jesus, our perfect friend, cannot be measured. His gift opens the door of resolve to one of humanity's most complex issues: the internal restlessness of our hearts.

The world's treasures, fame, and power do not provide lasting peace for the heart. Even the kindest of gifts from a well-meaning friend only provides a temporary fix. Lasting peace stems from a singular source: Jesus Christ. And not only does he give it, but he also resides forever as its guardian. Therein lies the inexplicable rest for the soul.

PRAYER

Lord, cause my eyes to fix firmly on you, your provisions, and promises.
Your promises leave no room for need if I will simply trust and obey what you have spoken. Thank you for your gift of peace through the power of forgiveness. Amen.

Forgive us our sins, as we have forgiven those who sin against us.

THE GREAT PROTECTOR

WORD

Every word of God proves true.
He is a shield to all who come to him for protection.

Proverbs 30:5

THOUGHT

What a wonder it would be if each promise made by an authority figure was filled with truth and pure motives. If a person in authority fails us, we can forgive the unforeseen, unavoidable challenges, and unanticipated delays when we know their truth and integrity remain intact. However, when a leader makes groundless fabrications and hollow promises, or has dark motivations and abuses authority, that is wrong.

Many of us have experienced the effects of authority abuse; it often leaves us hurt, wary, and angry. But be assured: every word of God proves true, regardless of how difficult or impossible those promises may first appear. I have heard it said, "No one speaks complete truth!" Yes, there is one—Jehovah God! His words stand without waivering in purity and promise, despite our own flaws or failures. Wise are those who hear and obey the true words of God.

We find ourselves lost, hopeless, and adrift without God and his Word, from individuals to entire nations. Remember, Ephesians 6:17 reminds us the Word of the Lord is a sword—powerful, protective, reliable, penetrative. Let the promises of his Word penetrate the depths of our hearts, govern our steps, and protect us as we seek his kingdom.

PRAYER

Without the truth of your Word, Lord, I am without hope.
Guide me today by the truth, accuracy, and effectiveness of your Word. Amen.

Don't let us yield to temptation.

January 13

DELIVERER

WORD

Those who live in the shelter of the Most High
will find rest in the shadow of the Almighty.
This I declare about the LORD:
He alone is my refuge, my place of safety;
he is my God, and I trust him.
For he will rescue you from every trap
and protect you from deadly disease.
He will cover you with his feathers.
He will shelter you with his wings.
His faithful promises are your armor and protection.

Psalm 91:1–4

THOUGHT

On the afternoon of May 20, 2013, a severe tornado with peak winds estimated at 210 miles per hour struck Moore, Oklahoma, killing twenty-four people and injuring 212 others. The tornado touched down and remained on the ground for close to forty minutes, creating a path that was seventeen miles long and over a mile wide at its peak.[6,7]

After the tragedy, sales for storm shelters in the Moore, Oklahoma, region surged substantially, as they do in any region following such destruction. In the aftermath of a storm, people realize its power and devastation—and their own vulnerability.

Horrible and fierce as storms can be, humanity has a far more formidable danger, more detrimental than nature's greatest force. This foe is Satan, and he desires our complete destruction. A tornado has power, but not ability to harbor ill will. The evil one has unmitigated hate and disdain for his victims and pursues their ruin.

However, there is good news! The enemy of our souls is no match for the Lord! There is rest for those who abide in the shelter of the Most High. He is their protector, strong refuge, and safety. Our God delivers us from the evil one.

PRAYER

My trust and my hope are in you, the God of my salvation and keeper of my soul. Amen.

But rescue us from the evil one.

THE HOLY ONE

WORD

Who will not fear you, Lord,
and glorify your name?
For you alone are holy.
All nations will come and worship before you
for your righteous deeds have been revealed.

Revelation 15:4

THOUGHT

Some time ago, I was hiking steep terrain on the southern coast of Australia on a trip with friends. We began to question whether the view atop the mountain would merit the climb. Once we reached the top, we found the work it took to reach the summit did not disappoint. The view was breathtaking: the summit overlooked the vast blue ocean, beautifully wild waves, and a rich golden beach. It was so striking that our first few moments contained only silence.

Just like the state of awe we can experience through an amazing view, there is no better way to begin a day than in awe of the Holy One. When we study his promises, rest in his presence, and commune with him through prayer, we cannot help but be amazed by his glory. He was here before we were, he made us for his purposes, and he will remain once we depart. His goal in creating all things, from you and me to Australian mountaintops, was for his good pleasure—for all created things revolve around him and his desires, not around us and what we desire. He is the highest, the purest, and the noblest. His character is flawless; his actions are justified. Indeed, he is the *only* one worthy of our worship.

It's impossible to even grasp a portion of all he is, has done, and will do. The grateful, humble heart is left speechless and in awe of this Ancient of Days.

PRAYER

Lord, there are many things I could pray today,
but I choose to be still before the glory of your beauty and power in honor and worship of you.
For you alone are God—you alone are holy and worthy of all glory!

For yours is the kingdom and the power and the glory forever.

January 15

LIKE NO OTHER

WORD

"To whom will you compare me?
Who is my equal?" asks the Holy One.
Look up into the heavens.
Who created all the stars?
He brings them out like an army, one after another,
calling each by its name.
Because of his great power and incomparable strength,
not a single one is missing..
The LORD *is the everlasting God,*
the Creator of all the earth.
He never grows weak or weary.
No one can measure the depths of his understanding.

Isaiah 40:25–26, 28

THOUGHT

These Scriptures describe God's greatness and limitlessness—and his glory renders us with little thought beyond humility, awe, and the call to worship.

We, unlike our heavenly Father, are full of limits. We grow weak and weary when faced with difficulty. We thirst, hunger, and tire. We are unable to approach God by our own might, and we are unable to make penance for our own sin. It's humbling to realize we deserve nothing; it's humbling when we realize God has chosen to love us and made a way for us to experience his good grace and favor through Christ; and it's humbling to realize he alone provides us with strength, protection, and the resources to do his will.

Left to our own means, approaching God is impossible due to our own sin, but the love, mercy, and grace we receive through the covering of Christ's sacrifice has provided a place for us at our heavenly Father's table. His love is limitless and gives us strength. There is no one like him.

PRAYER

Lord, you give strength to the weak and powerless. Those who trust in you will find new strength. They will soar high on wings like eagles. They will run and not grow weary, walk and not grow faint. You, Lord, have no equal. You are the Lord of all. Amen.

Our Father in heaven, may your name be kept holy.

FOR EACH, AN ADVENTURE

WORD

The LORD had said to Abram, "Leave your native country, your relatives, and your father's family, and go to the land that I will show you. I will make you into a great nation. I will bless you and make you famous, and you will be a blessing to others."

Genesis 12:1–2

THOUGHT

Whether we are pastors, worship leaders, physicians, plumbers, schoolteachers, stay-at-home parents, factory workers, or farmers, if we embrace the Christ-life, we are in full-time ministry. We are Christ's ambassadors wherever we live and whatever we do.

There was great weight in God's instruction to Abraham. Abraham's obedience would require leaving most everything familiar, perhaps forfeiting comfort, and launching into many things unknown. Abraham's security and future would lie in his trust in God. Wisely, he followed God, and—though not always the easy, rational, or humanly reasonable path—it was the right one because it was God's design for Abraham. The same is true of God's will for each of us.

We're often drawn to these words in God's promise to Abram: *I will bless you and make you famous.* We should note God's blessing, while always right, purposeful, and fulfilling, also requires trust when there is uncertainty. God's designed blessings may not always look like we feel they should, but they are always exactly what we need. The life given fully to loving and following God will, in the end, be found with no regret.

PRAYER

In my heart, Lord, I know your will, and your path for me is better than anything I could design for myself. You lead; give me wisdom and strength to follow you. You have called me to use my life for your purposes, to worship and honor you. I pray that I do just that. Amen.

May your kingdom come soon. May your will be done on earth, as it is in heaven.

THE ULTIMATE PROVISION

WORD

The Lord is my shepherd;
I have all that I need.

Psalm 23:1

THOUGHT

A cold winter's day in January concluded with freezing rain, a half inch of ice, and several inches of snow in my Arkansas town. Tens of thousands in the region were experiencing power outages. I knew our car wouldn't make it up our narrow country drive on the ice. I began to wonder how long we might be without power in below-freezing weather or if the water pipes might soon freeze and create additional concerns.

It was then that I looked out into our yard and noticed a sparrow retrieving seed from a bird feeder and retreating to the cover of a cedar tree limb. After a few moments the bird would again fly to the feeder, gather seed, and return to the same limb. It repeated this process several times. The bird did not appear to be cold, and it certainly had plenty of food. Nor did it appear stressed or fretful. I have a feeling it was indifferent to our electrical power outage.

We have the Lord God as our protector, provider, and guide. No other power exists with unlimited ability to care for those under its watchful eye. The Lord is our Shepherd. He knows our actual needs and nothing can prevent him from meeting those needs—except perhaps our own foolishness to refuse or neglect his gracious offer to be our Shepherd. He is the ultimate provisionary regardless of the situation. His offer as Shepherd of our lives is the promise of flawless provision.

PRAYER

Within your divine design, Lord, is my daily provision for all you have called me to do.
For everything you call me to do today, you've already provided a way for me to complete it,
and I'm grateful for that provision. You are my source as I follow your will;
you are all I need. You are the Lord, my Shepherd. Amen.

Give us today the food we need.

RESCUED

WORD

I waited patiently for the LORD to help me,
and he turned to me and heard my cry.
He lifted me out of the pit of despair,
out of the mud and the mire.
He set my feet on solid ground
and steadied me as I walked along.
He has given me a new song to sing,
a hymn of praise to our God.
Many will see what he has done and be amazed.
They will put their trust in the LORD.

Psalm 40:1–3

THOUGHT

Some time ago, I heard a report of a Los Angeles woman who tried to jump from the top of one roof to another eighteen inches away and fell between the two buildings. She had only minor injuries but was wedged upright between the two buildings with no hope of escape on her own. All she could do was cry out for help as she remained hopelessly trapped. The woman was later rescued by a firefighter who was lowered to her by rope and grabbed her arms, lifting her from what could have been a slow death. She expressed sincere gratitude for her rescue as onlookers cheered the process on.

Much like the woman who was hopelessly trapped, without Christ, we are hopelessly trapped in our sins—and helpless to change the situation on our own. God heard our cries for help, and through Christ, he lifted us from our hopelessness.

We are not only the joyful recipients of divine rescue, but the good news of our escape from impending peril becomes evidence and catalyst for others endangered. Our Christ-rescued lives become path markers for others to find safety.

PRAYER

Left to myself, Lord, I had no way to escape the captivity of sin, but you in your love and mercy granted me freedom. Today, lead me to share with others how I once was in despair but you rescued me. Thank you for your saving grace. Amen.

Forgive us our sins, as we have forgiven those who sin against us.

THE PERFECT GUIDE

WORD

I will bless the LORD who guides me;
even at night my heart instructs me.
I know the LORD is always with me.
I will not be shaken, for he is right beside me.

Psalm 16:7–8

THOUGHT

In 2013, a group of Algerian hostages planned and managed an escape from terrorists holding them. To elude their captors they fled through a treacherous desert and seemingly impossible circumstances using only the compass app on their smartphones as a guide. Fortunately, the app worked despite the lack of a cellular signal.[8] I can only imagine their feelings of fear, hunger, need for determination, and the extent of their mental and physical exhaustion.

The scripture reminds us, even in times of despair or uncertainty, the Lord has promised to always be with his children. He, as the Maker and Sustainer of all things, guides and protects. He selects our path, leads us within it, and in his limitless abilities to alter the natural if need be, promises success of arrival to his selected destination for us. He never calls us to a task or mission without provision to accomplish the mission to which he has called us.

Stronger and more reliable than any compass, God has promised to lead and instruct those who have given themselves to follow him and to care for his children who long to fulfill the desires of his heart. His are not promises offered only on good days; they are sure promises that can be relied upon during any difficult circumstance. The next time loneliness and uncertainty come calling, and surely they will, rest in his promise to always guide you and always be beside you.

PRAYER

I bless your name, Father God, for you are true north for my soul. You guide me flawlessly—
if I will allow you to do so. Holy Spirit, bring your holy conviction in my life when I am not
allowing the Lord to direct my steps. You are the God of my destiny; lead me this day
by the power of your truth on your path alone and in your perfect way. Amen.

Don't let us yield to temptation.

January 20

THE LORD OUR PROTECTOR

WORD

I love you, LORD;
you are my strength.
The LORD is my rock, my fortress, and my savior;
my God is my rock, in whom I find protection.
He is my shield, the power that saves me,
and my place of safety.
I called on the LORD, who is worthy of praise,
and he saved me from my enemies.

Psalm 18:1–3

THOUGHT

The forecast for our region was for "bitter and dangerously cold" weather. A rare Arctic event would occur, uncommon for our Southern state of Arkansas. The next morning outside our living room window I watched the wind push the snow briskly across a white field. The temperature was in the single digits and overexposure to the elements without proper protection would have had quick and harsh effects on the human body. I, however, was huddled inside near the warmth of a wood stove and sheltered from the external conditions capable of harm.

There is a far greater danger to us than the cruelest of weather elements: evil itself. Cold-heartedly deceptive, Satan—the enemy of our souls—seeks to draw us away from the Lord's love and the Lord's will. Without Christ, one's spiritual future is desperately dark; apart from him, we can get caught up in the tangles of sin and its painful consequences.

However, in Christ we are shielded from harm that leads to eternal death; in him, we have eternal life. We have the Holy Spirit to guide our hearts down the path of righteousness, a path filled with hope, abundant life, and true, lasting joy that cannot be found in the momentary pleasures of this world. Christ is our hiding place—he provides safety in the midst of treachery, danger, and deceit. He is our protector and conquering King!

PRAYER

Father, my heart rejoices with love for you this morning.
I praise you for your refuge from the one who would harm me. Thank you for guiding me
and keeping me safe. You are my God, my Rock, my fortress, and my Savior. Amen.

But rescue us from the evil one.

MORE THAN WE CAN IMAGINE

WORD

O LORD my God, you have performed many wonders for us.
Your plans for us are too numerous to list.
You have no equal.
If I tried to recite all your wonderful deeds,
I would never come to the end of them.

Psalm 40:5

THOUGHT

One summer's evening I was standing on an isolated beach in Florida looking out into the Gulf of Mexico. There's just something about the ocean that invites reflection, isn't there? After a long, mesmerizing gaze, I shifted my eyes to the waves breaking on the beach. A thunderstorm had passed through the area earlier, but now an exceptionally clear sky appeared, stretching across the horizon.

Though the stars were obviously always present behind the clouds, thousands more seemed to appear after the storm was over. The view was breathtaking, and the moment was a memory-maker. A deep sense of awe rose within me: I was so consumed with gratitude for the moment that I praised God for his greatness. In our individual journeys with the Lord, reverent moments like these are treasured for a lifetime.

The immensity of all God has done—and continues to do—far exceeds our capacity to take it all in. In my own life, there are times of reflection when I am amazed, overwhelmed, and astounded by all he has done and how much he loves me, *even* in my own failings and *even* through difficulty. As his children, we are invited to respond to his greatness by acknowledging him, following him as he leads, worshiping him wholeheartedly, and honoring him with all of our lives. He alone is the God of wonder!

PRAYER

Lord, you have done more for me than I am aware of, more than I can even imagine.
You have included me in your magnificent plans, and I am humbled and grateful.
Lead me to tell those in my path of the greatness of your glory, and provide me
with the words to share your good news with others. Amen.

For yours is the kingdom and the power and the glory forever.

HE IS EXALTED

WORD

All honor and glory to God forever and ever! He is the eternal King,
the unseen one who never dies; he alone is God. Amen.

1 Timothy 1:17

THOUGHT

In my opinion, there is no better time of day to experience the comfort and power of scripture verses such as these than a crisp fresh quiet morning. Starting the day with this exclamation of praise from 1 Timothy surely sets the tone and opportunity for a day well lived.

It's a powerful thing to have our hearts and minds washed by this reality of scripture our God—to whom all honor is due, who abides forever, who rules in absoluteness, who will never relinquish authority, and who will stand forever as the singular life-source for all eternity—cares dearly for us. *Us!* Little me and little you are loved and seen by the highly exalted eternal King.

Not only does he care dearly for us despite our weaknesses, failures, and imperfections, but he also has perfect and noble plans for each one of his children. We were created for his purposes! In fact, this day was already planned out for you before time began. Go forth knowing you are deeply loved by the one who is deserving of all glory and praise. What an amazing honor to worship such a one, what an amazing opportunity to serve such a one, what an amazing experience to abide with such a one!

PRAYER

May you, Lord, be honored and glorified through the activity of this day.
I acknowledge your perfect and powerful rule over the whole earth and my life. You alone are God,
the Lord of all life, the Lord of my life. You will accomplish what you have planned. Amen.

Our Father in heaven, may your name be kept holy.

January 23

SET APART TO BE LIKE JESUS

WORD

You must be holy because I, the LORD, am holy.
I have set you apart from all other people to be my very own.

Leviticus 20:26

THOUGHT

Christ is just. Christ is fair. Christ is righteous in all his ways. These are some of his divine qualities and by grace and his Holy Spirit, these are the qualities that are to be displayed in and through us as well.

To grow in depth and maturity of these qualities, we practice the disciplines of consistently seeking God in scripture, prayer, and corporate fellowship with other believers. These activities are not the writ of legalism or the harsh keeping of the law to stay in God's good graces. No, they are heaven's gifts and ways of worship. Consistently seeking the Lord, both individually and corporately, is the source of whole and hearty spiritual nourishment.

This is the Christian's pursuit: to be like Jesus and reflect his character and qualities. To deepen and intensify our knowledge of him, our love for him, and our service to him, is our deepest hunger and our holy passion.

PRAYER

Holy Father, cause me to go about my day with the discernment of your Spirit and standards of your kingdom. I truly desire to be just, fair, righteous, and good—like you.
May my actions reflect your glory and reveal the intent of your will.
I pray I would be more like you with each day that passes. Amen.

May your kingdom come soon. May your will be done on earth, as it is in heaven.

OUR SOURCE OF LIFE

WORD

For you are the fountain of life,
the light by which we see.

Psalm 36:9

THOUGHT

One spring morning, my sons were exploring the woods and fields surrounding our house. They returned after a hike to tell me they had located a spring bubbling from the ground. The water source was a wet-weather spring. Following a few very dry years, there was suddenly an abundance of rain that replenished the water tables and saturated the ground surface. The water continued to flow from that wet-weather spring for several days.

Spring and summer that year were some of the greenest we've experienced since living on our property in Arkansas. Field flowers bloomed well into August when, usually, the days are dry and hot and the fields turn mostly brown.

The psalmist describes God as a fountain of life, the steadfast source that never depletes. The Lord is the light that penetrates darkness in our world and hearts; he makes a way for all of humanity to see and avoid those things hidden and harmful.

Jesus Christ "gave life to everything that was created, and his life brought light to everyone. The light shines in the darkness, and the darkness can never extinguish it" (John 1:4–5).

PRAYER

Through you, Lord Jesus, I have discovered the one fountain of genuine life.
You are the never-ending source of living water. You are the light of the world—the singular source
for my eyes to be rid of spiritual blindness and see the paths of life on which you lead me.
I trust you and look to you as my life-source. Amen.

Give us today the food we need.

POWER OF FORGIVENESS

WORD

At that moment the Lord turned and looked at Peter. Suddenly, the Lord's words flashed through Peter's mind: "Before the rooster crows tomorrow morning, you will deny three times that you even know me." And Peter left the courtyard, weeping bitterly.

Luke 22:61–63

THOUGHT

I was eleven years old when I entered Boy Scout Troop 91 in Louisville, Kentucky. The scoutmaster was a great role model for young men, and I deeply respected and admired him. During one of the weekly scout meetings, he divided us into groups to participate in a game designed to encourage teamwork and trust. Each group sat on the floor with their backs to a table filled with a couple dozen objects. Each group was brought to the table, given a short time to look at the objects, and then returned to record as many objects that were sitting on the table as they could remember. Whoever remembered the most objects won.

At one point, I took an unfair second glance at the objects. As I turned around, my eyes met my scoutmaster's. I quickly felt shame and embarrassment—but the worst feeling was knowing I had betrayed the trust of a man I deeply respected. Although it was difficult, I went to him, confessed my deed, and asked for forgiveness, which he granted. While I regretted my foolishness and received a gentle rebuke, I also experienced the power of pardon.

How awful and empty Peter must have felt when, after his third denial of Christ, the Lord turned and looked at him. Peter had been told it would occur, but he insisted that he would remain loyal. Instead, he failed, was humiliated, and let down the one he loved and respected most.

Jesus, however, not only told Peter of his coming denials, but also of the coming provision, restoration, and honor of encouraging and ministering once again for Christ. Thanks be to God for his forgiveness.

PRAYER

Holy One, sufficient words to express your grace and forgiveness do not exist, yet this morning my heart is alive with gratitude. Amen.

Forgive us our sins, as we have forgiven those who sin against us.

MUCH-NEEDED LIVING WATER

WORD

As the deer longs for streams of water,
so I long for you, O God.
I thirst for God, the living God.
When can I go and stand before him?
...Why am I discouraged?
Why is my heart so sad?
I will put my hope in God!
I will praise him again—
my Savior and my God!

Psalm 42:1–2, 5–6

THOUGHT

One night as I rested my head on the pillow, I heard a dog howling in the distance, running through the surrounding hills and meadows. The next morning I discovered a very tired bloodhound asleep on our doormat. I opened the door, patted her head, and retrieved a phone number from her collar. I called the owner thinking he would want to immediately retrieve her, but instead he asked if I might give her water and let her rest.

"She knows the way home; she's just tired," he assured. So I placed a bowl of water by her side, and she stood, drank, and sat down to rest. After her time of respite, she headed home.

There is a reason the psalmist compares our own human longing to be with the Lord to a thirsty animal seeking water. The absence of God's presence leaves the heart dry, tired, vulnerable to temptation, and spiritually drained. Once a Christian experiences the presence of God, a thirst is forever embedded to remain there. And we should seek after him more eagerly than the bloodhound searching for physical comfort and rest, for Christ's presence alone provides true and complete refreshment.

Christ alone is much-needed living water to our souls; he delivers exactly what we need in this life, while the temptation of sin would like us to think otherwise. In his presence we abide in peace, joy, and in the fullness of life. Nothing quenches a Christian's thirst but the presence of God.

PRAYER

Lead me to your presence, oh God, for therein lies my refuge, strength, and hope.
Your presence is the path of refreshment, renewal, clarity, and peace. Amen.

Don't let us yield to temptation.

JEHOVAH:
THE IMPENETRABLE FORTRESS

WORD

The name of the LORD is a strong fortress;
the godly run to him and are safe.

Proverbs 18:10

THOUGHT

Fort Eben-Emael in Liege, Belgium, was once believed to be the strongest military fortress in the world. Built between 1932 and 1935 and connected by miles of tunnels, it was effectively self-sufficient, containing barracks, sick bays, and a communication center.

However, on May 10, 1940, the unimaginable happened. The fort fell under a German attack called *blitzkrieg*, or "lightening war." For all its strength, Eben-Emael had a weakness: vulnerability to an air attack. The Germans surprised the Belgian army by using armed gliders carrying troops, and the fort was quickly taken with a devastating blow to the confidence of Belgium and other European nations.[9]

Likewise, despite how grounded or ready we might feel against spiritual attack, our spiritual foe is very cunning to use speed, surprise, and distraction against the pale defenses of humanity. Without God, we are no match for the enemy.

Although the greatest human fortresses still have weakness and vulnerability, there is one safe fortress void of vulnerability: Jehovah Sabaoth, the Lord our protector.

PRAYER

Lord, without your protection, I am completely exposed to the enemy of my soul.
I know my efforts to defend myself on my own are futile. You, though, are my refuge and fortress,
an impenetrable stronghold in which I put my confidence and hope. Whatever strategy may be
formed against me today, you are able to keep me safe as I trust in you. Amen.

But rescue us from the evil one.

January 28

MUSIC'S GREATEST PURPOSE

WORD

Praise the LORD, for the LORD is good;
celebrate his lovely name with music.

Psalm 135:3

THOUGHT

Who doesn't love music? It can stir deep emotions and feelings we are unable to articulate through words alone. It can help change a dull, listless attitude into one of optimism. I once saw a quote beautifully framed and displayed on a wall. Attributed to Martin Luther, it read, "I am strongly persuaded that after theology there is no art that can be placed on a level with music; for besides theology, music is the only art capable of affording peace and joy to the heart."

The first chapter of Colossians tells us God made everything that exists through and for himself: "Everything was created through him and for him" (Col. 1:16). As wonderful and far-reaching as music is, it finds its highest value and purpose in worship to God.

Praise God from whom all blessings flow.
Praise him all creatures here below.
Praise him above ye heavenly host.
Praise Father, Son and Holy Ghost.
—Thomas Ken, 1674

PRAYER

I glorify you, God, for your goodness today, and I will sing the song of praise
you have placed within my heart. Amen.

For yours is the kingdom and the power and the glory forever.

OUR HIGHEST GOAL

WORD

*For everything comes from him and exists by his power and is intended
for his glory. All glory to him forever! Amen.*

Romans 11:36

THOUGHT

The old Westminster Catechism says, "Man's chief end is to glorify God and enjoy him forever."[10] These ancient words are bursting with timeless truth.

We find our beginning in God and our continued sustenance for all things in him. He is our provision for all things: breath, sunlight, rain, food, hope, peace, freedom, rest, love, and joy. He has freely given us all we need so we might use his provision—whatever form that may take in our individual lives—to facilitate his will and declare his glory.

We were created to glorify, worship, and honor him in all that we do. The purpose of our every breath—our highest goal—is to exalt him, to tell the world who he is and what he has done. Life originates from him and is sustained by him. All glory, acclaim, and recognition is to be directed to him forever. He is the amazing one, the awesome one, the Holy One, the only true God!

PRAYER

*Lord, reset my heart today for your purposes, for I know all things exist by your power
and for your glory. You are the one who has given me breath, and you have done so that I might be
liberated from darkness to declare your name and purposes. You made me and you sustain me.
Use me to honor you as I walk through this day. Amen.*

Our Father in heaven, may your name be kept holy.

COMMISSIONED FOR MISSION

WORD

God sent a man, John the Baptist, to tell about the light so that everyone might believe because of his testimony. John himself was not the light; he was simply a witness to tell about the light. The one who is the true light, who gives light to everyone, was coming into the world.

John 1:6–9

THOUGHT

John the Baptist was commissioned by God to announce the *arrival* of the Redeemer of mankind. Following thousands of years of prophetic words, John's voice would be the final one to announce the *arrival* of the Christ.

However, God is still sending all his children into and throughout the world to tell of the *coming* of Christ—that he walked on earth among us, gave us his Holy Spirit to guide us even today, and will be coming again. We live as witnesses of his light and the hope he brings to humankind.

Each believer in Christ is "sent," meaning each is on a mission commissioned by God to tell others of his light. This is God's will, his desire, and his mandate so the world might know his mercy, love, and grace. In a diminishing, darkening world, we have the privilege, empowered through the Holy Spirit, to share the good news of life in Christ.

PRAYER

Lord, use me today to tell those you place in my path that there is good news for them in the light of your salvation. Today, let my ears be sensitive to your leading, and guide me to sow the seed of your kingdom. Amen.

May your kingdom come soon. May your will be done on earth, as it is in heaven.

PROVISION WITHOUT PERISH

WORD

All praise to God, the Father of our Lord Jesus Christ. It is by his great mercy that we have been born again, because God raised Jesus Christ from the dead. Now we live with great expectation, and we have a priceless inheritance—an inheritance that is kept in heaven for you, pure and undefiled, beyond the reach of change and decay. And through your faith, God is protecting you by his power until you receive this salvation, which is ready to be revealed on the last day for all to see.

1 Peter 1:3–5

THOUGHT

My wife and I enjoyed a long walk in the small New England village of Woodstock, Vermont, one afternoon. We happened upon an old cemetery located beside the Ottauquechee River, which runs through the village. It was a beautiful, sunny day, and we decided to investigate the cemetery a bit. We stepped through a narrow gate within the native stone wall that surrounds it, and for a few moments we spent time reading some of the stone markers.

Most inscriptions were simple and dated from the 1700s. The weather over the years had faded many names, dates, and epitaphs, but some still remained legible. Strolling slowly and quietly, I began to wonder how some of those deceased once lived. What were their occupations? What were their days like?

I then wondered about their faith: how many of them would I someday have an opportunity to meet because of our common hope in Christ? The inheritance for all of us who are redeemed is eternal life worshiping God forever, and the relationship between the friends of God will also last for eternity.

The things of earth will fade and fail, but those whose faith is in Christ live with a hope that will not disappoint and the promise of an unfading inheritance protected by God eternal!

PRAYER

Heavenly Father, thank you for your provision of life.
Keep my eyes, my mind, and my heart focused on you and things of eternal value.
May your will be my purpose and my daily bread. Amen.

Give us today the food we need.

February 1

THE CERTAINTY
OF FORGIVENESS

WORD

*My sheep listen to my voice; I know them, and they follow me. I give them eternal life,
and they will never perish. No one can snatch them away from me, for my Father
has given them to me, and he is more powerful than anyone else.
No one can snatch them from the Father's hand. The Father and I are one.*

John 10:27–30

THOUGHT

In the distraction of our fast-paced and information-laden culture, we move quickly from one thing to the next, often without taking a moment to reflect on all we have been given in Christ. Because of this, we sometimes overlook some obvious and important things.

First, we forget how amazing our liberty in Jesus Christ truly is. No matter what each day looks like—whether our day is joyful, stressful, heartbreaking, or simple— we've been set free from the chains of this world, and that is something we can rejoice over in all circumstances.

Second, we forget to recognize his faithfulness in keeping and caring for those who hear his voice and follow him. How wonderful it is that our forgiveness in Christ is certain! We are truly undeserving, but he intercedes lovingly on our behalf.

And third, we fail to remember that our response to this certainty of forgiveness and freedom should be to tell others about his great salvation. His glory, greatness, and goodness must be known.

PRAYER

Lord, you are good and your love is everlasting. I am unworthy, but your great power has made me part of the flock under your divine care. I am overwhelmed and grateful. I will not be silent— and by your power, I will share your great grace with those willing to listen. Amen.

Forgive us our sins, as we have forgiven those who sin against us.

THE DIVINE GUARDIAN

WORD

He guards the paths of the just
and protects those who are faithful to him.

Proverbs 2:8

THOUGHT

On a visit one summer to London, we were able to watch the formality of the Changing of the Guard at Buckingham Palace. Though some visitors may mistake that the soldiers stationed there are just for show, in reality, they are some of the best-trained soldiers in the British Army. When guarding Buckingham Palace, their duty is to protect British royalty and the palace itself, a task for which these men and women are well suited and prepared.

The church, the body of Christ, is referred to in 1 Peter 2:9 as *a royal priesthood*, an honor and position we did not earn but were gifted by God through his grace as redeemed followers of Christ. Additionally, we enter a unique and sacred relationship set aside for those committed to the will and way of God and his kingdom. We become the sons and daughters of the Most High. Our protector is the good and perfect Father, and no one cares for us as he does. He is our divine guardian, and no one is more capable to steer us around pitfalls and temptations. Our Royal Guard has more authority and power than all the combined armies of the world. There is none his equal, none to whom he submits or bows. In Christ, we are divinely guarded—our protector is none other than the unconquerable Lord God Jehovah. To request his assistance to guide us away from temptation is to release the most powerful defender to set a course for us upon the right paths, and successfully along the narrow way.

PRAYER

Thank you, Lord, for being my protector and guide. The one who leads me faithfully through the paths of this day—and every day, with strength to resist the wiles of the evil one—for the glory of your name. Amen.

Don't let us yield to temptation.

LIVING FEARLESSLY

WORD

But when I am afraid,
I will put my trust in you.
I praise God for what he has promised.
I trust in God, so why should I be afraid?
What can mere mortals do to me?

Psalm 56:3–4

THOUGHT

This scripture notes *when* I am afraid, not *if* I am afraid. The psalmist David doesn't conceal his emotions; he confesses them and proceeds to realign his trust in God. Attempting to cloak our fear is not the answer, and David reveals the better course. When fear is sensed, acknowledge it and turn to the Source that alleviates and dismisses it: Jehovah God!

For the believer, time spent in God's Word and prayer builds and reaffirms trust, sending fear to flight. What can mere humans do to us in the realm of eternity? The apostle Paul in 2 Corinthians 5:8 told the church that when we are not in our physical bodies, we are present with the Lord. Therefore, even in death the enemy loses. Death itself is swallowed up in Christ's victory.

In this life, temporary discouragements and difficulties are certain, but for the child of God, *victory* is the final word written in our story.

PRAYER

Lord, when David called out to you, you heard him and freed him from his fears. I, too, ask that when fear invades my heart, you will deliver me as I put my trust in you. Amen.

But rescue us from the evil one.

WHOLLY DEVOTED

WORD

Let all that I am praise the LORD.

Psalm 104:1

THOUGHT

When Jesus was asked which was the greatest commandment, he exhorted us to love the Lord with all our hearts, all our souls, and all our strength and, equally, to love our neighbor as we would love ourselves (Mark 12:29–31).

His response revealed the purpose and design for humanity: our entire being is to be devoted to a lifestyle of worship, which is simply our expression of love to God. While our salvation through Christ is based solely upon his free gift of grace, our response to and manifestation of this great salvation is the display of our complete abandonment to him.

We are to worship him with our whole selves: mind, body, and spirit. We are to live with our hearts wholly devoted to his glory, and devotion to Christ should affect how we love one another. Christian worship looks like celebration—singing, dancing, and playing music for his glory. It looks like bowing low—praying, submitting, and calling out to God. It also looks like the works of our hands—serving, caring, and giving in his holy name.

Our entire being is to be consumed in adoration of God.

PRAYER

Lord, let my day be filled with the sense and knowledge of your presence. By your Holy Spirit, may I be close to you and hear your voice. May I boldly declare my adoration of you to all those who would hear. It is you, God, I praise. Amen.

For yours is the kingdom and the power and the glory forever.

February 5

AMAZED BY HIS GREATNESS

WORD

May you be blessed by the LORD,
who made heaven and earth.

Psalm 115:15

THOUGHT

One winter's morning while staying in a lakeside cottage in the Ozark hills, I was again reminded of how truly vast and varied is both the Creator of heaven and earth and thus his creation. On the first morning, I woke to a temperature of minus five degrees, snow-covered shorelines, and thin layers of ice scattered about the lake's surface.

Despite a cold, cloudy morning, the day was filled with serenity and beauty. I stared through the cottage window and watched as a slight breeze caused the smallest of sways in a large cedar tree. I thought how, in just a few weeks, the view from the window would begin to yield an entirely different landscape. Spring would come, introducing new colors and a variety of wildlife emerging from winter habitats.

When we ponder the Earth, the handiwork of God should amaze us and fill our hearts with awe and wonder. Indeed, God is the Maker of heaven and earth, the Creator of all that exists. Our world is full of his beauty and artistry. He is above all things and to be boldly praised, and yet, in all his beauty and power, he is greatly merciful and calls us his own children.

PRAYER

Praise to you our Father in heaven, Maker of heaven and earth. Who is like you?
There is no other. I worship you, Lord; I honor and bless your holy name. Amen.

Our Father in heaven, may your name be kept holy.

LIVING IN THE PLACE OF JOY

WORD

I take joy in doing your will, my God,
for your instructions are written on my heart.

Psalm 40:8

THOUGHT

With each technological breakthrough that allows us to see farther into space, scientists declare new discoveries. This trend will continue as long as technology advances, for the creation of God is inexhaustible. God designed the earth, all within and around it, and then blessed his children with wonderful plans too numerous to list.

Just as God's creation escapes our comprehension, *his* great plans escape our ability to understand as well. Therefore, we are wise to embrace his plans and *not* ours. Not only is his will perfect, but his unlimited resources and power also ensure his plans will come to fruition.

In serving God and doing his will, we experience internal fulfillment, deep privilege, a purposeful life, and the wonder of divine design. The Lord offers us opportunities and adventures we could never come to have on our own. His will for us is pure, perfect, destined to succeed, and fashioned to honor him.

PRAYER

I can rest in your design for my life, Lord, for it is right and good.
Knowing what you've called me to do in this life and carrying that out will bring me incredible joy.
I take pleasure in doing your will, my God. Lead me today into your will. Amen.

May your kingdom come soon. May your will be done on earth, as it is in heaven.

LIVE IN FULLNESS

WORD

Let the message about Christ, in all its richness, fill your lives. Teach and counsel each other with all the wisdom he gives. Sing psalms and hymns and spiritual songs to God with thankful hearts.

Colossians 3:16

THOUGHT

To pursue the world's riches to attain the fullness of life is to err. In the end, if our gathered objects of adornment and accumulated wealth were purposed to fill the heart with gratification, we will have run vanity's deceptive course. We brought nothing into the world and we shall depart the same.

God, by divine design, has made each within humanity to live fully purposed, vibrant lives. The experience, however, does not emanate from gaining the treasures of this world, but instead the treasures through and in Christ. When the heart is given to all things Christ, feasting on his graces, the soul is filled from the coffers of the Holy One. Our garments we once perceived knitted with golden thread were disclosed as wretched rags once the beauty and richness of God's grace were realized.

God has purposed for the follower of Jesus to maintain the fullness of life by daily feeding on his Word, prayer, and partaking in genuine Christian fellowship; fellowship that encourages growth in the grace and knowledge of our Lord and Savior Jesus Christ. These components, practiced consistently, provide the daily nourishment for the fullness of life.

PRAYER

Lord, thank you for awakening me to the genuine riches for life's fullness. As I daily nourish myself with you through the reading of your Word, prayer, and placing myself within the community of faith, your church, let me bring honor to your name and your causes. Amen.

Give us today the food we need.

FREE INDEED

WORD

LORD, if you kept a record of our sins,
who, O LORD, could ever survive?
But you offer forgiveness,
that we might learn to fear you.

Psalm 130:3–4

THOUGHT

I have good friends whose pasts were entangled in crime, who were arrested, convicted as charged, and then later discovered Christ and turned to him. They love him, serve him, and have followed him for many years now. However, because of their previous crimes and subsequent sentences, some of them are unable to accompany me on the short-term mission trips I take out of the United States. And many with difficult pasts have a hard time finding work or being accepted into their communities long after they've justly paid for their errors.

Unlike this world that keeps a record of our sin, Christ eliminates the record *and* sentence against us—completely, entirely, and forever. In his desire for us all to be in close, growing relationship with him, he rescued us from our hopeless situation to free us from the result of our sin.

Without the application of God's grace and his path to forgiveness, our record of offenses would still stand and lead to eternal separation from him. But within his provisional plan, he not only forgives us, but he also calls us one of his own—we are sons and daughters of God. God, through the redemptive work of Jesus Christ, has expunged the record of our sins. Doesn't this gift of forgiveness cause your heart to rejoice with gratefulness?

PRAYER

Thank you for your salvation, which I've received through confession, repentance,
and embracing your Son Jesus Christ, the Lord and Savior of the world.
Thank you for revealing to me the way to true and full life. I pray my actions would honor
you today and that you would use me to lead others to your path of freedom. Amen.

Forgive us our sins, as we have forgiven those who sin against us.

DEEP ROOTS

WORD

*Blessed are those who trust in the L*ORD
*and have made the L*ORD *their hope and confidence.*
They are like trees planted along a riverbank,
with roots that reach deep into the water.
Such trees are not bothered by the heat
or worried by long months of drought.
Their leaves stay green,
and they never stop producing fruit.

Jeremiah 17:7–8

THOUGHT

Louisville, Kentucky, sits along the banks of the Ohio River, and the city was my home until age twenty-one when I moved to attend a Bible college in Missouri. My childhood was lived out on the west side of town a few blocks away from the river. I would often take extended bike rides along the paths and trails that ran parallel to the river to enjoy the sights, sounds, and smells of the mighty Ohio River.

The riverbank was host to huge cottonwood, oak, and river birch trees—the roots of which would sometimes stretch far across walking paths to reach the water's edge. Even during hot, dry summers, these trees remained green and seemingly unscathed during seasons of drought because their roots drew from the river when rain was lacking.

Jesus told us to seek first the kingdom of God and his righteousness. As we do, the provisions and strategies we need to carry out God's plan for our lives will be supplied as we follow him. The Bible instructs us to place our trust and hope in him and not to be ruled by natural circumstances. During times of trial, our deep roots will hold fast to the life-source that is Christ. We are to draw what we need from him, and he will lead us through the challenges of this life.

PRAYER

Lord, you are my source of life. You are my protector, and your provision gives me strength to follow and honor you according to your will. Keep me deeply rooted in you and able to stand against those temptations designed by the evil one to distract me. Amen.

Don't let us yield to temptation.

February 10

STEADFAST

WORD

*Hold firmly to the word of life; then, on the day of Christ's return, I will be proud that
I did not run the race in vain and that my work was not useless.*

Philippians 2:16

THOUGHT

There was a season at our house when each morning at first light, a male cardinal
would repeatedly fly into one of our windows. While persistence is often presented as a
virtuous characteristic, in this case it was better defined as obnoxious. A bit of research
revealed this little fellow was in a battle with himself. Ornithologists believe this action
occurs when the male sees his refection in the glass, and because he is territorial, he
attempts to challenge the "other male" invading his region. The tenacious little fellow
outside my window was in a battle of vanity he could not win.

Another battle of vanity is the attempt of the evil one to alter God's ultimate plan
of eternal restraint and imprisonment for the prince of darkness and his cohorts. In
the meantime the deceiver continues his wiles aimed toward humanity's separateness
from the love of God.

Those who have become followers of Christ and pursuers of God's kingdom realize
a unique position. Though vulnerable in the weakness of their flesh, through faith in
Christ, they abide on the one immovable foundation within the divine impenetrable
covering of the Almighty.

Jesus Christ is our steadfast protector and victor. To attempt battle against human-
ity's foe on our own is a vain struggle—no matter the intensity of our persistence. The
Christian's protector, however, is *The Lord, strong and mighty…invincible in battle* (Ps. 24:8).
He is a warrior undefeatable.

Our part is to hold firm, steadfast in him, for he has said…*apart from me you can do
nothing* (John 15:5). In Christ, however, we stand resolute as Paul declared *indeed, nothing
in all creation will ever be able to separate us from the love of God that is revealed in Christ Jesus our
Lord* (Rom. 8:39). Nothing!

No foe exists who can overcome Christ the King. Remain steadfast in him!

PRAYER

*Help me to understand, Lord, that you are mightier than the enemy planning my demise. I trust in
you, your strength, and your promises of hope! Amen.*

But rescue us from the evil one.

February 11

FOREVER EXALTED

WORD

All heaven will praise your great wonders, LORD;
myriads of angels will praise you for your faithfulness.
For who in all of heaven can compare with the LORD?
What mightiest angel is anything like the LORD?
The highest angelic powers stand in awe of God.
He is far more awesome than all who surround His throne.
O LORD God of Heaven's Armies!
Where is there anyone as mighty as you, O LORD?
You are entirely faithful.

Psalm 89:5–8

THOUGHT

Located in the Central American jungle on the banks of the beautiful Belize River is the small village of More Tomorrow. Within a clump of trees at the village's edge stands a tiny house. And within that tiny house lived a frail-framed, humble gentleman I considered a friend. His face was leathery and wrinkled, and his life was a long, difficult struggle to provide for himself and his family.

I had the privilege of spending time with him on trips to his village, and I was honored on several occasions to visit his home. Each time he would greet me with a smile and say, "My friend, you have returned." Sitting in his living room, a square space of about ten feet by ten feet, we spoke of how he was getting along. He slowly pointed his crooked and shaking finger upward and said, "He always takes care of me." In his lengthy and hard life, he had fully experienced that the Lord is entirely faithful.

I was sad when I heard he had passed; on my next trip to his village, I would not be greeted again by his beautifully wide smile.

Losing a friend never ceases being difficult. But when we lose a friend in Christ, we can have hope in knowing it is not the end. I will again see my friend's smile one day when all of heaven's host, along with all of God's redeemed, will proclaim together in worship: God is the Almighty, he is our faithful Father forever, he is all glorious, he is Jehovah God!

PRAYER

May you, Lord God, Maker and Sustainer of the heavens and the earth, be honored in worship today. May you, Father, Son, and Holy Spirit, be exalted! You are glorious and faithful. Amen.

For yours is the kingdom and the power and the glory forever.

OVERWHELMING GREATNESS

WORD

Exalt the LORD our God,
and worship at his holy mountain in Jerusalem,
for the LORD our God is holy!

Psalm 99:9

THOUGHT

There is no one equal to our God, for there is no one and nothing like our God. Though he made all things—galaxies, mountains, seasons, forests, animals, people, oceans, *everything*—and though they are made for him, his glory, and his enjoyment— he is separate from all created things. He is the singular self-existent life form whose depth, complexity, and mystery immediately leave our minds exhausted in attempts to comprehend his greatness. He is God, Jehovah God.

Yet in all his vastness and power—although he's in need of nothing and no one—he chose to allow us an intimate relationship and friendship with him. He invites us close, so we can know him as our Father in heaven.

PRAYER

Father, you have done more for me than I am aware of and more than I can imagine.
You have included me in your magnificent plans, and I am humbled and grateful.
I worship you in your perfect holiness. Amen.

Our Father in heaven, may your name be kept holy.

February 13

PERSISTENCE

WORD

One day Jesus told his disciples a story to show that they should always pray and never give up.

Luke 18:1

THOUGHT

Despite multiple career and political failures, not to mention great personal loss, rejection, and stress, Abraham Lincoln is recognized as one of the greatest presidents in United States history.

We think of him as a great man and prestigious orator, but during his life he held countless job positions—most of them physically laborious and incredibly unpresidential.[11] He was known to be a man of humility and persistent faith, and regarding prayer, he's quoted as saying, "I have been driven many times to my knees by the overwhelming conviction that I had nowhere else to go. My own wisdom, and that of all about me, seemed insufficient for the day."[12]

Truly, we are insufficient apart from the Lord. His wisdom, strength, and power are great, and we must ask him, in humility, to provide what we need to carry out his will. When it comes to seeking the Lord and persistently following his call on our life, application of Luke 18:1 is necessary: "always pray and never give up."

PRAYER

Lord, you have called me and I am yours. You have made it clear your grace
is sufficient in all things. You have given evidence of your faithfulness and encouraged me
to pray and never give up. I embrace your will and, by your grace and for your glory,
I will persistently pursue your heart and will for this day. Amen.

May your kingdom come soon. May your will be done on earth, as it is in heaven.

GOD OF GOODNESS

WORD

You have done many good things for me, Lord,
just as you promised...
You are good and do only good;
teach me your decrees.

Psalm 119:65, 68

THOUGHT

During my Christian experience, I have often awakened during the night with a thought of concern. Most times these thoughts are quickly dismissed and I return to sleep, but there have been moments when I cannot easily dismiss them, so I get up, get my Bible, and pray.

In one of these moments I discovered the wealth of these words from Psalm 119, for indeed God has done so many good things.

God, who watches over us and leads us, does *only* good. He has done many good things for us, none of which we are worthy of, yet he gives goodness because this is his *nature* and *desire*.

In the truth and light of God's word, we will gain a changed perspective. When we know that God only does good, we can have hope in knowing that the trials we experience in this life are overseen and commandeered by him with the ultimate goal of bearing fruit for his kingdom. What we may interpret from our vantage point as trial may one day be revealed as God's hand of good provision to bear fruit for his good purposes.

PRAYER

Indeed, Lord, you have provided me with goodness—and my heart knows it well. Lead me through this day with a heart of gratefulness. You've done many good things for me. Amen.

Give us today the food we need.

FORGIVENESS FOR ALL

WORD

What mighty praise, O God,
belongs to you in Zion.
We will fulfill our vows to you,
for you answer our prayers.
All of us must come to you.
Though we are overwhelmed by our sins,
you forgive them all.
What joy for those you choose to bring near,
those who live in your holy courts.
What festivities await us
inside your holy Temple.

Psalm 65:1–4

THOUGHT

A man once told me he could not measure up spiritually to other Christians he had met. His life was simply too ridden with dysfunction, his situation too complex to repair, and his transgressions beyond forgiveness. Without disclosing identities, I shared the stories of others around him in the church he attended who had once thought the same about themselves—but who were now experiencing the freedom of forgiveness.

I observed the power and beauty of God's mercy in this man as he realized the grace of Christ and power of his forgiveness. This man became one of my good friends and has since helped redirect others who thought as he once did, showing them God's invitation to life is open to all who would turn toward Christ's forgiveness.

The enemy would have us think we're too much a mess for God to forgive us. God's love, grace, and salvation is for all who say *yes* to the redeeming sacrifice of the Father's only Son, Jesus Christ, and repent of their sin. There are no exceptions.

God's forgiveness is the gateway to genuine freedom and inexpressible joy—and it's offered equally to all. God shows no favoritism. Our release from the power of sin and death give all who believe a reason to celebrate the love, mercy, power, and glory of God.

PRAYER

Apart from you, Lord, we have no hope of forgiveness and are locked away in a place that only you can liberate us from. You are the only way, and all must come to you for salvation. There is no sin you cannot forgive. In your forgiveness, I have great joy and a reason to celebrate for all time. Amen.

Forgive us our sins, as we have forgiven those who sin against us.

UNFAILING LOVE

WORD

Let me hear of your unfailing love each morning,
for I am trusting you.
Show me where to walk,
for I give myself to you.
Rescue me from my enemies, Lord;
I run to you to hide me.

Psalm 143:8–9

THOUGHT

Great Christian men and women of the past stressed the importance of seeking the Lord in scripture and prayer first thing in the early morning. We see others throughout the Bible, like the psalmist here, proclaiming the early hours of the day as the first choice for searching fresh input from the Lord.

Seeking the Lord at the beginning of the day allows *him* to set the tone for the day—instead of our own circumstances, feelings, or attitudes steering us. By spending time at the start of the day in scripture and prayer, we are reminded of God's unfailing love, his care, and his protection from the enemy.

In this atmosphere is gained the wisdom, strength, and discernment to avoid seeking vain ambitions, self-gratifications, and other worldly snares.

In this earth-life, we will face many challenges to walking in God's will. Being reminded first thing in the morning of Christ's unfailing love, power, mercy, and truth will equip us for whatever the day ahead may hold.

PRAYER

Father, your great gift of grace delivered me from a fate of darkness.
You are my Savior and Lord, and I'm grateful for your unfailing love that upholds me.
I trust you to guide me through this day, and deliver me from the plans of the evil one who would
cause me to fail. Show me where to walk; I give wholeheartedly to you. Amen.

Don't let us yield to temptation.

February 17

SEND YOUR RAIN

WORD

I lift my hands to you in prayer.
I thirst for you as parched land thirsts for rain.

Psalm 143:6

THOUGHT

I once read an article about a long period of severe drought in the western portion of the United States. The story contained two pictures: One was of several people gathered in a small church praying for relief from the long drought. The second was of a handwritten sign attached to a section of barbed wire fence that read "Pray for Rain." The lack of precipitation was so concerning, the state farm bureau asked the public to join together in prayer and fasting for relief from the drought.

For three consecutive summers, my region was very hot and dry—with one span of temperatures rising daily above 100 degrees. There were multiple effects and several beautiful large trees on our property died. Drought brings the realization (and desperation) of our dependence upon rain to sustain life.

The psalmist raised his hands not simply to express thanks but to express his desperate desire for relief from the weight he was carrying. He thirsted for God's presence so greatly that he compared his situation and need of God to that of parched land in need of rain.

And what of you? Have you or are you experiencing a season of spiritual drought? These are the seasons the evil one attempts to prey on our weakness. Respond as Christ did in his forty day desert experience, "People do not live by bread alone, but by every word that comes from the mouth of God" (Matt. 4:4). Seek God's presence, God's deliverance, God's holy rain.

PRAYER

Father, my spirit is fed only by the refreshment of your presence. Without you I am a hopeless, parched, and weary soul. I thirst for your presence and the life contained for me there. Amen.

But rescue us from the evil one.

BEYOND BOUNDARIES

WORD

"To whom will you compare me?
Who is my equal?" asks the Holy One.
Look up into the heavens.
Who created all the stars?
He brings them out like an army, one after another,
calling each by its name.
Because of his great power and incomparable strength,
not a single one is missing...
The LORD is the everlasting God,
the Creator of all the earth.
He never grows weak or weary.
No one can measure the depths of His understanding.

Isaiah 40:25–26, 28

THOUGHT

God's greatness and his unlimited abilities draw the worshiper of Jehovah into a state of glorious admiration and exaltation. The Lord cannot be compared to anything or anyone else, for there is no one or nothing his equal. Humanity is unable and unworthy to approach God in his purity and holiness.

Our heavenly Father's power is beyond boundaries, and his love is pure and limitless. As sons and daughters of God, this gives us great hope and trust in him. Family may fail us, friends may dishearten us, and authorities in the church may disappoint us, but the Lord's faithfulness, purity, greatness, and loving kindness *never* fail. His kingdom is one without blemish, and his rule is just, reliable, and merciful.

Our just and merciful King, our Lord in his great love and grace, made a way for humanity to experience his good gifts, receive favor, and live in divine relationship through Christ Jesus. In Christ we are strengthened, protected, and armed to do the Lord's will.

PRAYER

Lord, you are trustworthy, and you give power to the weak and strength to the powerless. Those who trust in you will find new strength. Because of your boundless power and love, I can soar high on wings like eagles. I can run and not grow weary. I can walk in your will for my life and not grow faint. All glory, honor, power, and praise are yours. Amen. (Adapted from Isaiah 40:29–31.)

For yours is the kingdom and the power and the glory forever.

AWE AND WONDER

WORD

In the beginning the Word already existed.
The Word was with God,
and the Word was God.
He existed in the beginning with God.
God created everything through him,
and nothing was created except through him.
The Word gave life to everything that was created,
and his life brought light to everyone.
The light shines in the darkness,
and the darkness can never extinguish it.

John 1:1–5

THOUGHT

This is one of scripture's most familiar passages. Although sometimes overlooked because of their familiarity, these words are filled with precious and priceless spiritual gems for the hearts and souls of those who strive for a life grounded in truth. We benefit when we slow down, quiet ourselves before the heavenly Father, and—to borrow an antiquated but wonderful term—*bask* in the beauty and life found in his Word.

Welcome to the edge and mystery of the *other-world* of God as seen in today's reading. Although we can get a glimpse, we will never exhaust the boundless landscape that is the mysterious truth of Christ. For those whose lives are found in him, this passage provides a serene place of security and trust.

Within the beautiful sea of absolutes contained in the first five lines of John is the solution for humanity's plight: the Word, Jesus Christ, the light for our dark world. Christ is the giver of life and light; he is the surety for our souls. The wise will embrace him in worship and service.

PRAYER

Lord, I sit in wonder this morning as I dwell on your inexhaustible power, infinite wisdom, and mysterious ways. What more can my finite mind do than marvel in reverence at your greatness? What more can my heart do than humbly bow before you in gratitude for the abundance and generosity of your perfect love? It is you I worship and adore, mighty God. Amen.

Our Father in heaven, may your name be kept holy.

REFINED FOR THE BEST

WORD

My gifts are better than gold, even the purest gold,
my wages better than sterling silver!

Proverbs 8:19

THOUGHT

Refining gold, according to *Encyclopedia Britannica*, is commonly done in two ways: either by high-temperature flame or by introducing strong chemicals. Both methods work to purify the precious metal, removing pollutants and imperfections so that the purest gold possible is left. However, experts tell us that even 24K gold, at 99.999 percent purity, contains imperfections.[13] Despite the extensive refining process, producing completely pure gold is a physical impossibility for humans at this point in time.

God alone can refine to perfection—whether that is a precious metal such as gold or our own human hearts. Although we may strive for self-perfection, it is work done in vain. We may get close to feeling purified by making morally upright choices, checking all the boxes of church membership, and keeping our promises. However, apart from Christ and his kingdom work in our hearts, we are useless in our own attempts at redeeming and refining our actions to earn the righteousness that can be found only in submitting our whole selves fully to him.

The will of God—the principles of his kingdom, his wisdom, and his ways—is to be desired by those who love and serve him above the earth's wealth, riches, reputation, and honors. His abundant gifts of freedom, peace, joy, and rest are better than the purest gold and are given freely to us—they cannot be earned through our earthly striving. He alone is capable of truly refining our hearts and giving us the good and perfect gifts that come with complete, grace-filled redemption.

PRAYER

Lord God, I seek you and the treasure of your kingdom above all else. Thank you for making a way in Christ for me to enjoy all your good and perfect gifts that I'm unable to earn in my own right. You are generous and loving, and I give you all the glory and praise. Amen.

May your kingdom come soon. May your will be done on earth, as it is in heaven.

TRUST FOR PROVISION AND PEACE

WORD

For the word of the LORD holds true,
and we can trust everything he does.

Psalm 33:4

THOUGHT

Within our culture, the enemy strives to spawn doubt that truth in a pure, accurate, and absolute form exists within God. However, God and the promises of his Word are absolute, even though the very word *absolute* is often troublesome to the doubting secular academic mind. Adherence to this value by Christians can sometimes produce aggression from doubters when an unyielding apologist persists.

For the sons and daughters of God, however, Psalm 33:4 and passages like it are treasures to their hearts and produce great comfort and peace. To know everything our heavenly Father says and does is flawless in design and destined to unfold in his perfect timing is a deep well flowing with fresh encouragement for the soul.

Within his perfect truth abides his enduring promise to facilitate his will for us. If the Lord asks a task of us that seems overwhelming or intimidating, because of his unwavering truth we know that he has already planned to provide us with everything we need to walk in his will. We can have rest and assurance in the fact that his will is good and his promises hold true.

PRAYER

Thank you, Lord God, for reminding me this morning that all things were created for your purposes
and will materialize as you have planned. There is no reason to question anything you do,
for all you do is right. But in times when I do have questions and doubts, thank you for the comfort
of knowing you are my provider and you love me dearly. I am abiding in your refuge,
and you will perform your will with perfection to the end of my days. Amen.

Give us today the food we need.

February 22

SEEING THROUGH EYES OF FORGIVENESS

WORD

Love prospers when a fault is forgiven,
but dwelling on it separates close friends.

Proverbs 17:9

THOUGHT

The love of God is flawless: it never diminishes, and it is without prejudice. Love—in its purest form—is God, for God is love. In fact, we are told not only do we not know God without love, but we also cannot know him until we love as he loves. According to 1 John 4:7–8, "Anyone who loves is a child of God and knows God. But anyone who does not love does not know God, for God is love." No need of a theology degree—this truth is clear and simple. Love prospers when we forgive others as he has forgiven us.

Have you experienced the truth of today's scripture in your own life? I've not only observed good friendships suffer in the hands of a fault-finding spirit, but I myself have also been on the receiving end of a fault-finding and critical spirit. And to my dismay, I have been a dispenser of it; I've witnessed the wounds I produced because of my anger or jealousy toward others and experienced the shame it brought to my heart. I'm so grateful that the Lord sees me through the eyes of forgiveness.

Thankfully, I've also seen and known the power of forgiveness in relationships when we offer the same grace and mercy extended by Christ to one another. Forgiveness is first an act of obedience: God expects nothing less from us than what he has offered each of us. The effects of obedient forgiveness then heal the deepest of wounds, rebuild trust, and restore life.

PRAYER

God, thank you that you see me through the eyes of forgiveness because of the grace of your Son, Jesus Christ. May I walk in your spirit of forgiveness and extend it to others as you have instructed, for it pleases and honors you as I walk in obedience. Amen.

Forgive us our sins, as we have forgiven those who sin against us.

DISCIPLINED AND SUCCESSFUL LIVES

WORD

These are the proverbs of Solomon, David's son, king of Israel.
Their purpose is to teach people wisdom and discipline,
to help them understand the insights of the wise.
Their purpose is to teach people to live disciplined and successful lives,
to help them do what is right, just, and fair.

Proverbs 1:1–3

THOUGHT

God is overwhelmingly mysterious, and the depths of his knowledge are inexhaustible. He requires honor, worship, and obedience, but he also desires personal relationship, fellowship, and close intimate friendship.

The Christian, however, discovers security and encouragement in knowing God is both complex and beyond understanding yet simple and approachable for those of childlike faith. How can the words *simple* and *complex* be used to describe the same person? Not easily, unless the subject of discussion is God.

If the Lord is so vast and great, how are we able to still please him? How can we bring him honor and glory in our lives, even though the best we have to offer amounts to filthy rags?

We can look to his Word to see what God loves and finds honorable. In a modern culture confused about values and how to treat one another, Proverbs is clear in revealing "what is right, just, and fair." At the end of our days, our worldly success will be of no value; instead, we will be measured by how well we represented Christ and loved our fellow man.

PRAYER

Lead me in your paths by your Word, Lord Jesus. Amen.

Don't let us yield to temptation.

STAND COURAGEOUSLY IN CHRIST

WORD

So humble yourselves before God. Resist the devil, and he will flee from you.

James 4:7

THOUGHT

I was on a walk in the field in front of our home, nearing a group of trees, when suddenly I heard a screech. Startled, I looked up. Coming from the direction of a nearby wooded area was a large red-tailed hawk. Quickly and desperately, it was flying to distance itself from the attack of another bird. This other bird was not a larger predator, but instead was a lone, squawking, aggravated, and very persistent mockingbird. Whatever the hawk did to invade or threaten the mockingbird's space, the little guy would have none of it, and it was tenaciously (and successfully) chasing the much larger and more dangerous enemy from its territory.

We have a dangerous and well-skilled enemy we know as Satan. His goal, as told to us by Jesus, is to "steal and kill and destroy" (John 10:10). However, our protector and fortress is the Lord God Almighty, and our shield is trust and faith in who he is and what he has said he will do.

Are you in a battle you feel you are fighting on your own? Remember, stand courageously in Christ, knowing the battle is his. Since he fights on our behalf and goes before us, we become a force to be reckoned with. He is our front and rear guard. When the enemy attempts to intrude into territory given us by God—no matter the enemy's reputation and size—those who trust in the Lord God Almighty become the winners. We are like the mockingbird against a bigger enemy, small but powerful due to our identity in Christ and God's position in the battle.

PRAYER

You, oh, Lord, are God and you are mighty in battle against your enemies. Thank you that the battle is yours, and you go before me as my king and protector. In your name and by your might, Holy Spirit, I will resist the wiles of the enemy—and as I do, I am promised the enemy will flee. Amen.

But rescue us from the evil one.

MOST HOLY

WORD

Praise the LORD!
Yes, give praise, O servants of the LORD.
Praise the name of the LORD!
Blessed be the name of the LORD
now and forever.
Everywhere—from east to west—
praise the name of the LORD.
For the LORD is high above the nations;
his glory is higher than the heavens.
Who can be compared with the LORD our God,
who is enthroned on high?

Psalm 113:1–5

THOUGHT

Everyone who calls on the Lord for redemption has the task, privilege, and honor of praising the Lord now and through eternity. Worship is the one thing we will do both in this earthly life and life eternal.

As his sons and daughters, we should glow with the complete and full love of Christ. Proclaiming his glory and goodness should be such a part of our natural makeup that it spills out of our mouths as easily as reciting our own names and street addresses. When was the last time you privately or publicly raised your hands in worship? Do you recall the last time you bowed low on your knees in a prayer of thanks and deep, humble gratitude?

He is deserving of all honor. There is none greater in existence than Jehovah God! Let us worship him today.

PRAYER

You are above all things. Nothing and no one can compare to you my Lord, my God, and my king!
Let me carry my thoughts of praise to you throughout the day and into the night from this day,
each thereafter, and into eternity. Praise your name, Most High! Amen.

For yours is the kingdom and the power and the glory forever.

NEW SONGS OF PRAISE

WORD

Let the godly sing for joy to the LORD;
it is fitting for the pure to praise him.
Praise the LORD with melodies on the lyre;
make music for him on the ten-stringed harp.
Sing a new song of praise to him;
play skillfully on the harp, and sing with joy.
For the word of the LORD holds true,
and we can trust everything he does.
He loves whatever is just and good;
the unfailing love of the LORD fills the earth.

Psalm 33:1–5

THOUGHT

People love music! It can change the mood of one individual or an arena of thousands. Music comes in myriad styles and forms, but its zenith experience is in worship to God. God created music and humanity with the intent of both to glorify him. When we worship God through music, we, in turn, experience the mystery of internal fulfillment through rhythm, lyric, and melody.

Martin Luther wrote: "Next to the Word of God, music deserves the highest praise."[15]

For those who have discovered genuine life in relationship with Christ, the first verses of Psalm 33 call us to joyfully exalt him with multiple instruments in a new song of praise. We praise him because he alone is worthy of worship, because his truth is flawless forever. His decisions are perfect, trustworthy, fair, and just. His love is absent of prejudice, darkness, and selfishness. It never fails.

He alone offers relief and fulfillment to the human soul. Let the redeemed sing joyfully, confidently, and often!

PRAYER

Be exalted, oh God, with the melody of a heart set free to worship you.
My source of hope, joy, and the Lord of my life, you are my song! Amen.

Our Father in heaven, may your name be kept holy.

MISSION OF HONOR

WORD

"How beautiful are the feet of messengers who bring good news!"

Romans 10:15

THOUGHT

Few things have the capability to instantly relieve feelings of discouragement than someone arriving with good news. Although everyone handles challenges and difficulties differently, receiving good news universally brings some level of joy to even the most negative situation. While *receiving* good news is a blessing, anyone who has had the experience of *delivering* good news will tell you what a joy it is to do so.

Christians are not only recipients of the good news, but we also have the most honored and glorious assignment in all the earth: we are privileged to take the good news to the broken, wounded, and disenfranchised. For every outcast and wanderer, for every person in despair or overcome by hopelessness, this news offers genuine and lasting hope. This is the gospel of Christ, and we have been granted the honor and joy of sharing it with the world—from the most remote rural village to our neighbors next door.

PRAYER

Father, you have given me freedom and great purpose for this life. I'm honored to be your messenger, to bring hope to the hopeless with the message of your great love, mercy, and grace. Let me be attentive to the leading of your Holy Spirit today; lead me to someone who's waiting for your good news. Amen.

May your kingdom come soon. May your will be done on earth, as it is in heaven.

BEYOND OUR IMAGINATION

WORD

Now all glory to God, who is able, through his mighty power at work within us,
to accomplish infinitely more than we might ask or think. Glory to him in the church and in Christ
Jesus through all generations forever and ever! Amen.

Ephesians 3:20–21

THOUGHT

Did you know that the brain is the most complex organ in the human body? Incredibly, it contains over one hundred billion nerve cells, and it creates a million new connections between cells every second in our lives.

According to physicist Sir Roger Penrose, "If you look at the entire physical cosmos, our brains are a tiny, tiny part of it. But they're the most perfectly organized part. Compared to the complexity of a brain, a galaxy is just an inert lump."[16]

God is the Creator of this complex organ and the thoughts it is capable of producing. Yet when it comes to the power of God working within us to accomplish his purposes, our minds can't compare to his. His thoughts surpass our deepest, most complex, and most creative thoughts.

The wise will acknowledge the truth that his thoughts are beyond ours—in him we find knowledge and life. When it comes to his ability to work his will in and through us, our greatest effort in imaginative thought is in no way measurable to his.

When Christ encourages prayer to our boundless God for provision of daily needs, we should rest in his limitless abilities to do so.

PRAYER

Lord, my desire is to do great things of significance for your glory and your kingdom.
I have imagined much of what I might do, yet I surrender my desires to you,
for your vision for my life exceeds what I can imagine. Amen.

Give us today the food we need.

DIVINE DELIVERANCE

WORD

*Let them praise the LORD for his great love
and for the wonderful things he has done for them.*

Psalm 107:15

THOUGHT

Psalm 107 gives thanks while reflecting on the history of God's relationship with his people, Israel. The verse above is repeated *four* times in this psalm. It exhorts thanksgiving from those to whom the Lord has rescued, delivered, and given favor. It's repeated amid the story of Israel finding themselves in a predicament, their response being to turn to God for his help.

Each of the four times this verse is written, the Lord's response is documented: he rescued them from distress and led them straight to safety (Ps. 107:6–7); "Lord, help!" they cried in their trouble, and he saved them from their distress. He led them from the darkness and deepest gloom; he snapped their chains (Ps. 107:13–14); he healed them by his word, saving them from death (Ps. 107:20); and he calmed the storm (Ps. 107:29). Throughout Psalm 107 alone, many proclamations are found of the Lord's loving and redemptive works for Israel, his people.

The final portion of Psalm 107 concludes by acknowledging God's ability to turn the grimmest of situations around for good—for he is good and desires to forgive us and liberate us from the clutches of sin. He redeems and restores through his divine deliverance.

PRAYER

*Lord, you change deserts into pools of water. There is no dark situation beyond your reach
and ability to deliver. You have been faithful when I have failed to be faithful.
Thank you for hearing my cry when I said, "Lord help!" Thank you for your rescue, your
deliverance, and the light of your salvation. Thank you for your forgiveness.
Great are you Lord! Amen.*

Forgive us our sins, as we have forgiven those who sin against us.

March 2

THE PATHMAKER

WORD

For the LORD watches over the path of the godly,
but the path of the wicked leads to destruction.

Psalm 1:6

THOUGHT

If you enjoy hiking, you probably frequent several favorite trails. I have a few familiar routes I routinely enjoy, and since I frequent them often, I know what's ahead: steep inclines, tree roots that have grown across the trail, a cliff that can cause hazards, places where snakes rest.

Although we can be familiar with what is ahead our own regular hiking trails, unfortunately it is not so with life. But God is familiar with our paths. He is acquainted with every step. He is the divine trail guide. We can rest knowing that God is the maker of the path on which he leads us—and he's familiar with every detail ahead.

We are limited in our ability to process and prepare for everything that may come. However, God knows the way and is prepared to assist us at each step and every challenge. The Bible instructs and encourages the follower of God to trust him without reservation for this very reason: we will never know our path like he does. However, Jesus said, "I am the way," and indeed he is. Follow him. Trust him.

PRAYER

Lord, you have made a path for my feet to walk. You are the God of all creation, and you know every facet and feature before me this day. I ask for your guidance as you watch over my steps and lead me away from the evil one. May I accomplish each task you have designed for me, and may I worship and honor you as I enjoy the beauty of your magnificence. Amen.

Don't let us yield to temptation.

LIVING EXPECTANTLY

WORD

*You have given me greater joy
than those who have abundant harvests of grain and new wine.
In peace I will lie down and sleep,
for you alone, O Lord, will keep me safe.*

Psalm 4:7–8

THOUGHT

David, writer of this psalm, reveals a threefold outcome from his trust in the Lord: joy greater than the abundance of material things, safety or security from whatever would endanger him, and peace, the most sought-after treasure of heart and soul.

Worldly recipes and tactics to bring peace, wealth, power, and reputation are to no avail. God alone—with his unlimited wisdom, power, and resources—is capable of delivering genuine peace. He alone is capable of fending off the wiles of the evil one, and he alone is worthy of our complete trust.

Because of God's goodness and power, and because we are his children, we can live expectantly, knowing that he holds us, provides for us, and gives us a joy that is greater than anything this world can offer. David's experience of trusting the Lord can also be our experience—if we will place ourselves before and within the care of Almighty God.

PRAYER

Father, when I think of you and all you have done for me, my heart fills with joy, for whom have I in heaven but you? Who but you, Lord Jesus, can bring peace, the result of your perfect and eternal provision. When I genuinely rest, it is because of my trust in you. I choose today to trust in you alone, for you alone can deliver me from the evil one. Amen.

But rescue us from the evil one.

CREATION REVEALS THE GLORY OF GOD

WORD

In the beginning God created the heavens and the earth.

Genesis 1:1

THOUGHT

There's just something about contemplating creation. When we take the time to do so, it humbles us, leading us to worship and adore the Lord.

As I write this, the view through my window reflects the handiwork of the Lord, an unfolding canvas created by a skilled artisan. Just above the wooded hilltops, the slow-moving and shape-changing cloud formations reflect dawn's early rays, creating brilliant colors of blue, white, and gold. An almost translucent mist hovers above the yellow and brown winter landscape though a few, pale green patches are slowly emerging, signifying spring is near. Songbirds that grace the trees seem like they're working to outsing one another.

All creation reveals the glory of God. True, you do not have to be a believer in Christ to appreciate the beauty of nature, but only a believer in Christ can appreciate the beauty, depth, and majesty of nature's Creator. Without him, there would be no beginning. Without him, light would have not pierced the darkness. Had he not spoken, "Let there be," the word *emptiness* would describe the darkness, void, and absence of life. But God did say, "Let there be," and the result is indescribable beauty, brilliance, and the holy presence of divine creative pageantry.

PRAYER

Glory to God in the highest! You are God the Father, Jesus Christ the only Son, and the Holy Spirit. There is no other God but Yahweh! May all the heavens and earth declare your glory! Amen.

For yours is the kingdom and the power and the glory forever.

March 5

GOD, FATHER OF ALL

WORD

The heavens are yours, and the earth is yours;
everything in the world is yours—you created it all.

Psalm 89:11

THOUGHT

God our Father made everything and maintains everything—and all of it, including humanity, exists for his good pleasure and glory.

Some time ago on a mission trip to Central America, I was being driven to a small village on a narrow, winding road through a hilly region. Along the way, you could find a few small dwellings next to cleared fields for livestock or crops where there were breaks in the thick flora. Other than these tiny domesticated areas, the region was covered by lush, captivating, wild jungle.

In contrast, on a separate trip in a completely different part of the world, I found myself overlooking a massive Alaskan glacier that stretched through a valley and extended into the sea. The valley was framed by a rugged mountain range—all sheltered under the deepest blue sky I had ever seen.

As wonderful and vastly different from one another as these places were, they are only *two* of the countless stunning locations within this massive earth. The diversity and majesty of the heavens and earth are captivating and breathtaking. Our attempts to capture and replicate the beauty through film, photo, and artwork escape us—it is too wonderful, too magnificent.

The earth—and humanity, in all its diversity—were created to glorify and please God.

PRAYER

Lord, you are majestic in all your ways and in all you have made. You are alone God, and you have no equal. You alone are worthy of glory, honor, and worship.
I praise your name this morning, oh, Most High! Amen.

Our Father in heaven, may your name be kept holy.

THE LIGHT OF RIGHTEOUSNESS

WORD

The way of the righteous is like the first gleam of dawn,
which shines ever brighter until the full light of day.
But the way of the wicked is like total darkness.
They have no idea what they are stumbling over.

Proverbs 4:18–19

THOUGHT

The sky was cloudless and star-filled above the little valley just outside the small town of Van Buren, Arkansas. The only sounds were a few crickets and tree frogs creating a tranquil mantra for the moment.

First, light slowly unveiled the silhouette of the oak, cedar, and sweet gum trees hosted by the hilltop to the east of the valley, and prelude to a beautiful sunrise. The slowly emerging light was beginning to descend the hillside. Soon the entire valley was visible revealing a heavily dew-covered meadow. As the sunrays interacted with the water droplets on the winter grass it created the effect of hundreds of thousands of tiny LED lights spread upon the ground.

This scene serves well to illustrate the desire in the heart of the Father to illuminate his good paths for each person. The beauty of his will is before all and waits to be revealed by his light.

Some discover this light as it is Christ who illuminates the unfolding adventure of the Father's will for all who would seek him. Others sadly do not as they doubt or resist the light of the world, missing what he has prepared for them as it remains hidden by the darkness.

The wise embrace, submit, and follow the will of the Lord, making their way as bright as the clearest of days. The will of God is perfect in every way for every individual. It is divine destiny so brilliant and abundant in design, it causes perplexity as to why anyone would rather walk about in the absence of light.

The Christ-life is the intended heart of the Father for all; it is his architecture for us to know and experience the way, the truth, and the life.

PRAYER

My heart, Lord, is to honor you in rightly identifying and walking the path
you have designed for me to follow. Illuminate the unfolding steps that best serve you
and your will. Amen. May your kingdom come soon.

May your will be done on earth, as it is in heaven.

WE LIVE IN HOPE

WORD

"Lord, remind me how brief my time on earth will be.
Remind me that my days are numbered—how fleeting my life is.
You have made my life no longer than the width of my hand.
My entire lifetime is just a moment to you;
at best, each of us is but a breath."
And so, Lord, where do I put my hope?
My only hope is in you.

Psalm 39:4–5, 7

THOUGHT

Our life is short, fleeting, and best lived when our hope is placed fully in Christ.

In almost a half century of ministry, graveside visits to honor the departed have been numerous and have included both the very young as well as those who lived exceptionally long lives.

Each memorial service brings the reminder of the fragility of life and the uncertainty of its conclusion as well as the importance of investing the time in our lives wisely. Death is inescapable and this earth life ends for everyone. Whether rich, poor, powerfully important, or little-known by earth's measurement, we all pass from this life and leave our borrowed earth-shell behind.

Each human life is valuable because each has as their Creator, Jehovah God. Each is given opportunity to allow the optimum stewardship of life by entrusting it into the care of God the Father through a relationship with Jesus. Whether then the days in our life are many or few, their value is assessed by how devoted we were in our love and service to the Lord.

We will discover in seeking his kingdom and righteousness, accompanied with following his will, is his daily provision to accomplish it. We are instructed by the Lord not to seek the wealth of this world or worry about sustenance, but to seek his kingdom and his righteousness, and to pray for daily provision.

PRAYER

Lord, you say in your Word, "Our days on earth are like grass; like wildflowers, we bloom and die"
(Ps. 103:15). But I'm grateful that your Word also tells us that your love remains forever
with those who fear you I trust in you to lead me and to provide whatever needed
to fulfill your will. You are my hope for all things. Amen.

Give us today the food we need.

THE FREEDOM OF GRACE

WORD

When people work, their wages are not a gift, but something they have earned. But people are counted as righteous, not because of their work, but because of their faith in God who forgives sinners.

Romans 4:4–5

THOUGHT

No power of man could have ever provided release from the lethal grip of sin on humanity. There existed no armada, no massive army, and no weaponry sufficient enough to deliver us from the clutches of the evil one. Our own works to self-heal and self-purify are insufficient. Only the hand of God, only the redemption of Christ, provide escape from sin's dark dungeons.

True freedom is unearned and undeserved, and it is through God's grace alone that we are welcomed into it. True freedom came as the result of love and mercy—in the unlikely form of a man—from the heavenly Father and Creator himself. Forgiveness came in the life, death, and resurrection of Jesus Christ.

The most wonderful truth is this: freedom and forgiveness are available to as many as who receive the Son of God as their Lord and King. Christ's lavish grace welcomes us in as sons and daughters—and that is surely a reason to always be rejoicing.

PRAYER

You and you alone, Lord Jesus Christ, have given me freedom—motivated by your love and accomplished by your sacrifice. Covered by your grace, I am no longer condemned to death but now live in the hope of your glory. Amen.

And forgive us our sins, as we have forgiven those who sin against us.

ONE APPROVED BY CHRIST

WORD

Greet Apelles, a good man whom Christ approves.

Romans 16:10a

THOUGHT

At the end of our days, when we come face-to-face with Christ himself, we can only hope to hear the same accolade that the apostle Paul writes about Apelles.

This truly is a most honorable commendation from Paul concerning the character of Apelles, a fellow believer in the Roman church. Paul begins his Roman letter declaring himself a slave of Christ and confirms the good news to those in Rome: that they are loved by God and called to be holy. In the latter portion of the letter, Paul sends personal thanks and greetings to several individuals, and this is where he esteems Apelles.

Paul wrote with conviction, sincerity, and passion, but he also was straightforward and used words economically. Consider the honor to have been mentioned with such a positive tone in an open letter, for Paul was not one given to idle words. He obviously knew the heart of Apelles and saw the fruit of his service to Jesus.

What more encouraging and affirming words could be said of any humble follower of Christ than he or she *is a good person of whom Christ approves.*

PRAYER

I pray, Lord, that you would continue to lead me—through the power of your Holy Spirit—and make my life one that is honorable and approved by you. Amen.

Don't let us yield to temptation.

ABIDING IN HIS PRESENCE

WORD

How lovely is your dwelling place,
O LORD of Heaven's Armies.
I long, yes, I faint with longing
to enter the courts of the LORD.
With my whole being, body and soul,
I will shout joyfully to the living God.
Even the sparrow finds a home,
and the swallow builds her nest and raises her young
at a place near your altar,
O LORD of Heaven's Armies, my King and my God!
What joy for those who can live in your house,
always singing your praises.

Psalm 84:1–4

THOUGHT

Each spring a small bird called an Eastern Phoebe visits our home and builds a nest under the covering of our front porch. There is a lot of other activity in our home throughout the year: small-group meetings, counseling appointments, visits from missionaries, and stopovers from family and friends. Although the front door is quite busy with many comings and goings, the Eastern Phoebe still finds a home and raises her young on our porch.

Perhaps the heart of the psalmist was captured by a similar notion or scene in the house of the Lord; possibly, he visited the temple and noticed a bird on its nest in one of the most sacred of places. He recalls the internal loveliness and joy he experiences when he is there, and he longs, not only to visit, but also to abide within it to experience the presence of God continually.

Oh, to be even a sparrow that I could find a place of continual habitation in your house!

PRAYER

Oh, Lord, your Word reveals there is joy found in your presence. Because of Christ, your tabernacle is now in the hearts of those you have redeemed. In your presence is safety, refuge, and deliverance from evil. May I abide in the life of your abundant presence. Amen.

But rescue us from the evil one.

GOD OF THE AGES

WORD

...all glory to him forever! Amen.

Romans 11:36

THOUGHT

I completed a ministry event one evening at Boston University in a mid-sized room just off Commonwealth Avenue. The students had been kind and receptive, and the evening was enjoyable. Afterward, the event coordinator drove the two of us to his home where his wife had prepared a meal, and we sat talking about the evening and rich heritage of the area.

At some point the topic arose of antiquated hymns and my newly discovered appreciation of them. The husband left the room and returned with a gift, a very slender small book, an old Methodist hymnal published October 1779.

I remember carefully turning through its pages the next day on my flight home. I was amazed at its age, the rich prose contained on each page, and wondered of the history of its past owners. The songs it hosted were poetic, contained depth of meaning, and were grounded in solid theological moorings.

The hymn composers were obviously given to lifestyles embedded in and narrowly focused on God's matchless superiority and his intent and interaction with humankind. The number of compositions alone in this hymnal indicated their commitment and time investment to proclaim the glory of God. One of the writers in the hymnal was Charles Wesley, who is attributed to penning over 6,000 songs with some historians estimating upward to 8,000.

The hymnal sits with several others in an antique bookcase in our home. They are one of the many reminders to me of the wealth of creativity inspired by the Holy Spirit to give honor to the majestic one, the Ancient of Days.

THE PRAYER

Lord you are the inspiration for all genuine and pure creativity.
You are indeed glorious from eternity past to eternity future and worthy of all our worship. Amen.

For yours is the kingdom and the power and the glory forever.

THE IMMENSITY OF GOD

WORD

The LORD merely spoke,
and the heavens were created.
He breathed the word,
and all the stars were born.
He assigned the sea its boundaries
and locked the oceans in vast reservoirs.
Let the whole world fear the LORD,
and let everyone stand in awe of him.
For when he spoke the world began!
It appeared at his command.

Psalm 33:6–9

THOUGHT

These can be difficult verses for those who conclude the earth is the result of random natural development. However, if we believe only in what we *can* understand or *choose* to understand, then we are destined to live a limited and less fulfilled life on this earth. God, who is immense in power and unlimited in creativity, has indeed made and sustains all things. The finite mind will never fully comprehend God's unlimited capacity.

We are granted only limited insight into the vastness of the Holy One. Yet we are invited into an intimate relationship with the Creator and Sustainer of all things. Passage and permission into this rarest of relationships is through the mysterious but wonderful way of faith.

THE PRAYER

Lord, when I dwell on the whole of creation, I discover quickly the finite manner of my humanness. I am in awe of your greatness, and I'm grateful for my part in your vast plan I am grateful to have you as my protector and provider, my Lord and Savior. There is none like you, you alone are holy, you alone are worthy of praise. Amen.

Our Father in heaven, may your name be kept holy.

COMMUNION WITH GOD

WORD

He sends the snow like white wool;
he scatters frost upon the ground like ashes.

Psalm 147:16

THOUGHT

Snow causes an unusual stillness and silence. When it falls, the few sounds that do occur are subdued. As I'm writing this, I am enjoying the beauty and calm of an early spring snow that has blanketed our small valley in Arkansas.

Truly, the whole of Psalm 147 is a song of the handiwork of God. He is the Creator and Sustainer—he is the Lord of all, in all, and over all. While reflecting on this truth, a quiet, snowy morning became filled with new depths of respect and appreciation for God as Creator, and a greater understanding of the holiness of his presence was realized. All heaven and earth—every creature, every element, and every moment—is under his command. And somehow still in his greatness, God is always ready to enjoy deep communion with any child of his who is willing.

We can rejoice in this: the Lord seeks to commune with us and reveal aspects of his greatness to us—even through simple acts of creation like snow. He invites us into his presence so that he can gently introduce us to his revelation and glory and love, wanting us to enjoy it with him.

PRAYER

Praise to you this morning, Lord Jesus. I am under your care, in the loving hands
of the living God whose ways are infinite and endless. You abide with your children,
and you bless them with your presence. Thank you. Amen.

May your kingdom come soon. May your will be done on earth, as it is in heaven.

FROM NOTHING TO SOMETHING

WORD

...Abraham believed in the God who brings the dead back to life
and who creates new things out of nothing.

Romans 4:17

THOUGHT

Only God can create something new from nothing. The proof of God's love for us was sending his only Son, Jesus Christ, to set us free from the sentence of death. Believing by faith in Christ and his redemptive work is the key to being made new and entering into eternal life with the Father. This is the promise of promises, the gift of gifts, and the miracle of miracles!

Because of the Father's love for us and because of his desire to be in lasting relationship with us, he did what no one else could do: he made *something* of us when we were *nothing*. How? When we were unworthy because of our sin, Christ died for us and made us heirs in his kingdom. And this is God's nature and character: to make something from nothing. He made the world and all it contains when there was not the least bit of substance to do so. He made a way for hope when nothing but hopelessness existed. He takes worthless people and gives them destiny, divine purpose, and genuine life!

Be humble in this day. Be grateful in this day. Stand on the great promises God has given, for he took our "nothing" lives and created us beautiful in his sight.

PRAYER

This morning, Lord, awaken within me the everlasting joy of knowing you as my heavenly Father.
Your great work on the cross has taken a worthless thing and made it a vessel of beauty
in your eyes. You created in me a new heart, a new life! Amen.

Give us today the food we need.

SET FREE

WORD

Oh, what joy for those whose disobedience is forgiven, whose sin is put out of sight!

Yes, what joy for those whose record the Lord has cleared of guilt, whose lives are lived in complete honesty!

When I refused to confess my sin, my body wasted away, and I groaned all day long.

Day and night your hand of discipline was heavy on me. My strength evaporated like water in the summer heat.

For you are my hiding place; you protect me from trouble. You surround me with songs of victory.

Psalm 32:1–4, 7

THOUGHT

Located in the trees some thirty feet from our home sits a small, self-contained eight-by-ten-foot room. We call it "the Nook," and its purpose is to provide a quiet place to rest, read, and pray. One morning I noticed a small bird had squeezed through a slightly opened door and was desperately attempting to escape. It flew from end to end and side to side but found no way out. When I approached the Nook to attempt to free it, the bird became more frantic, slamming into the windows. I stood still; the bird was tired and breathing rapidly, all its energy exhausted.

I slipped through the door and gently cupped my hands over the small, fatigued animal now perched on a window ledge. There was little struggle to escape my grasp, and once outside, I released the bird. Now free, it flew quickly into the wooded area behind our home.

Without Christ, we are hopelessly trapped in our own sin with attempts to escape being futile. But God's mercy and grace await, offering us freedom and forgiveness. As David illustrates in Psalm 32, when we realize our dilemma and surrender to the Lord's salvation and will, we become a soul set free.

PRAYER

Lord, like the bird, I was hopelessly trapped in my sin with no possible way to escape on my own. When I confessed my sin and my helplessness, you came and rescued me, covered me with grace, and delivered me. All glory to God: my help, my hope, my deliverer, my sustainer. Surrounding me are the songs of victory. Amen.

Forgive us our sins, as we have forgiven those who sin against us.

REVEALING THE PATH OF PEACE

WORD

You will tell his people how to find salvation
through forgiveness of their sins.
Because of God's tender mercy,
the morning light from heaven is about to break upon us,
to give light to those who sit in darkness and in the shadow of death,
and to guide us to the path of peace.

Luke 1:77–79

THOUGHT

Here in Luke 1, we find the final words in Zechariah's prophecy concerning John the Baptist's privileged mission to pave the way for Jesus's ministry. *Because of God's tender mercy, the morning light of heaven is about to break.* What a beautiful image of the Word becoming flesh. Jesus, the Good News of the kingdom of heaven, was about to embark on his earthly mission to bring light to humankind. Darkness would no longer be the conqueror, but instead it would be conquered through the unbeatable power of the cross of Christ. What an honor for John to declare that heaven's light was coming to penetrate the darkness and lead all who were willing to the path of peace.

When we ask the Lord to steer us from temptation, we are revealing our desire to be led by God in the ways of Christ. Christ's arrival to his completed mission has given the ultimate guidance from darkness to light if we choose. The intensity of that light has led (and still leads) all who say *yes* to the truth of Christ.

PRAYER

Thank you, Father, for sending your Son as the light to the world. Thank you for leading me
to the path of peace and delivering me from the darkness. I pray for your continued leading
to all things Christ, and may I be found until my last breath telling the story
of Jesus Christ, his path to peace as the giver of life. Amen.

Don't let us yield to temptation.

March 17

GOD'S RESCUING POWER

WORD

He is my loving ally and my fortress,
my tower of safety, my rescuer.
He is my shield, and I take refuge in him.
He makes the nations submit to me.

Psalm 144:2

THOUGHT

The psalmist David knew the rescuing power of the Lord. It almost seems that David was always being chased down by a foe, but the Lord provided for him and protected him throughout his life. Through God's will and power, even nations submitted to David. In our own times of trouble, our first response may not always be to seek the Lord, but it is true that he still provides us with his rescuing power today.

In January 1992, I met an outstanding young man while on an extended visit to Moscow, Russia—we'll call him Martin. He was a strong, energetic believer in Christ with a robust yet childlike personality and faith. He told me of an event that occurred during the fall of communism in his country. Marxist loyals within the military had commandeered a large number of tanks and were bound for a government building, intent on expelling the young democratic patriots, fueled by hope for a better future for their country, holed up inside.

When Martin saw the potential setback from the recent advances toward liberty, he boldly proceeded to the location where the column of tanks was prepared to attack. He ran to the lead tank, placed his hands on the vehicle, and prayed a brief but effective prayer to rebuke the advance of evil in the name of Jesus Christ. God answered his prayer, providing protection and rescue. The column of tanks ceased to advance at that very spot, with the lead tank remaining there to this day as a symbol of victory and the fall of communism.

PRAYER

Lord, our enemy is intent on preventing the advancement of your kingdom, but you have no equal and victory is yours. Deliver us from the plans of the evil one as we stand in the victory of your grace, declaring your glory. Protect us from the enemy as we do your will. Amen.

But rescue us from the evil one.

THE WONDER OF THE CREATOR

WORD

When I look at the night sky and see the work of your fingers—
the moon and the stars you set in place—
what are mere mortals that you should think about them,
human beings that you should care for them?
Yet you made them only a little lower than God
and crowned them with glory and honor.
You gave them charge of everything you made,
putting all things under their authority—
the flocks and the herds
and all the wild animals,
the birds in the sky, the fish in the sea,
and everything that swims the ocean currents.
O LORD, our Lord, your majestic name fills the earth!

Psalm 8:3–9

THOUGHT

Have you ever had one of those moments where you're so overcome with God's glory that the only sufficient response is to rest in wonder and awe of his majesty?

The Creator of the heavens and earth, the Lord we love and serve, is incomprehensible in his majesty, filling the heart of his sons and daughters with awe and wonder. We're able to see but a small portion of his handiwork from where we stand this side of heaven, yet—much as the psalmist in these verses expresses—it is often still more than we can take in.

Though we're mere mortals, products of his divine creation, somehow this incomprehensible God desires close relationship with us and made a way for us to experience it. He is like no other—he's one who cannot be understood or measured—yet he has created a way for us to communicate with him, be in his presence, and call him *friend.* Yes indeed, the wonder and awe of it all!

PRAYER

Father, there are times when I see but a small portion of your handiwork and it overwhelms me because of how great you really are. I worship you, the Lord of glorious wonder. Amen.

For yours is the kingdom and the power and the glory forever.

OUR INCREDIBLE GOD WHO IS WORTHY OF WORSHIP

WORD

*Now all glory to God, who is able to keep you from falling away and will bring
you with great joy into his glorious presence without a single fault. All glory to him who alone is
God, our Savior through Jesus Christ our Lord. All glory, majesty, power, and authority are
his before all time, and in the present, and beyond all time! Amen.*

Jude 1:24–25

THOUGHT

Contained in this closing benediction of the book of Jude, we find verses that
remind us of God's unequaled authority, singularly held position, and unparalleled
power. These scriptures underscore his ability to keep us safely protected through the
perils of this earth-life as we go about his will, and then they reassure us that, in Christ,
we will be brought before God's eternal presence in heaven without a single fault.

Through Christ, God has gifted us righteousness and purity, allowing us to enter
the gates of his holiness and enjoy him forever. Our incredible God alone is worthy of
our worship and praise! All glory, power, and authority are his through eternity past,
present, and in the ages to come—beyond all time.

PRAYER

*My dear Lord and Savior, I glorify your name this morning. Without you I would be lost, alone,
and abiding forever in darkness. You brought me light and life. I am humbled, grateful,
and I worship your name in these early morning hours. Thank for your grace, for forgiving me,
and for leading me to your salvation. Amen.*

Our Father in heaven, may your name be kept holy.

WORKING FOR CHRIST

WORD

Work willingly at whatever you do, as though you were working for the Lord
rather than for people. Remember that the Lord will give you an inheritance as your reward,
and that the Master you are serving is Christ.

Colossians 3:23–24

THOUGHT

We can often spend far too much of our Christian lives waiting for some grandiose idea, plan, or expectation to unfold as God's will instead of simply following these instructive words from the apostle Paul.

Paul tells us to cultivate the message of God's kingdom wherever we are at the moment. If we are sincerely given to Christ as his servants, trusting him for his divine leadership, we should understand he is always working in and through us. No matter our vocation or current circumstances—whether we are serving in full-time ministry, leading a company, cooking in a kitchen, recovering in a hospital, cleaning office spaces, servicing machinery, or are simply unable to work—the Lord places us right where he wants to use us most.

Whatever we do, we should bring him honor in our work. We are always somewhere in the process of his will, and ultimately, he is our inheritance.

PRAYER

Holy Spirit, I ask you to guide my steps today, knowing you will unfold the will of the Father
before me. I thank you for the day that you have provided for me, and I'm grateful
for every breath on this earth that I'm able to do your will. Amen.

May your kingdom come soon. May your will be done on earth, as it is in heaven.

GENUINE, ABUNDANT LIFE

WORD

The Spirit of the Lord is upon me,
for he has anointed me to bring Good News to the poor.
He has sent me to proclaim that captives will be released,
that the blind will see,
that the oppressed will be set free,
and that the time of the Lord's favor has come.

Luke 4:18–19

THOUGHT

With the forty-day desert experience behind him, Jesus was now in a synagogue in Nazareth reading from Isaiah. When he finished, he handed the scroll to the attendant and sat down. With all eyes in the room on him, he said, "The Scripture you've just heard has been fulfilled this very day!" (Luke 4:21)

With his own death and resurrection yet ahead of him, Jesus could confidently announce the path to freedom and abundant life had arrived because he knew the flawless, unfailing plans of his Father.

Because of Christ, we get to enjoy genuine life as God intended for it to be lived: released from the captivity of sin, granted full spiritual sight, freed from the pain of oppression (even in times of oppression) with our value grounded in him, and granted his favor in every moment. Without argument, his plan for us is the best, and it leads to genuine, abundant life.

PRAYER

Father, through your redeeming grace, I've found the unfailing path to freedom and eternal life.
This is the ultimate provision, and I gratefully, thankfully, praise you. Amen.

Give us today the food we need.

THE GRACE-FILLED LIFE

WORD

But very early on Sunday morning the women went to the tomb, taking the spices they had prepared. They found that the stone had been rolled away from the entrance. So they went in, but they didn't find the body of the Lord Jesus. As they stood there puzzled, two men suddenly appeared to them, clothed in dazzling robes.

The women were terrified and bowed with their faces to the ground. Then the men asked, "Why are you looking among the dead for someone who is alive? He isn't here! He is risen from the dead! Remember what he told you back in Galilee, that the Son of Man must be betrayed into the hands of sinful men and be crucified, and that he would rise again on the third day."

Luke 24:1–7

THOUGHT

For two millennia, the resurrection of Jesus Christ has been surrounded by controversy. This should come as no surprise since what we believe about Christ, his life, mission, and our position with him are life-altering decisions of the highest magnitude.

Those who embrace him have the undeserved privilege of living a grace-filled life. Because of God's great grace—displayed in the giving of his Son—we have forgiveness of our sins, unlimited provision to complete his will, peace that passes all understanding, and so much more. Jesus Christ, motivated by love, willingly sacrificed his life for the sins of the world. He lived among us, was crucified, rose from the dead three days after he was killed, remained for forty days with his disciples sharing with them about the kingdom of God, and then in the clouds to the right hand of the Father where he reigns forever.

The grace of God made a way for all who believe in him to turn from our sin, be forgiven, receive eternal life, and abide with him forever.

PRAYER

Father, you are the risen King of glory, the only one deserving of honor and worship. Thank you for loving me in your abundant mercy and grace. Because of your life, I have life. Amen.

Forgive us our sins, as we have forgiven those who sin against us.

LETTING GO OF SELF

WORD

Those who love their life in this world will lose it. Those who care nothing for their life in this world will keep it for eternity. Anyone who wants to serve me must follow me, because my servants must be where I am. And the Father will honor anyone who serves me.

John 12:25–26

THOUGHT

Here Jesus reveals the pathway to genuine freedom with a heart of compassion, love, and deep longing for people to understand the impact of his message.

Human history is filled with stories of selfishness—self-preservation, self-centeredness, self-exaltation. Jesus reveals the eventual destruction that comes when we make self-seeking our goal and purpose. He exposes that chasing fame and fortune eventually lead to feelings of emptiness, purposelessness, and hopelessness. There is no greater tragedy than gaining the whole world while losing the soul (Mark 8:36).

In contrast, Jesus teaches that all who lay aside self-agendas and take up the causes of his kingdom would be honored by our perfect Creator, our Father in heaven.

Selfishness is a common temptation among most of us. It rears its pathetic head all too often, and is a foe best avoided in remembering Christ's humility to defeat it and our access to the humility of Jesus through the Holy Spirit and his fruit (Gal. 5:22–23).

PRAYER

My God and my King, I dedicate my life solely for your glory. Holy Spirit, please bring your holy and grace-filled conviction in my life so I'm able to clearly see areas of myself that need to be fully submitted to Christ. I desire to do your will, and I truly want to set aside my own selfishness for your kingdom work. Amen.

Don't let us yield to temptation.

NEVER ALONE

WORD

Who will protect me from the wicked?
Who will stand up for me against evildoers?
Unless the LORD had helped me,
I would soon have settled in the silence of the grave.
I cried out, "I am slipping!"
but your unfailing love, O LORD, supported me.
When doubts filled my mind,
your comfort gave me renewed hope and cheer.

Psalm 94:16–19

THOUGHT

Many are the stories of people of faith who have been weak, vulnerable, and struggling with doubt. Perhaps the cause was an illness, the death of a loved one, deep concern for future provision, or a prodigal son or daughter.

Jesus told us to allow him to provide for whatever circumstance might occur, to seek his kingdom first, and not to worry. However, in our humanity, we are often deceived by the evil one, and like the psalmist in the preceding verses, we sense we are slipping. Then our great God of mercy, like the arrival of rain in a drought, renews hope within us when doubt had nearly conquered us. The faithful love of the Lord introduces his spirit of comfort, ensuring that we are never alone—*even* in our doubts.

Can you recall times in your life when despair led your thoughts to doubt instead of trust? And when the Spirit of God, through his unfailing love, gently whispered, "When have I not cared for you?" He, indeed, has always been there with adequate provision.

PRAYER

Lord, you are the one who corrects my thoughts. You are the Lord of all, including what lies before me. Where there is doubt and distress, remind me of your faithful love and goodness and restore me to the hope which comes from you. Thank you for always being by my side. I'm grateful that, in you, I am never alone. Amen.

But rescue us from the evil one.

FILLED WITH GREAT JOY

WORD

Then Jesus led them to Bethany, and lifting his hands to heaven, he blessed them. While he was blessing them, he left them and was taken up to heaven. So they worshiped him and then returned to Jerusalem filled with great joy. And they spent all of their time in the Temple, praising God.

Luke 24:50–53

THOUGHT

How awestruck the disciples must have been to see Jesus ascend into heaven before their very eyes. The disciples had observed him as he talked by the sea and on hillsides. They watched as he touched the eyes of the blind and suddenly those eyes could see. They walked along roads with him, listened to his wisdom, heard his stories of the kingdom of God, and received instruction from him to continue the mission of sharing the good news. They experienced agony and emotional turmoil as he entered Jerusalem for the final time, and they watched him submit to the events leading to his death.

Oh, but the victory and wonder of his resurrection!

Now, after forty days among them again since his resurrection, he was ascending, his physical form disappearing as they strained their eyes against the sky in the hope to catch a final glance of his form. Saddened by his departure, but with hearts overflowing with great joy and expectancy, they worshiped the risen King.

PRAYER

Savior, I pray for my heart to be filled with the same joy, wonder, and expectancy of those who beheld you as you ascended. I worship you this morning, for you have shown me mercy and given me hope. I worship you in gratitude, for I will see you someday in all your glory. May I display genuine joy to all in my path today, for you are my God, my Savior, and my Lord, and I have much to rejoice in. Amen.

For yours is the kingdom and the power and the glory forever. Amen.

March 26

IT'S ALL FOR HIM!

WORD

*Oh, how great are God's riches and wisdom and knowledge! How impossible it is for us to
understand his decisions and his ways! For who can know the LORD's thoughts? Who knows enough
to give him advice? And who has given him so much that he needs to pay it back? For everything
comes from him and exists by his power and is intended for his glory. All glory to him forever! Amen.*

Romans 11:33–36

THOUGHT

We are limited and lack the ability to accomplish anything of lasting kingdom value
on our own. This truth, instead of spurring disappointment, should actually encourage
a spirit of gratefulness and peace in us through knowing God's wonderful adventure is
sourced by his unlimited riches and wisdom—and not by our own might.

Today's verses remind us the Lord is above us in all ways—even his way of thinking
cannot be understood. He is mighty, glorious, wise, and powerful beyond all measure.
And not only is this is the glorious wonderful God we are honored to worship, but we
are also honored to be called his children.

Everything which has existed, presently exists, and will exist is because of the Lord
and for the Lord. It's all for him—even our own lives!

PRAYER

*Lord God, you are my hope and my salvation. I rest in you this morning
as I dwell on the words of this passage. I have nothing and can do nothing without you
that is anything of true worth. You have shown me mercy and the way to life,
and I submit myself to your will and desire to be used for your glory. Amen.*

Our Father in heaven, may your name be kept holy.

March 27

DO THIS TO REMEMBER ME

WORD

Jesus took some bread and gave thanks to God for it. Then he broke it in pieces and said, "This is my body, which is given for you. Do this in remembrance of me." In the same way, he took the cup of wine after supper, saying, "This cup is the new covenant between God and his people—an agreement confirmed with my blood. Do this to remember me as often as you drink it."

1 Corinthians 11:23–25

THOUGHT

Without Christ's coming, and without Christ establishing the new covenant, all of humanity would have been hopelessly lost in the entrapment of sin, separated from God. In the moment recorded in these scriptures—Holy Communion—our remembrance of his provisional gift overflows with sincere, humble gratitude, for his love and mercy are immeasurable.

By participating in Holy Communion, we remember the empty, shallow, fruitless vanity of our once self-focused lives. We remember the helplessness we felt when attempting to redeem ourselves from the result of our sin. We remember the moment of our own salvation, a moment that transformed a familiar story in history into a personal, experiential encounter with the living God. We remember when our prison bars were destroyed, allowing us to escape into the genuine freedom of a life with Christ.

Yes, we remember when compassion and perfect affection led us to repentance; and we remember the escape from darkness through a threshold of grace by the power of Jesus Christ, the Son of God, the only way to salvation.

PRAYER

With a heart full of love and gratitude, Lord, I remember. For without you, I would be absent of hope and life. You I worship, you I honor and adore, and before you alone I bow. Amen.

May your kingdom come soon. May your will be done on earth, as it is in heaven.

PROVISION FROM THE FATHER'S HEART

WORD

From his abundance we have all received one gracious blessing after another.
For the law was given through Moses, but God's unfailing love and faithfulness came through Jesus
Christ. No one has ever seen God. But the unique One, who is himself God,
is near to the Father's heart. He has revealed God to us.

John 1:16–18

THOUGHT

With Jesus Christ as our Savior and Lord, we are no longer spiritual beggars and orphans, no longer spiritually homeless or abandoned. With Christ, we are no longer helplessly exposed to the elements of darkness that seek to harm us and bring us despair. We have protection *in* him, and we have provision *through* him.

In Christ, we are embraced by God's unfailing, fatherly love and faithfulness. The prince of this world and his plans for destruction were interrupted and thwarted by the Prince of Peace. Grace triumphed over injustice and goodness triumphed over evil. And in his abundant love, we have all received one gracious blessing after another!

PRAYER

Father, you are my provision for all things—beginning with the provision for the salvation of my soul. Thank you for delivering me from darkness and death, and thank you for abundant life. Amen.

Give us today the food we need.

DEALING WITH THE DIFFICULT

WORD

A servant of the Lord must not quarrel but must be kind to everyone, be able to teach, and be patient with difficult people. Gently instruct those who oppose the truth. Perhaps God will change those people's hearts, and they will learn the truth. Then they will come to their senses and escape from the devil's trap. For they have been held captive by him to do whatever he wants.

2 Timothy 2:24–26

THOUGHT

This may be the very day someone rudely challenges or opposes your faith. At some point, this happens to anyone committed to honor God with their lives.

Pride, criticism, and opposition will challenge the person given to fulfilling the will of God. There will be resistance and arguments, and they will seem—and may actually be—unfair. Difficulties will come to the believer in the form of insolence and perhaps from unexpected sources. When it happens, for surely it will, this passage instructs us how to respond in a way that will cause us to grow, honor God, and in the end, possibly invite the attacker to change their heart.

When dealing with difficult people or those who harshly oppose the faith, remember to answer with a kind word and extend the same grace that has been given to you through Christ Jesus.

PRAYER

Lord, your Spirit conducts your will upon the earth in all things. My desire is to honor you. Should there appear in my path someone set to cause harm, please guide me through the circumstance in such a manner to become more like you, and provide me with the words to say in that time. Amen.

Forgive us our sins, as we have forgiven those who sin against us.

EFFECTIVE WEAPONS

WORD

We are human, but we don't wage war as humans do. We use God's mighty weapons,
not worldly weapons, to knock down the strongholds of human reasoning and to destroy false
arguments. We destroy every proud obstacle that keeps people from knowing God.
We capture their rebellious thoughts and teach them to obey Christ.

2 Corinthians 10:3–5

THOUGHT

When it comes to dealing with the enemy, we are instructed by scripture not to engage defensively or offensively in our natural abilities. Our worldly weapons prove worthless as we wage war in the supernatural. The battle belongs to the Lord, and his methods against the enemy manifest differently than the strategies formed in the minds of people. In fact, God's ways often appear unrealistic and impractical. However, if they are the methods of God, they will prove effective.

Napoleon Bonaparte, the famous and often quoted military strategist, said this concerning Christ: "I know men, and I can tell you that Jesus Christ is no mere man," and "between him and every other person in the world there is no possible term of comparison."

Napoleon, along many other historical military figures before him and after him, founded empires through the use of force. Jesus Christ, however, establishes his kingdom through love. He is no mere man. God's ways are not our ways, and his "weapons" that lead him to victory are *not* our weapons.

PRAYER

Father, teach me your ways so I might see the things in my life that are obstacles to bringing you glory fully destroyed. Thank you that you are all-knowing and all-loving. I rejoice in being able to serve the one true God, who builds his lasting kingdom on the foundation of on love and mercy. Amen.

And don't let us yield to temptation.

OPEN TO ALL, YET ALL ARE NOT WILLING

WORD

You can enter God's Kingdom only through the narrow gate.
The highway to hell is broad, and its gate is wide for the many who choose that way. But the
gateway to life is very narrow and the road is difficult, and only a few ever find it.

Matthew 7:13–14

THOUGHT

"On our journey today we will walk through a very narrow passage."

Though these words might have been borrowed from a pastor's Sunday morning sermon, they were not. Instead, they were from an older gentleman who was our tour guide at Mammoth Cave the day my youngest son and I were caving in Kentucky. The two-hour trip would certainly not challenge a true spelunker, but it was an enjoyable, leisurely father-and-son adventure. On one part of the tour, there was a narrow passage—and, indeed, the passage with its low ceiling was a challenge. It was so narrow and low some of the cave visitors were notified ahead of the tour of the difficulty; the narrow passage was the only way through this portion of the cave.

Unlike the narrow passage at Mammoth Cave that eliminated some visitors from the tour, clearly God wants us all to know his saving grace—and all are invited to join. Jesus shows us the entrance to his kingdom is open, yet he also reveals the way as difficult. The only thing that disqualifies us is our own unwillingness to fully submit our lives to the Lord, not age, ethnicity, history, background, or income.

Unfortunately, those who are *unwilling* to take the narrow way of escape far outnumber those who are *willing*. Yet this is the only way of deliverance and rescue from the evil one.

PRAYER

Lord, may my life be a beacon this day pointing to you and the hope you provide.
I pray for those I come in contact with, may they see your kindness,
mercy, and grace, and choose the narrow way. Amen.

But rescue us from the evil one.

FOREVER FAITHFUL

WORD

Shout with joy to the LORD, all the earth!
Worship the LORD with gladness.
Come before him, singing with joy.
Acknowledge that the LORD is God!
He made us, and we are his.
We are his people, the sheep of his pasture.
Enter his gates with thanksgiving;
go into his courts with praise.
Give thanks to him and praise his name.
For the LORD is good.
His unfailing love continues forever,
and his faithfulness continues to each generation.

Psalm 100

THOUGHT

Each spring reminds me of regeneration, the renewal of life, the sense of time's passage, and the introduction of new beginnings. For me, spring is an annual reminder of the Lord's continued faithfulness and goodness. Everything exists for God's glory and divine enjoyment, including the changing of the seasons.

When I see the first glimpses of spring—leaf buds on trees, birds busily building nests, early spring flowers budding—I give thanks for the rhythms that God has put in place. He made the seasons, and they are his. And although seasons shift and the earth changes, his unfailing love and faithfulness continue through each generation.

Let us come before him with gladness and songs of joy, for we are his people and he is our Good Shepherd. He is forever faithful!

PRAYER

You, Lord, are faithful to all, through all generations. From the smallest to greatest of creation,
all is yours for your good pleasure. I worship you, Lord, for you have given me life.
You are holy, worthy, and forever my Lord and Savior. Amen.

For yours is the kingdom and the power and the glory forever.

HIS WONDERFUL WORD

WORD

How great you are, O Sovereign Lord! There is no one like you.
We have never even heard of another God like you!

2 Samuel 7:22

THOUGHT

We need only to dwell a few moments in the life-giving gift of God's Word to get a sense of his indescribable wonder, goodness, and greatness. From his Word, we discover simple and practical instructions for daily living, but we are also confronted with the unfathomable depth of his unexplainable mystery. For example, we do not deserve his love, yet he loves us. He is rightly justified to bring judgment on us, yet he has shown mercy. We were condemned to punishment, but he extended grace.

Who can understand why the Lord decided to extend his grace, to invite us into relationship with him? No one—but we are wise to humbly, repentantly, and gratefully embrace him in all his glory while submitting to his sovereignty and will.

Our relationship with him begins with us finding ourselves in him and trusting in his infallibility and perfect care. We will never completely understand or exhaust his depth, but spending time in his Word will give us a greater understanding of the mystery of who God is. Knowing him more intimately allows us to rejoice in his holiness and faithfulness.

PRAYER

I am overwhelmed by you, Lord. Sufficient words do not exist to honor your greatness.
Holy Spirit, I ask that you speak to me throughout my day and also when I take the time
to study your Word. Illuminate the scriptures so that I may more intimately know your love.
To you be all glory and honor forever. Amen.

Our Father in heaven, may your name be kept holy.

JOY, THE WILL OF GOD

WORD

Always be joyful. Never stop praying. Be thankful in all circumstances,
for this is God's will for you who belong to Christ Jesus.

1 Thessalonians 5:16–18

THOUGHT

Our daily roles are filled with positions, titles, and tasks given to us by the Lord. In today's Scriptures, Paul is directing us how we should live out our faith as we work in those positions, titles, and tasks. Going about our day's work with genuine joy—no matter our circumstances—testifies to the character of Christ.

When the Bible commands us to *always* be joyful and be grateful in all circumstances, does that mean we display a shallow and carefree happiness? Or that we smile to cover up the genuine sadness and grief experienced in our life here on earth? By all means, no.

Our day-to-day circumstances may weigh down our hearts, and although we are not exempt from experiencing real pain and suffering in this life, we can hold fast to the truth that even death itself cannot defeat the sons and daughters of God. The heart belonging to Christ is filled with joy and fueled with the knowledge of being eternally loved and provided for.

Never stop praying and being thankful, for this is the will of God!

PRAYER

Jesus, because of your grace and power in my life, you have given me great and lasting joy.
Please increase the kind of qualities you want to see in me so that I become more and more like you.
I want to clearly bear your name in a world needing to know your redemptive love. Amen.

May your kingdom come soon. May your will be done on earth, as it is in heaven.

NEW LIFE

WORD

Once we, too, were foolish and disobedient. We were misled and became slaves to many lusts and pleasures. Our lives were full of evil and envy, and we hated each other. But—When God our Savior revealed his kindness and love, he saved us, not because of the righteous things we had done, but because of his mercy. He washed away our sins, giving us a new birth and new life through the Holy Spirit. He generously poured out the Spirit upon us through Jesus Christ our Savior. Because of his grace he made us right in his sight and gave us confidence that we will inherit eternal life.

Titus 3:3–7

THOUGHT

Early one morning I saw two does and four young fawns eating berries and chasing one another around the field in front of our house. Most of us are typically fascinated by new life, whether fawns, puppies, kittens, or any baby animal. And when it comes to human babies, even the grumpiest adult can have a tender heart in the presence of a newborn.

This fascination with new life comes from a deep place within us. As adults, we consider baby humans and animals adorable or enthralling as they experience new life and explore the world, and we sometimes long for the innocence or simple joy we experienced in childhood. But thanks be to God, we do get to experience new life and simple joy in Christ Jesus!

Although our sins separated us from God, Christ provided a way through his body and blood for us to experience the redemption and freedom we couldn't earn on our own—new life! Love, grace, confession, and repentance result in spiritual new birth. When we experience new life in Christ, we are overwhelmed with gratitude, for spiritual new birth always brings joy to the family of God.

PRAYER

Father, I thank you this morning for the new life you have given me through your love, mercy, and provision of your redeeming grace. I'm beyond grateful for new life and fresh joy. This morning, I give all praise to you, the lover of my soul and giver of new life. Amen.

Give us today the food we need.

THE PRAYER OF FORGIVENESS

WORD

Jesus said, "Father, forgive them, for they don't know what they are doing."

Luke 23:34

THOUGHT

Christ was mocked, betrayed, falsely accused, humiliated, unjustly tried, cruelly beaten, and then nailed to two coarse wooden beams in the shape of a cross. Most of us would find it completely justified if Jesus had decided his tormentors should be destroyed for their actions. Yet in this unbearable moment of suffering found in Luke, Jesus prays the unthinkable, something that goes against our natural humanity: *Forgive them, for they don't know what they are doing.*

The word *forgiveness* means "to cancel a debt, to be freed of an obligation, or to receive pardon." And who are the subjects of Christ's prayer here? The Roman soldiers hammering nails through his flesh into the wood? The temple guards who arrested him in the garden? Was it Judas, the betrayer, or maybe Herod, Pilate, or the false witnesses who led to his crucifixion? His disciples who ran? Or the crowd that was yelling for him to be crucified? Yes, this prayer was for all who were involved in his death—including you and me.

Sin—yes, our own—caused the death of God's Son. But thanks be to Christ, he made the way for *all* to be forgiven and justified through his selfless, redemptive, sacrificial act.

PRAYER

Most gracious and merciful heavenly Father, may your name be forever praised and honored for your immeasurable love and abundant grace. I am unworthy, but through Christ you extend mercy and grace to a sinner like me. Thank you for forgiving me and welcoming me in as a child of God. Amen.

Forgive us our sins, as we have forgiven those who sin against us.

April 6

TO BE LIKE JESUS

WORD

Those who say they live in God should live their lives as Jesus did.

1 John 2:6

THOUGHT

Often the briefest, simplest statements contain the most weight and depth of truth and power—such as this single scripture. In 1 John 2:6, we're reminded the benefits of God's mercy and grace are found in following and emulating his Son by the power of the Holy Spirit.

John clearly tells us the proof of our Christianity is in living life as Jesus did. He loved perfectly, and his focus was the will of his Father. He was selfless, with pure motives and character. All who say they are of Christ will look and live as he did.

By our own might and strength, we are unable to live such a righteous life. However, through the guiding love of the Holy Spirit—which brings holy conviction and direction to us—and by the wisdom of God's word, we are able to clearly see how to live like Christ. May we serve, love, forgive, and include others the same way that he does.

PRAYER

Lord Jesus, I find myself with this simple prayer to you this morning: please,
by enabling your Holy Spirit, cause me to look and live like you.
I desire to honor you with my life, that it may be of genuine value in your kingdom. Amen.

Don't let us yield to temptation.

IN MY DISTRESS

WORD

For the glory of your name, O LORD, preserve my life.
Because of your faithfulness, bring me out of this distress.

Psalm 143:11

THOUGHT

Christians are not promised a life free of distress. Both Old and New Testament passages reveal the possibility, if not the *certainty*, of facing challenges and trials in this life. Despite this truth, wonderfully abundant are God's promises of peace and grace to meet our every need.

In today's scripture, the psalmist prays to the Lord for rescue. The writer asks God to intervene in the face of despair and danger so God will be glorified by others knowing the Lord comes to the aid of his children.

When difficult times come, we may not be able to change our circumstances—but the Lord will prevail. He is faithful to come to our aid and bring us out of our distress for his namesake.

PRAYER

Lord, when I am in despair, you tell me to trust and rest in your faithfulness. You deliver me
from fear and distress. I fix my eyes on you, my source of strength. When I am distressed,
you comfort me. You are the Shepherd of my life, the one who leads and protects me. Amen.

But rescue us from the evil one.

LET ALL CREATION PRAISE HIM

WORD

Let every created thing give praise to the LORD,
for he issued his command, and they came into being.
He set them in place forever and ever.
His decree will never be revoked.

Psalm 148:5–6

THOUGHT

Every created thing was given life through the Lord, and our response is to give him all the glory and honor and praise. However, our God is so amazing, words cannot supply us with sufficient expression for our adoration and awe.

The book of Psalms is full of countless praises to our King, but in all their lyrical beauty to assist us in our praise to God, we will never exhaust the list of reasons to worship God as the list is endless. In Psalm 40:5, the writer reveals frustration when attempting to fully express God in all his wonder, proclaiming God's plans are "too numerous to list" and that "if I tried to recite all your wonderful deeds, I would never come to the end of them."

We are given sufficient means to worship while living constrained in these earth shells. However, these passages hint of far more to come once we've stepped beyond this limited realm of the flesh and through the threshold into eternity. Absent there will be the constraints and limitations of all things temporal. God in his boundlessness will be forever worshiped in limitless fashion.

The awe-inspiring being who is praised within this psalm is Yahweh, our God and Creator. He is the great Commander of all created life and time—past, present, and future. He is Jehovah God, the Lord of all, and he's worthy to be praised!

PRAYER

Father, while I could never fully express my honor and respect for you or my love and gratitude,
I bow before you in worship. I desire to please you with my life as your servant,
and I humbly submit myself before you today. Let everything praise your name, Mighty King! Amen.

For yours is the kingdom and the power and the glory forever. Amen.

I LOVE YOU, LORD

WORD

I love you, LORD;
you are my strength.

Psalm 18:1

THOUGHT

Some days I find myself reading large portions of scripture, attempting to take in as many practical instructions and kingdom principles as I can so that I can apply them in my daily life. Other times, reading a section of scripture opens my heart to the Lord in new ways, providing me with revelations of his immeasurable qualities and great love.

Then there are the mornings—like this one—where I read but a few words and pause to drink in their simple beauty and truth, discovering I am unable to continue beyond what I have read. Eight simple words—*I love you Lord; you are my strength*—and I am undone.

Have the courage and patience to sit with small portions of God's Word and drink deep. These eight words speak to our identity as Christians and illuminate our destiny. We love him; he is our strength.

PRAYER

Lord, thank you for treasured and holy moments like this one where your Holy Spirit
provides an unexpected, deeper understanding of a brief and beautiful phrase.
It is the truth: I love you, Lord. You have my heart. Amen.

Our Father in heaven, may your name be kept holy.

April 10

ALONG THE WAY

WORD

As Jesus was walking along, he saw a man who had been blind from birth.

John 9:1

THOUGHT

Jesus was devoted to the will of the Father. He knew the mission was to liberate humanity from the darkness and death of sin. And he knew he was authorized and empowered by the Holy Spirit to do so. We, too, are commissioned by Christ and empowered by the Holy Spirit to continue his mission as we are "walking along" and going about our daily lives.

When Jesus would set out to new locations, he would watch, discern, and minister along the way—and so should we throughout our day. And whenever Christ was confronted by those in need, he would come to their aid.

As modern-day Christians, our pattern should be that of Christ. We, too, should discern and watch for the opportunities to serve and minister to people *along the way* within all chapters of our life's earth journey. We should attempt spiritual vigilance always, in hope for opportunities to bring help and encouragement to those in need whom we encounter.

We may design plans of noble opportunities and destinations in our lives; ones we think contain the best potential to honor God. But he may have opportunities *along the way* not within our playbook that might possibly yield the greater fruit for his kingdom.

PRAYER

Lord, may I see and hear you as you lead me through the day. Guide me to minister to others along the way just as you did. Lead me to the needs of those around me, and provide me with careful discernment and the words for each situation. Amen.

May your kingdom come soon. May your will be done on earth, as it is in heaven.

April 11

NEW MERCIES EVERY DAY

WORD

The faithful love of the LORD never ends!
His mercies never cease.
Great is his faithfulness;
his mercies begin afresh each morning.

Lamentations 3:22–23

THOUGHT

My mornings typically feel fresh and filled with peace and the excitement of new opportunities offered by our Father in heaven. How precious it is that the Lord's mercies toward us never cease; in fact, they are fresh with each sunrise. When we wake up, no matter what the day ahead contains, he has already lavished his mercy upon our life with our first morning inhale, a picture of favor and grace.

However unholy and undeserving we were before we met Christ, however unfit and unlovable we've been made to feel by the world's standards—all of that is dissolved in the light of Christ's mercy. Through the provision of the cross, he deems us worthy, lovable, righteous, and welcome as the children of God.

God's faithful love toward us never ends! Other sources of love will cease, but we are promised his love and his mercies never end. No wonder the writer's next words declare with increased energy, "Great is his faithfulness; his mercies begin afresh each morning" (v. 23). What sweet provision indeed!

PRAYER

Father, this morning my heart is overwhelmed by your goodness and
the magnificent beauty of your awesome promises. In your presence I am humbled;
my heart is grateful beyond words. Thank you, Lord, for loving me,
for being my Shepherd, and for being my Redeemer. Amen.

Give us today the food we need.

HONOR THE GIFT OF GRACE

WORD

How can I know all the sins lurking in my heart?
Cleanse me from these hidden faults.
Keep your servant from deliberate sins!
Don't let them control me.
Then I will be free of guilt
and innocent of great sin.
May the words of my mouth
and the meditation of my heart
be pleasing to you,
O LORD, my rock and my redeemer.

Psalm 19:12–14

THOUGHT

As Christians, we're recipients of God's great grace and cannot earn a more favorable position with him than we already experience. He has liberated us, he guides us by his Holy Spirit, and he is continually working to form us into the image of his only Son. Such is the way of grace.

While God does see us through the redeeming power of Christ's work, we are living in a fallen world, and we still experience all the weaknesses and flaws that come with that. Though covered in his robe of righteousness, we humbly come before him and pray the words of this great psalm, asking that he would cleanse us from the things hidden, guide us to follow his way, and not let us fall into any snare set for us by our enemy.

May the words of our mouths and the meditations of our hearts bring pleasure to God and honor him and his wonderful gift of grace.

PRAYER

Lord Jesus, you are my strong, solid Rock, and you are my Redeemer—for you alone were able to pay the price for my sin. Holy Spirit, please bring your holy and gentle conviction in my life, so that I would be aware of the places in my heart that do not honor you. By your grace, keep me from anything that would cause you dishonor. Instead, lead me in your strong and righteous path. Amen.

Forgive us our sins, as we have forgiven those who sin against us.

A LIFE WORTH ABANDONING EVERYTHING FOR

WORD

*Later, as Jesus left the town, he saw a tax collector named Levi sitting
at his tax collector's booth. "Follow me and be my disciple," Jesus said to him.
So Levi got up, left everything, and followed him.*

Luke 5:27–28

THOUGHT

Through the ages, many have heard of Jesus Christ, the forgiveness he extends, and the new life he offers through the gift of grace. It is the offer of a lifetime: redemption from our reckless choices and trespasses, from the guilt and shame of hurting others in the past, from our pain and loneliness.

To enjoy this gift, however, means to leave our old lives and to follow Jesus, to embrace him and his lifestyle, and to commit to a life of serving him.

In today's scriptures, Levi provides us an excellent example of the proper response to this great invitation. Jesus invites Levi to follow him, and upon the invitation, Levi gets up, leaving behind every hindrance, and commits himself to serving Christ. Our response to the love of Christ should be the same: leave our life as we know it and follow him. It may not be easy, but it is the wise, right, and life-giving choice. Nothing in this world compares to—or is worth forfeiting—the invitation to follow Jesus.

PRAYER

Father, you have extended the offer to follow you. May I never hesitate to receive you as my Savior and Lord, and may I never waiver on any request you would ask of me during my lifetime. Amen.

Don't let us yield to temptation.

April 14

MY REFUGE AND STRENGTH

WORD

Have mercy on me, O God, have mercy!
I look to you for protection.
I will hide beneath the shadow of your wings
until the danger passes by.

Psalm 57:1

THOUGHT

One spring, we experienced widely varying weather patterns that resulted in a series of severe thunderstorms, most of which produced tornadic conditions. One evening when the storms were particularly intense, we took shelter as a family in a small space under the staircase. The following day resulted in another storm: the wind blew fiercely and dime-sized hail pelted the ground. In a moment of fearlessness and curiosity (note, I did not say *wisdom*), I stepped out onto the front lawn with wind, rain, and hail blowing into my face and began to pray and rebuke the storm. Within a few seconds, the winds quieted and I returned to my work, giving thanks to the Lord for the gift of safety.

A similar situation occurred some days later; this time the hail was larger. I ran inside for shelter and prayed the Lord would cause the storm to pass without damage to anything. It did pass, but this time my prayer was sent from underneath the stairs and not bravely from the front lawn.

Psalm 57 was written when David was in danger. Honestly, there are times I feel as bold as a lion in my walk as a believer (much like when I went outside into the dangerous storm and prayed), but other times I find myself confused in dangerous situations, and I simply run to God for mercy and protection, praying for the danger to pass over me. In either response, God is there, providing me with refuge and strength.

PRAYER

Lord, my trust, my hope, and my strength are in you. I am reminded in my weakness that you are the source of my refuge and protection. When I face danger, I pray you will hide me in the shadow of your wings until it has passed. Thank you for your life-giving protection. Amen.

But rescue us from the evil one.

TAKE TIME TO PONDER

WORD

How amazing are the deeds of the Lord!
All who delight in him should ponder them.
Everything he does reveals his glory and majesty.
His righteousness never fails.

Psalm 111:2–3

THOUGHT

Although *ponder* is not a word often used anymore, it is the perfect word to describe a slow morning reflection on the deeds of the Lord. We are told not only to ponder the deeds of the Lord, but to take delight in *every* single one.

In our hurry to meet our daily responsibilities, we don't often stop to deliberately consider the incredible works of our King. Not only is his glory seen in the small things—the tiniest spring flower, a baby expressing joy for the first time, the majesty of a routine sunset—but we also see his glory in the big things—a person healed from sickness, a new Christian's first encounter with the tangible presence of God, the ever-enduring redemptive work of the cross.

This day, create room in your schedule to ponder the majesty of his work in your own life. From birth to this present moment, he has held you in his loving mercy and kindness. He deserves all power and honor and glory forever for his goodness toward us.

PRAYER

Indeed, Father, my heart is filled with awe, wonder, and gratitude.
The works of your hands are great and awe-inspiring, even in my own life. Your goodness knows
no bounds, and I directly benefit from that truth. You, Lord, are great and glorious.
You are righteous and holy. You alone are God and King forever. Amen.

For yours is the kingdom and the power and the glory forever.

HIS MASTERPIECE

WORD

For we are God's masterpiece. He has created us anew in Christ Jesus,
so we can do the good things he planned for us long ago.

Ephesians 2:10

THOUGHT

I was slowly driving the narrow lane up from our house toward the paved country highway. About halfway there, I caught a glimpse in front of me of some small animal in the middle of the dirt road. I stopped the car and realized it was a small bird. It was motionless at first, but then quickly darted into one of the many trees lining the old barbed-wire fence beside the lane. The little fellow's brightly colored blue, red, yellow, and green feathers were breathtaking. I thought to myself, *What a masterpiece God has made in creating this small, graceful bird.*

I have been infatuated with the animal kingdom for as long as I can remember. And as easy as it is for many of us to find the animal kingdom wonderfully creative, beautiful, and awe-inspiring, it's a lot harder for us to feel that way about our own humanity. However, although we live in a fallen world, the Lord created us *in his image* as his greatest masterpiece.

Through the redemptive work of Christ and our obedience to him, we get to step into a realm of things he has planned for us: good things that bring glory and honor to him as we walk where he leads us. He takes the bruised and broken parts of us and makes them new. He looks upon his sons and daughters with joy and the proud heart of a dad. Our God and Father of life does make beautiful things.

PRAYER

God, you have created me for good purposes and redeemed me through your Son,
the Savior for all humankind, Jesus Christ. I am the result of your divine craftsmanship
and exist for your great pleasure. Let this day, all you have planned for me
to accomplish and encounter, be done according to your will. Amen.

Our Father in heaven, may your name be kept holy.

FOR THIS IS THE WILL OF GOD

WORD

Jesus replied, "The most important commandment is this: 'Listen, O Israel!
The Lord our God is the one and only Lord. And you must love the Lord your God with all your
heart, all your soul, all your mind, and all your strength.' The second is equally important: 'Love
your neighbor as yourself.' No other commandment is greater than these."

Mark 12:29–31

THOUGHT

There is much to be gleaned from the words of Jesus contained in the four gospels.
They reveal his ministry and plans for his kingdom. But from all his teaching, we can
find a solid summary in today's passage of his heart and instruction while he was here
teaching us on earth.

Jesus conveyed that God's principal goal is for us to love him with unconstrained
devotion and with the whole of our being—and obeying this commandment produces
abundant life. Truly, loving God is the ultimate human experience; all other loves fail
to compare.

Jesus also instructs us to love our neighbor as much as we love our own self. Ultimately, how do we live out that commandment to its fullest extent? By sharing the love
and freedom found in Christ with others.

PRAYER

I love you, Lord, and I want to love you more. You said if I loved you then I should obey your
commands, and what you have commanded is that I love people as you do. Help me, Lord Jesus,
to be like you and share the good news of your kingdom with others. Amen.

May your kingdom come soon. May your will be done on earth, as it is in heaven.

HE DECIDES WHEN IT IS FINISHED

WORD

Jesus knew that his mission was now finished, and to fulfill Scripture he said,
"I am thirsty." A jar of sour wine was sitting there, so they soaked a sponge in it, put it on a hyssop
branch, and held it up to his lips. When Jesus had tasted it, he said, "It is finished!"
Then he bowed his head and gave up his spirit.

John 19:28–30

THOUGHT

One of the reasons it is essential to spend time in the Bible and in prayer is to develop a keen sensitivity to the Spirit of God, to develop the ability to distinguish his voice from the many other voices clamoring, competing, and attempting to distract us from him. God is sovereign, providential, and has purpose in his every action.

Jesus knew his mission well and how it was to unfold on this earth. It was one of great difficulty. It would have been easier for him to abort this mission, but he endured the cross until completion. Christ alone decided when his mission and his earth-life were complete, not his accusers, the Romans, or anyone else. Jesus alone had the power to declare *"It is finished."*

As his children, we are in his care—which means we are a part of his unstoppable divine plan that is playing out in our own story. Let him decide the chapter changes and conclusions, and allow him to write the epilogue. He alone has the power to decide what happens next.

PRAYER

Father, I pray my life would follow your way by your provision and for your glory. Help me to be obedient to what you ask of me, and provide me with what I need to accomplish your will. Amen.

Give us today the food we need.

April 19

THE FAITHFUL ONE

WORD

Jesus Christ is the same yesterday, today, and forever.

Hebrews 13:8

THOUGHT

When I was a young boy the signal for dinner was when my father pulled into our driveway at the end of his workday. He would walk in the back door, greet the family, put his lunch box on the kitchen counter, wash his hands, and then take his place at the table.

Then is when we would often discover how the mood of his supervisor had been during the workday, whether he was unreasonably grumpy or cordial. The frustration for my father was his supervisor's inconsistent and unforgiving temperament. On the rare days his boss was cordial, my dad would comment about the positive atmosphere in the shop.

It can be difficult to follow a leader who is erratic in their mood and decision-making, and who is also unforgiving.

Unlike fragile and broken humanity, Jesus Christ has, is, and will be consistently the same in character and leadership. He leads us with compassion, mercy, and grace, and his abilities and expectations are the same *always*. No changes or mood swings occur in him as a result of circumstance. His *yes* is yes, and his *no* is no, and his decisions are flawless.

He will never disappoint us, but should we disappoint him, he forgives the genuine heart who asks. Truly, Jesus is the always-faithful Rock upon which to build our lives. He does not recant his forgiveness of sin, and his love is permanent.

PRAYER

Thank you, Lord, for your faithfulness, forgiveness, and consistency. Thank you for your unwavering guidance and care. I always know what to expect from you. I know that what is best for your glory will ultimately also be best for me. Amen.

Forgive us our sins, as we have forgiven those who sin against us.

April 20

THE RIGHT PATH

WORD

Those who follow the right path fear the LORD;
those who take the wrong path despise him.

Proverbs 14:2

THOUGHT

Some scriptures seem to elude clarity at times, perhaps because they are tied to the old covenant or an ancient cultural practice long forgotten. There are also scriptures, such as those found in the book of Revelation, where the meaning will remain somewhat veiled until we arrive at the moment of fulfillment.

Then there are the many verses, such as Proverbs 14:2, where the purpose appears bright and clear with no room for misinterpretation. Scriptures like this one directly remind us of how we should be living in order to please our heavenly Father and bring him glory. It's simple: if we love him, we will follow him; if we choose to disobey, we are declaring boldly that we despise his good gift of grace.

Jesus said, "The gateway to life is very narrow and the road is difficult, and only a few ever find it" (Matt. 7:14). May we be the ones who hunt down the narrow way and follow it wholeheartedly.

PRAYER

Lord Jesus, you alone are the only way to the Father, to life.
Thank you for your mercy and revelation. I praise you for your love, grace, and
continued care over my life as I trust and follow you. Amen.

Don't let us yield to temptation.

April 21

FREEDOM FROM FEAR

WORD

I prayed to the LORD, and he answered me.
He freed me from all my fears.

Psalm 34:4

THOUGHT

We often do not need to look far beyond our own backyard to discover something that could cause us concern, discomfort, or fear. The local evening news is filled with enough trouble to keep us full of worry as we travel through our neighborhoods. However big or small, however global or local our fears may be, the Lord promises to deliver us from *all* fear.

But can this promise be taken literally? How is this possible?

The key is in this sentence: *I prayed to the Lord, and he answered me.* Prayer is encouraged throughout the Bible as a normal and vital part of the Christian life, but unfortunately, it's often the most neglected spiritual practice. A church dinner will often pack a room, but a call for a prayer meeting practically empties it.

Prayer is absolutely necessary for a healthy, growing, balanced spiritual life. Jesus told his disciples they should always pray and never give up (Luke 18:1), and the apostle Paul urges us to "never stop praying" (1 Thess. 5:17). When we pray, we are putting everything in God's hands and recognizing him as our true Deliverer and King, banishing our fear with a simple act of faith.

PRAYER

Father, thank you for the gift of prayer, and thank you for delivering me from my fears. Any strength that I would have lies in trusting you and seeking your answers and protection as I pray. Amen.

But rescue us from the evil one.

April 22

WHO BUT THE LORD?

WORD

You are my God, and I will praise you!
You are my God, and I will exalt you!
Give thanks to the LORD, for he is good!
His faithful love endures forever.

Psalm 118:28–29

THOUGHT

We were created to experience emotions—even in our relationship with the Lord—and we can easily see the full spectrum of emotional experience throughout the psalms. There are days we don't seem to "feel" him, but in our love for, trust of, and devotion to him, we keep marching forward. By faith, we place one foot in front of the other, following where God leads, simply because he is to be obeyed.

Then there are the days when our emotional experience feels overwhelmingly full and charged. We might feel like the psalmist in Psalm 73:25 who writes, "Whom have I in heaven but you? I desire you more than anything on earth."

In our journey of faith, there are times we're overcome with an awareness that nothing else can provide comfort or contentment other than the Lord's sweet presence. Who but the Lord can satisfy our hearts?

PRAYER

All else leaves me wanting, my Lord and my King. You have captured my heart,
and you've exposed my earthly desires as vanity when compared to life with you.
Wealth and fame do not satisfy the soul. Only you, and the hope of being in your presence,
bring peace. You are my God and I praise and exalt you! Amen.

For yours is the kingdom and the power and the glory forever.

April 23

HOLY

WORD

Exalt the LORD our God!
Bow low before his feet, for he is holy!

Psalm 99:5

THOUGHT

The most excellent way to begin each day is to acknowledge and honor the One who was here before us, made us for his purposes, and will be here when we leave this earth. We were created for his good pleasure. It's truly humbling to recognize everything—even our own existence—revolves around him and what he desires, not what we desire. He is the highest, the purest, the noblest. His character is flawless and all he does in thought and deed is wholly justified and righteous. Indeed, the Holy One alone is worthy of our worship.

This verse explodes with the command to worship the Lord, followed by the instruction to show adoration in a physical manifestation—expressed in the humblest of forms—by bowing low before the Lord's feet. Also revealed is the sheer delight of the worshiper, as the Lord is *our God*, the focal point and passion of the believer's heart.

What appears to be—and is—a command to worship could be perceived as a legalistic act, but it is actually the opposite for those who are after God's heart and presence. The heart given to the Lord finds honor, anticipation, privilege, and fulfillment in exalting the Holy One in worship.

PRAYER

Lord, though there are many things I could pray today, I choose instead to be still in honor
and worship of you, for truly you alone are God. You alone are holy,
and you alone are worthy of all glory!

Our Father in heaven, may your name be kept holy.

OUR SOURCE OF LIFE

WORD

Those who desert him will perish,
for you destroy those who abandon you.
But as for me, how good it is to be near God!
I have made the Sovereign LORD my shelter,
and I will tell everyone about the wonderful things you do.

Psalm 73:27–28

THOUGHT

The substance, character, and nature of God is love. He is the singular source of pure love, and he defines its very essence. His grace, originating from the depth of his love, moved him to extend mercy to us and provides us with the possibility for salvation. Refusing or denying his gracious and extravagant offer of forgiveness is like walking into an unforgiving desert with no provision for survival. Without the Lord, we perish.

In contrast, the psalmist says it is good for him to stay near God—his refuge, protection, and life-source. May we make it our goal to let everyone know the great wonders of our God, who gave his one and only Son so that we may enjoy eternal life with him. He alone is the true source of life.

PRAYER

I desire to remain in your presence, oh, Lord, for you alone are able to give abundant life and love.
You sustain me and give me breath. Please lead me to tell those in my path
of the wonders of your love, for this is your will. Amen.

May your kingdom come soon. May your will be done on earth, as it is in heaven.

April 25

OUR PLACE OF SAFETY

WORD

But as for me, I will sing about your power.
Each morning I will sing with joy about your unfailing love.
For you have been my refuge,
a place of safety when I am in distress.
O my Strength, to you I sing praises,
for you, O God, are my refuge,
the God who shows me unfailing love.

Psalm 59:16–17

THOUGHT

Each morning I will sing with joy about your unfailing love. I'm drawn to this psalm often, but when I really grasp the gravity of what's being said here, I am tempted to ask myself, *Seriously?*

What are we to do on the mornings we feel defeated or overwhelmed by our circumstances? What about the days we don't have enough energy to get ourselves out of bed, let alone enough joy to break out in song?

On difficult days, we can look back at our past and remember how God has been our deliverer and protector, faithfully rescuing us and leading us time and time again with his unfailing love. When we are distressed and overwhelmed, he is our hiding place, refuge, and place of safety. Whatever the cause of our concern, the provision to endure is found in God's unfailing love.

PRAYER

Father, I give sincerest thanks that each day, through your sufficient grace,
you provide the resources to meet whatever challenges I endure.
Thank you for being my place of safety and the source of all I need. Amen.

Give us today the food we need.

THE MESSAGE TO DECLARE

WORD

Then he opened their minds to understand the Scriptures. And he said, "Yes, it was written long ago that the Messiah would suffer and die and rise from the dead on the third day. It was also written that this message would be proclaimed in the authority of his name to all the nations, beginning in Jerusalem: 'There is forgiveness of sins for all who repent.' You are witnesses of all these things.

"And now I will send the Holy Spirit, just as my Father promised. But stay here in the city until the Holy Spirit comes and fills you with power from heaven."

Luke 24:45–49

THOUGHT

The phrase "you are forgiven" is powerful and liberating. Genuine and sincere forgiveness releases the heart from captivity and the weight of sin. When we repent and receive God's forgiveness, our hearts are released from oppression and we're filled with emotions beyond measure as we enter the life God intended for us.

In this passage, Jesus is addressing his disciples after the resurrection and before his ascension into heaven. He gives his disciples a great responsibility: as witnesses of the Scriptures coming to pass, his disciples were to proclaim Christ's message of redemption to all the nations through the power of the Holy Spirit.

Praise God there is forgiveness available for all who repent, and praise God the disciples obeyed, spreading the good news of Christ throughout the earth. Today, thousands of years after the death and resurrection of Jesus Christ, the experience of full and complete forgiveness remains relevant, alive, and ready for any open heart. The good news is always available for hearing ears, and the power of forgiveness is ready to free the imprisoned soul. May we not take our own salvation for granted, and may we share the truth of Christ with others.

PRAYER

Lord, a redeemed and grateful heart bows before you this morning. Fill me with your Holy Spirit, that I would be ready to boldly declare your good news to those who are willing to hear it. Amen.

Forgive us our sins, as we have forgiven those who sin against us.

April 27

UNTROUBLED

WORD

But all those who listen to me live in peace, untroubled by fear of harm.

Proverbs 1:33

THOUGHT

Peace is the promise to everyone who listens and takes heed to the wisdom and guidance of God. Based on my own struggles, as well as the observations of others over the decades, temptation has two traveling companions: one is named unrest and the other, anxiousness. Both are troublesome and neither is a good neighbor to peace.

Peace was designed by God to present the best functioning, healthy, spiritual heart. The advice and offer of Christ are to allow his peace to take up residence in us. His is an offer of permanence, unique from any temporal worldly counterfeits; his is the peace the world cannot offer. His is the peace so wonderful it cannot be fully understood.

Temptation is recognized by the absence of peace, so may all whose hearts find life in allegiance to Christ, pray well to be steered far from the abodes of temptation.

PRAYER

Lord Jesus, without you, peace is a mere concept—but in you, peace is certainty, as is hope. Lead me toward all things honoring of you. Amen.

Don't let us yield to temptation.

THE LORD, OUR FORTRESS

WORD

The LORD is my light and my salvation—
so why should I be afraid?
The LORD is my fortress, protecting me from danger,
so why should I tremble?
When evil people come to devour me,
when my enemies and foes attack me,
they will stumble and fall.
Though a mighty army surrounds me,
my heart will not be afraid.
Even if I am attacked,
I will remain confident.

Psalm 27:1–3

THOUGHT

Sometimes there is a mist lying low in the small valley near our house. On these misty mornings, when the light has yet to arrive, even though I peer carefully across the familiar landscape, everything seems foreign when cloaked in the darkness and fog. It's almost as if I were looking out onto a setting for a mystery novel or film. However, as soon as dawn casts enough light to shine on the valley, it's converted into a beautiful and peaceful scene.

In the Lord, we have unending light that penetrates the darkness. His light brings hope, peace, and the ability to see the path he leads us on. We need not fear what is hidden to us if our trust is in the Lord, for he is our protector from danger.

We learn from today's scripture that we are not exempt from the enemy's attack but are still sustained by Christ Jesus, the victor! He is our fortress: who shall we fear?

PRAYER

Lord, the psalmist David wrote that he could sit at your table in the very presence of his enemies
and be at peace for you were with him there. You are my light and my salvation; you are my refuge,
stronghold, and fortress. I should not fear because I rest in your strength and peace.
I am confident that, regardless of the enemy's strategy to do me harm this day,
you will deliver and protect me. Amen.

But rescue us from the evil one.

MAGNIFICENT!

WORD

The heavens proclaim the glory of God.
The skies display His craftsmanship.
Day after day they continue to speak;
night after night they make him known.
They speak without a sound or word;
their voice is never heard.
Yet their message has gone throughout the earth,
and their words to all the world.

Psalm 19:1–4

THOUGHT

Have you ever woken up early enough to enjoy a clear moon and starlit morning? Perhaps you did so today. The air during this time of year and at this time of day is often crisp and smells unusually fresh. On early predawn mornings, myriad brilliant stars and the moon's bright light reveal the handiwork of God, both above us and as they gently illuminate the earth below.

Day after day and night after night, the heavens continue to speak of God's faithfulness and majesty. Who but God could imagine and create such beauty? Who but God could make something so vastly wonderful that humans are unable to measure or catalog it?

Certainly, no human intelligence could ever have imagined or developed something of such indescribable immensity. Did God first create it in his mind's eye, or did he merely speak and it appeared? There is only one source who could accomplish such magnificence: his name is Yahweh, and he alone is God! His is the glory forever!

PRAYER

Father, you alone are magnificent. The only word I have to describe how I feel in moments of awe like these is speechless. *I love witnessing your majesty. Thank you for the moon, the stars, and the sky that all work to make your glory known. May I also make your glory known as I sincerely and humbly worship you in all I do today. You alone are worthy to receive worship. Amen.*

For yours is the kingdom and the power and the glory forever.

April 30

HIS MIGHTY WORKS

WORD

Praise him for His mighty works;
praise his unequaled greatness!

Psalm 150:2

THOUGHT

The child of God humbly honors and exalts God as the source of life, both now and into eternity. It is our privilege and call to honor God's greatness and praise him for his mighty works. While the enemy attempts to discredit and defame God, his works, and his Word, we have the honor of sharing true stories with others of God's goodness, provision, kindness, and forgiveness in our own lives.

Do not underestimate the power of humbly telling others the good news of what God has done in you or through you. You don't have to be a pastor, missionary, minister, or seminary student for this to have a meaningful and lasting effect in the lives of others around you. It honors our heavenly Father when we share with others how we've seen his glory in our life, and it builds faith in our communities.

The redeemed people of God will forever praise the Lord for his mighty works and his unequaled greatness. When all temporary things in this world fade and are forgotten, the Lord and his works will stand.

PRAYER

I humbly bow my heart before you this morning, my Savior and God. You are my life-source.
By the power of your Holy Spirit, help me tell the story of your mighty works—not only the ones
found in your Word, but also those I've experienced in my own life. You took a broken wretch
separated from your goodness, and drew me into the place where I could see your mercy
motivated from your love. There I laid aside failure, selfishness, and sin. There is where your grace
covered over this heart boundlessly. Glory to your name my Lord and my King! Amen.

Our Father in heaven, may your name be kept holy.

THE IRREVERSIBLE PROMISES OF GOD

WORD

The Spirit of the Sovereign LORD is upon me,
for the LORD has anointed me to bring good news to the poor.
He has sent me to comfort the brokenhearted
and to proclaim that captives will be released and prisoners will be freed.
He has sent me to tell those who mourn that the time of the LORD's favor has come,
and with it, the day of God's anger against their enemies.
To all who mourn in Israel, he will give a crown of beauty for ashes,
a joyous blessing instead of mourning, festive praise instead of despair.
In their righteousness, they will be like great oaks that the LORD has planted for his own glory.

Isaiah 61:1–3

THOUGHT

The entire Bible speaks truth, power, and life. This passage is one of tremendous power as it reveals the coming liberation for all people through the Savior Jesus Christ. Motivated by his boundless love and mercy, God will fulfill his promises not only to his people, Israel, but to all people. Whether Hebrew or otherwise, all can enter into the family of God through Christ.

When Christ appeared on the earth, he fulfilled this scripture and successfully completed the Father's plan for the reconciliation of humankind into the family of God. When God makes a promise, he keeps it! Once the promise was completed, all who would repent and believe in God's only Son would be freed from the bleak sentence of eternal darkness and death and welcomed into eternal light and life.

The will of God is for all to be liberated from darkness into God's marvelous light. Those who surrender their hearts and lives to Christ and the glory of his cross are adopted sons and daughters of Jehovah, God Most High. His promises are irreversible, and those who enter into the family of God will forever abide in his presence, worshiping and honoring him.

PRAYER

Lord, I was poor in spirit and you came to me with the good news of salvation. You brought comfort and healed my broken heart. You liberated me from a prison of darkness and poured your mercy and favor over me. I received beauty for ashes, joy in the place of sadness, and praise for despair. Through your grace, I am yours. Amen.

May your kingdom come soon. May your will be done on earth, as it is in heaven.

LOVED BY GOD

WORD

Therefore, since we have been made right in God's sight by faith,
we have peace with God because of what Jesus Christ our LORD has done for us.
Because of our faith, Christ has brought us into this place of undeserved privilege where we now
stand, and we confidently and joyfully look forward to sharing God's glory.

We can rejoice, too, when we run into problems and trials, for we know that they help us
develop endurance. And endurance develops strength of character, and character strengthens our
confident hope of salvation. And this hope will not lead to disappointment. For we know how dearly
God loves us, because he has given us the Holy Spirit to fill our hearts with his love.

Romans 5:1–5

THOUGHT

What a wonderful and powerful promise, to have a confident hope in Christ that does not disappoint! In this passage in Romans, Paul reminds us we have the undeserved privilege and honor of being taken care of, developed, and provided for by God, our heavenly Father.

Whatever we may endure in this earth-life, we have security in knowing that God will use trials and tribulations to refine our endurance, develop our character, and, ultimately, strengthen our hope in him. Although we may feel uncomfortable, afraid, or even lost and depressed when experiencing difficulty, nothing we experience will go unused by God for our good and his glory—and nothing can separate us from the love of God. We can trust in him and his plans, for his Word makes it known that he loves us dearly, he is with us in every moment, and he has provided the incredibly lavish gift of his Holy Spirit to guide us and fill our hearts with his love.

PRAYER

Father, I rejoice in the truth that you use every difficulty to refine my character,
strengthen my hope, and increase my faith. I'm grateful for the gift of your Holy Spirit
who reminds me of your love and truth. I stand in awe of you this morning asking
for the faith to follow you anywhere and always. Amen.

Give us today the food we need.

UNDERSTANDING FORGIVENESS

WORD

And forgive us our sins,
as we have forgiven those who sin against us.
And don't let us yield to temptation,
but rescue us from the evil one.
If you forgive those who sin against you, your heavenly Father will forgive you.
But if you refuse to forgive others, your Father will not forgive your sins.

Matthew 6:12–15

THOUGHT

When I reflect on the above scripture, I immediately have three thoughts: First, without exception, we are all in need of forgiveness to become right with God. Second, though we do not deserve forgiveness, God extends it and has made it available to us through Christ. And third, our own forgiveness is linked to forgiving *others*.

As boundlessly merciful and forgiving as our Lord and Savior is, it is a truly terrifying reality that we would not be forgiven ourselves if our hearts are hardened toward others. There have been shameful times in my life where I have had an unforgiving heart. Praise God, the Holy Spirit brought his kind and gentle conviction into my life and I repented, simultaneously receiving forgiveness for my own sin while forgiving someone else for their sin against me.

If the Lord himself—the most holy Creator, Sustainer, and King of all—can forgive through his merciful love, then who are we, as mere human beings, to withhold forgiveness from others? As we forgive those who have trespassed against us, we're not only forgiven by the Father, but we're given a greater understanding of the power, depth, and undeserved mercy of God's forgiveness. Oh, the glory of his love and mercy in our lives!

PRAYER

Lord, I am undeserving of your forgiveness, yet you have extended mercy.
May I live as Christ lived and extend mercy and forgiveness to others. Amen.

Forgive our sins, as we have forgiven those who sin against us.

May 4

THE WISDOM OF FOLLOWING

WORD

*Your word is a lamp to guide my feet
and a light for my path.*

Psalm 119:105

THOUGHT

I was once on a daylong hike in an unfamiliar state park and, although I started my hike at sunrise, due to my poor planning, I ended up having to make it back to my campsite after sunset using a paper map and flashlight alone. Needless to say, my small flashlight hardly made an impact in the deep darkness of the woods.

At one point on this hike, I was dangerously near a steep cliff I couldn't see. After a successful realization of the hazard—and a quick move away from the ledge—I thought that if I had been wise enough to turn around while the sun was still high, I could have avoided the threat of danger, not to mention a long, uncomfortable hike back to the camp.

Thankfully, as sons and daughters of God, we don't have to navigate our lives apart from the light of Christ. There is wisdom in following him as our protector and guide. His love leads us gently in and through his will, and his Word illuminates his character and instructs us to model him in all we do. His Holy Spirit, his light—a light brighter and more permanent than that of the sun, moon, and stars—will steer us away from the hazards of temptation and the dangers the enemy lays in our path. God's Word shows us the way—follow him wholeheartedly.

PRAYER

*Father, I pray this morning that you would lead me in your right path
and do not let me wander or stray into harm's way. Let your way be made plain to me through
the guidance of your Holy Spirit and your Word. Amen.*

Don't let us yield to temptation.

CONCEAL ME IN TROUBLED TIMES

WORD

For he will conceal me there when troubles come;
he will hide me in his sanctuary.
He will place me out of reach on a high rock.

Psalm 27:5

THOUGHT

Have you ever looked back on a difficult season or a terrible event and realized how the Lord protected you and provided for you despite its difficulty, perhaps even concealing and shielding you from greater troubles? Whether it was a car accident, a difficult stretch at work, the loss of a loved one, or a time of doubt in your Christian walk—whatever the circumstance—he was right there with you.

The other day, I experienced a moment that illustrated today's scripture in a new way. I heard a loud thump on the window not far from where I was reading. When I investigated, I discovered a female cardinal lying outside on the ground below the window. My guess is, she was startled by something while eating from a bird feeder nearby and flew into the window while trying to escape whatever scared her.

I gently scooped her into my hands, placed her on top of a retaining wall under some covering, and placed a few leaves over her to conceal the bird from open view, eliminating the risk of attracting larger predators as she recuperated. After about thirty minutes, she had fully recovered and flew off.

It dawned on me some time later that this moment was a fitting, although small, example of the heavenly Father's great care when it comes to protecting his children. He's able to conceal us from dangers we see—as well as the ones we often do not know are there. He will put us in his place of safety.

PRAYER

Father, you hide me from the things that would destroy me and are aware of the troubles
the enemy has designed to overwhelm me. You are my hiding place and my rock of refuge.
Thank you for your protection and love. Amen.

But rescue us from the evil one.

SUPREMACY

WORD

Christ is the visible image of the invisible God.
He existed before anything was created and is supreme over all creation,
for through him God created everything in the heavenly realms and on earth.
He made the things we can see and the things we can't see—
such as thrones, kingdoms, rulers, and authorities in the unseen world.
Everything was created through him and for him.
He existed before anything else, and he holds all creation together.
Christ is also the head of the church, which is his body.
He is the beginning, supreme over all who rise from the dead.
So he is first in everything. For God in all His fullness was pleased to live in Christ,
and through him God reconciled everything to Himself.
He made peace with everything in heaven and on earth by means of Christ's blood on the cross.

Colossians 1:15–20

THOUGHT

The passage contained in Colossians 1:15–20 is one of the most illuminated presentations in the Bible of who Christ is and his realm of authority. Paul presents Christ along with all of Christ's accomplishments—his unparalleled power, ultimate authority, and unstoppable purpose and will—as God Almighty!

For those who adore Christ, these Scriptures bring great hope and security. For God was pleased to dwell within Christ *and* was Jesus Christ himself, and Jesus loved us so dearly that he gave his life for us on the cross, Who can separate the believer from God or his promises? No one and nothing!

Rejoice in the Father's supremacy and authority, in Jesus Christ the only Son of the Father. Rejoice in the completed work of the cross!

PRAYER

Lord. I praise you today for your divine gift of grace through Christ—and I worship you, for you
reign over all things justly and supremely. You—in all your glory, wisdom, and power—
are the Lord over my life, and you have already ordained my steps through this day. Amen.

For yours is the kingdom and the power and the glory forever.

EXALTING TOGETHER

WORD

I will praise the LORD at all times.
I will constantly speak his praises.
I will boast only in the LORD;
let all who are helpless take heart.
Come, let us tell of the LORD's greatness;
let us exalt his name together.

Psalm 34:1–3

THOUGHT

There is such beauty found in spending solitary time in the mornings studying God's Word, praying and seeking his presence, and worshiping him. While leading ourselves in worship to our heavenly Father is a vital discipline in our Christian walk, there is nothing that can replace the joy, encouragement, and wonder that come from worshiping God corporately and exalting his name together as a body of believers. In Psalm 34:1–3, we see just that: David leads himself in worship and then calls out to others, inviting all to exalt the Lord and celebrate God's greatness together!

With countless congregational worship styles, we're able to see the diverse beauty in all the ways our God is worthy to be worshiped. From raising hands or dancing during contemporary songs to kneeling during recited liturgies, from gathering in large modern buildings to huddling around a dusty campsite with no electricity, from the most urban cities to the most remote developing villages, our God will be exalted in all things and all ways.

Singing songs together in praise to our Lord and Savior, despite our different life experiences, upbringings, political beliefs, or language and cultural barriers, remind us that we are all one in the body of Christ, and we have all been loved and saved by his merciful, unchanging grace. The fruit of our lips is praise, and one day, all nations and tongues will praise the Lord at all times. What a blessed day indeed!

PRAYER

I praise you Lord, and I am grateful to be a part of the gathering of worshipers you have been assembling since the beginning of creation. May my words and deeds exalt your holy name. Amen.

Our Father in heaven, may your name be kept holy.

OUR LIST OF PRIORITIES

WORD

Then I pray to you, O LORD.
I say, "You are my place of refuge.
You are all I really want in life."

Psalm 142:5

THOUGHT

Early in my Christian experience, I heard someone teach that God is to be first on our list of priorities. The teacher's intent was to encourage and direct his audience toward the singular focus of godly living. His thoughts and comments were very helpful for me personally at that time.

Years later, a friend who was living and ministering in Minnesota told me of a recent experience he'd had in the midst of a severe physical challenge that landed him in the hospital for several days. One early morning while lying in his hospital room alone he prayed, "Lord, I want you to be the number one thing in my life." My friend said he immediately sensed this as the Lord's response: *I don't want to be the* first *thing on your list; I want to be the* only *thing on your list.*

Yes, there are certainly biblical responsibilities concerning family, friends, work, and other concerns we are to rightly prioritize as followers of God. Doing so not only honors God but becomes a form of worship as well. Jesus tells us to "seek the Kingdom of God above all else" (Matt. 6:33), and we honor him by living our lives this way. But in Matthew 10:37–39, Jesus also instructs us to love him above our own families and take up our cross and follow him wholeheartedly. Living our lives in honor of Christ and the furthering of his gospel is the *only* thing that truly matters.

The revelation my friend had from his hospital bed was both deeply convicting and encouraging for me, for truly all other right, good, and meaningful earthly relationships pale in comparison to our love for and devotion to the Lord—and rightfully so. He is the mighty and wonderful King of our hearts!

PRAYER

Father, you have designed me to discover my purpose in relationship with you,
and this is your will. Holy Spirit, guide me to live a life fully submitted to God's will and his glory,
that I would take up my cross and follow Christ wholeheartedly and truly be able to say,
Lord, you are all I really want in life. Amen.

May your kingdom come soon. May your will be done on earth, as it is in heaven.

THE INVITATION TO FLOURISH

WORD

Trust in your money and down you go!
But the godly flourish like leaves in spring.

Proverbs 11:28

THOUGHT

After a long cold winter we finally get to enjoy the bright, fresh green leaves and vibrant flowers that develop in spring. It is life-giving to be surrounded by such healthy growth, and this scripture reminds us that godly people who lead lives honoring the Lord flourish like the new, healthy leaves in springtime. However, this proverb also reveals the vanity and foolishness of trusting in the world's wealth. In our modern Western culture, it's tempting to consider our annual household salary and the numbers in our savings account as markers that we are doing things "right" or as evidence of our value to society. It can also be tempting to find security and safety in our earnings. Granted, financial wisdom and health are good things from the Lord and tools for his glory, but the truth is that money is not a marker of our significance, worth, or security.

The Lord alone provides us with identity, security, and safety. We are his children, and no matter what he asks of us in this life or what our earnings are, he is our kind and generous provider. He is where we find our hope. God always *knows* what is best for us and always *does* what is best for us. In Christ, we are invited to find true security and flourish like leaves in spring.

PRAYER

Lord, I desire your will for my life. Provide me with the wisdom and faith to trust in you for all that I need. By your Holy Spirit, guard my heart and don't let me be tempted to chase after the temporal and valueless treasures of this world. May I seek and serve you with my whole heart, for you are the true treasure. Amen.

Give us today the food we need.

GENUINE FREEDOM

WORD

So if the Son sets you free, you are truly free.

John 8:36

THOUGHT

In a busy shopping mall, I saw a young boy returning to his mother with a bucket of buttered popcorn he had been sent to purchase. Just as he reached his mother and other siblings, he slipped and spilled the entire contents of the bucket on the floor. He immediately received a loud scolding that the entire area could hear. The boy apologized for his mistake profusely, all while attempting to gather the popcorn into the bucket. The mother did not stop condemning her young son for his mistake, telling him how foolish and stupid he was—even as he continued to apologize.

Many of us have experienced the unforgiveness of others—perhaps from our parents, our close friends, or even our Christian brothers and sisters. In our own sin, there are times we have even been unforgiving to those who have hurt us. However, by the mercy, grace, and greatness of God, we have been fully, completely, entirely forgiven in Christ Jesus.

If we have been set free by Christ, we are free indeed. God does not continue to remind us of our failures, holding them against us. God does not embarrass or chastise us for tripping and falling when temptation comes our way. Surely, by his Holy Spirit, God brings his holy and loving conviction in our lives to teach us and steer us away from the disaster of sin—but when we repent of our sin, he welcomes us in joyfully as a forgiving, loving, grace-filled parent. There is no retaliation from our heavenly Father. The cross of Christ, the redemptive completed work of grace, is a finished work!

PRAYER

Father, I deserved punishment for my sins, yet you sent your Son to die for them to give me genuine freedom and abundant life. I am unworthy of this gift, but I treasure it and ask that I would be a good steward of your forgiveness, freely giving forgiveness and mercy to others. I praise you with an overflowing heart of gratefulness. Amen.

Forgive us our sins, as we have forgiven those who sin against us.

HE BENDS DOWN TO HEAR

WORD

*I love the LORD because he hears my voice
and my prayer for mercy.
Because he bends down to listen,
I will pray as long as I have breath!*

Psalm 116:1–2

THOUGHT

How humbling and wonderful it is that when we pray, God actually hears us! He loves and cares for us so much that he *bends down* to listen to what we have to say.

God Almighty, in all his power and glory, brings himself closer to us in order to hear our prayers for mercy. Why does he bend down? It's not because God has hearing difficulties. He does this to let us, his sons and daughters, know that he cares, is involved in our concerns, and is deeply committed to the relationship he has with each one of us.

Because of his kindness and listening ear, we know he's committed to loving us, guiding us, and leading us faithfully upon his paths, the good paths of his will for our lives. Let us never underestimate the value of the gift of prayer! He bends down to hear and lead us on good paths for his name's sake.

PRAYER

Merciful and loving heavenly Father, there is no rest or peace apart from your great and wonderful presence—and so it is you I seek and to you I pray as long as I have breath. Amen.

Don't let us yield to temptation.

FINDING LIFE

WORD

If you love your father or mother more than you love me, you are not worthy of being mine; or if you love your son or daughter more than me, you are not worthy of being mine. If you refuse to take up your cross and follow me, you are not worthy of being mine. If you cling to your life, you will lose it; but if you give up your life for me, you will find it.

Matthew 10:37–39

THOUGHT

This passage is uncomfortable, as it seems opposed to the many passages speaking of refuge, safety, and deliverance from danger—not to mention the command to honor your father and mother. We prefer avoiding hardships, and often Christianity is presented as the place to avoid adversity as well as experience prosperity. This appeals to my flesh, but I would have to ignore many of the Bible's verses that speak of challenge and difficulty.

After telling his disciples of the challenges they would encounter, Jesus clearly moves on to say there should be nothing held dearer to us than him. We are to honor earthly relationships in a Christlike manner, but they should pale in comparison to our relationship with him. In losing our lives, we will find life.

There is only one to be wholly trusted. Only one who speaks absolute truth, holds the keys to life and death, and decides who will live eternally in heaven or hell. Trust him and the words he has spoken. Follow him, for his advice flows from his pure compassionate love for those he came to save.

PRAYER

Obedience is better than sacrifice. There should be none before you, Jesus, for you alone have the words of life; you alone are my Deliverer. May you find in me, by the enabling power of your Spirit, a heart given completely to you and your will. Amen.

But deliver us from the evil one.

May 13

I LOVE YOUR SANCTUARY

WORD

I wash my hands to declare my innocence.
I come to your altar, O Lord,
singing a song of thanksgiving
and telling of all your wonders.
I love your sanctuary, Lord,
the place where your glorious presence dwells.

Psalm 26:6–8

THOUGHT

We have no way to be forgiven of our sin but through Jesus Christ. His redemptive work of grace—grace that is the result of his boundless love—purchased our freedom. We would have never known God's mercy the way that we do today had Christ not responded to our dilemma of being separated from our heavenly Father because of sin.

Because of Christ's lasting work of salvation, we can now come into God's presence with hearts full of gratitude and amazement. We can sing songs of worship and thanksgiving with sincerity, understanding each lyric. Like the psalmist in today's scripture, we have no fear in approaching the altar of God, for our sin has been paid for and we are fully, completely redeemed. Now we get to rejoice, telling all of our deliverance from darkness and of God's endless wonders. What a privilege!

As God's children, we long for his presence above all else. We love his sanctuary, the place where his glorious presence dwells. No matter what difficulties or disappointments we encounter in this life, where the Spirit of the Lord is, we are home—and we are loved.

PRAYER

With you, my Lord and glorious King, is where I desire to dwell. In your presence is where I long to be now and forever. Help me to feel your presence throughout my day in whatever I do. Amen.

For yours is the kingdom and the power and the glory forever.

May 14

WE EXIST FOR HIM

WORD

All glory to God forever and ever! Amen.

Galatians 1:5

Do not be afraid, for I am with you.
I will gather you and your children from east and west.
I will say to the north and south,
"Bring my sons and daughters back to Israel
from the distant corners of the earth.
Bring all who claim me as their God,
for I have made them for my glory.
It was I who created them.

Isaiah 43:5–7

THOUGHT

From the beginning of humanity, the goal of the Father's heart has been to gather a people for his glory. The Lord created us in *his* image for his glory, and he created his people—us—to glorify him and tell the world about his goodness, grace, and salvation.

Often in the bustle of daily life, we can feel as if we exist for mundane reasons: we wake up, go to work, commute home, feed the kids, feed ourselves, go to bed, and repeat it all again the next day. But we are playing a much larger part in God's purposes, and we exist to glorify God in our whole lives, even the moments that feel mundane.

As sons and daughters of God, we are created to tell the story of God's holiness, humanity's separation from him, and his gift of salvation through Christ for reconciliation. We were destined for darkness and separation from God, yet Christ freed us from our sin, released us from the grips of death, and we now have eternal hope.

Each Christian is commissioned to share the story exceeding all stories. The story of the Holy One whose purity prohibited communion with corrupted flesh, but whose love and grace made a way to know righteousness. The redeemed live no mundane lives; they exalt, declare, and worship the Holy Father.

PRAYER

On bended knee and with yielded heart, I declare the praise you are worthy to receive, heavenly Father. Teach me how to give you glory in all that I do. I exist for you. Amen.

Our Father in heaven, may your name be kept holy.

May 15

SEND ME

WORD

...then I heard the Lord asking,
"Whom should I send as a messenger to this people? Who will go for us?"

I said, "Here I am. Send me."

Isaiah 6:8

THOUGHT

God had a message for Israel, and he chose to send it through a human agent. *Whom should I send?* God asks. Isaiah responded to God's request with a resounding, *Send me!*

We have much to glean from Isaiah's encounter with God and the circumstances surrounding these words, but let's focus on the following: Isaiah boldly raised his hand to help spread the Word of God. Likewise, each of us who has said yes to Christ and his grace are enlisted as his agents, whether we're a pastor, factory worker, student, CEO, retail clerk, athlete, or stay-at-home parent.

Jesus told us the harvest is plentiful, yet the workers are few. Although the cure for the hopeless and tired heart is readily and abundantly available, where are those who will deliver the message? *Send me!* God produced the way to experience abundant life, and we are God's message delivery system, no matter what our day job is. We are to be the hands and feet of Christ—his strategy to make his good news known.

PRAYER

Father, you have showered me with grace in abundance, so I will go and tell others
of your goodness and salvation. Here I am. Send me. Amen.

May your kingdom come soon. May your will be done on earth, as it is in heaven.

THE WAY, THE TRUTH, AND THE LIFE

WORD

Jesus told him, "I am the way, the truth, and the life. No one can come to the Father except through me. If you had really known me, you would know who my Father is. From now on, you do know him and have seen him!"

John 14:6–7

THOUGHT

In these verses, not only is Jesus Christ ensuring us that he is the Son of God, but he's also declaring there's no other way to come to the Father except through him. As John 14 goes on, the disciples request Jesus to show them the Father, and then they "will be satisfied" (John 14:8). Then Christ quickly replies that anyone who has seen him has seen the Father, that they are one (John 14:9–11). Such mystery is revealed in these scriptures!

Can you imagine how the disciples must have felt? They were looking at and talking with God himself in the flesh, yet were still confounded by the mysterious truth that Son and Father were and are one and the same.

Today we can give thanks that we have these accounts of Christ's time on earth in order to help us get just a minuscule glimpse into the mystery. God himself has declared that he is the way, the truth, and the life. May we be ever grateful to him for revealing himself and his love for us, providing us a way into eternal fellowship with him.

PRAYER

Father, you drew me into the place of knowing you. Before you, I was living deceived by my own sin about my value and purpose, and you showed me your truth. Before surrendering to you, what I thought was true life was, in reality, just fleeting, temporal satisfaction. You gave me genuine life and the hope of abiding with you forever. I am humbled, and I am grateful. Amen.

Give us today the food we need.

READY TO FORGIVE

WORD

O LORD, you are so good, so ready to forgive,
so full of unfailing love for all who ask for your help.

Psalm 86:5

THOUGHT

At some point, we have all been in the position where we have either caused a disagreement in a relationship or have been in a relationship with someone who has caused a disagreement with us. Christians know we are to forgive, but sometimes the wounds caused by offenses linger unattended, and when they do, so do the tension and discomfort in relationships. Hopefully both people quickly realize the need to extend forgiveness to bring restoration to the situation.

In our earthly relationships, there may be a hesitance to seeking forgiveness. Sometimes we wonder if our request will be readily received and if forgiveness will be granted. But not so with the Lord! He is full of unfailing love, ready to forgive, and he wants to see a right relationship with him established. The heart of Christ desires us to be in unhindered, perfect, intimate fellowship with him. Praise the Lord, he will not refuse or ignore the sincerely repentant heart.

PRAYER

Thank you, Lord, for your great love. Thank you for your willingness and readiness to forgive.
I'm forever grateful. Amen.

Forgive us our sins, as we have forgiven those who sin against us.

LEARNING TO LISTEN

WORD

Pay close attention to what you hear. The closer you listen, the more understanding you will be given—and you will receive even more.

Mark 4:24

THOUGHT

In a wooded area close to our home lies an old stock pond constructed in the 1940s. The decades of tree growth now conceal its presence from plain view. My sons loved this pond when they were younger, and we would often take walks there together. In early spring evenings, the voices of dozens of frogs would sing—"spring peepers" as we like to refer to them in Arkansas—on the edges of the pond's banks.

At first, you can only faintly hear a few, but when they start their song, I know the evening atmosphere will soon be filled with the sound of their croaking. For me, it's a pleasant and restful sound. But more important, if I pay attention and learn to listen for them, the presence of the spring peepers will clue me in to winter's end.

When we quiet ourselves before the Lord, poised for spiritual listening, we will learn to recognize the signs and distinguishable voice of our Great Shepherd and the way he leads us through life. Though his voice may not be audible, he still speaks. He reveals himself in nature, he leads through circumstances, confirms things through the voice of our friends, but I believe those quiet times where we have his Word opened before us and our hearts are poised in prayer are his favorite times to give of revelation. When we position ourselves as Christ often did in the places void of crowds and distractions, we learn to recognize the holy, distinguishable tones, signals, and inflections of his voice.

God still speaks today; we just have to stop and learn to listen.

PRAYER

Father, teach me to listen, understand, and follow as you lead. Amen.

Don't let us yield to temptation.

ENCOURAGING THE DISCOURAGED

WORD

When we arrived in Macedonia, there was no rest for us. We faced conflict from every direction, with battles on the outside and fear on the inside. But God, who encourages those who are discouraged, encouraged us by the arrival of Titus.

2 Corinthians 7:5–6

THOUGHT

Most of us can relate to how the apostle Paul feels in this situation. Although it's unlikely in the Western world that, like Paul, we would be imprisoned or hunted down because of our faith, there are seasons during our spiritual lives when pressures and conflict seem to come at us from all directions and leave us with the feeling of no escape.

In many places throughout scripture, the Word of God tells us to be strong, courageous, and not worry, but even so, Paul confessed that the constant resistance from the pagan community, unbelieving Jews, and imposters imitating Christianity in Macedonia caused him and his companions to begin to experience fear. God used the arrival of Titus, a brother in Christ, to alleviate the tension of their situation. And God may do the same for us when we are feeling similarly; he may send a special person or persons at just the time we need to be encouraged.

Ultimately, we can take a very important promise away from this passage: God himself will encourage the discouraged. As we go through life as his children doing his work, no matter what conflict designed by the enemy comes our way, the Lord himself will be our comfort.

PRAYER

Thank you, Father, for the promises of your love for me. Rescue me from the plans of the enemy, and thank you for providing your encouragement as I do your kingdom work. Amen.

But rescue us from the evil one.

JOY FROM HIS HANDIWORK

WORD

May the glory of the LORD continue forever!
The LORD takes pleasure in all he has made!

Psalm 104:31

THOUGHT

Before the sun gives sufficient morning light to reveal the beauty of the earth, I sit with the Lord, anticipating the arrival of dawn. Although not everyone in my household enjoys getting up this early, I enjoy it as time alone with my heavenly Father. Whether you wake up at 4 a.m. or 9 a.m., you can enjoy a precious time of reflection like this too.

On one particular spring morning, the air was comfortably cool and fresh, and our entire property was full of the wonderfully pleasant sounds of an Ozark spring morning. I could even hear a rooster in the distance in addition to a variety of wild birds chirping from the surrounding woods. Everything seemed perfect on this particular morning, as though God had prepared it just for humanity to experience it so we would praise the Father of all creation for his greatness.

Just as you and I enjoy a beautiful, bright summer day, a peaceful, grey-skied autumn rain, or the simple majesty of another sunrise, the Lord also takes pleasure in all he has made. He looks on each new morning in this small valley in the Ozarks and smiles on the quiet, peaceful beauty of his creation. He does the same over the exact place where you're sitting. He can see our love and appreciation for what he has made. In his omnipresence, he simultaneously receives joy each day from his handiwork around the entire planet—joy over the birds, the sunrise, the hills, and you and me.

PRAYER

Lord, your handiwork is displayed over all the earth. You have made all things for your good pleasure.
May I, too, in my submission to your will, bring you good pleasure throughout the day. Amen.

For yours is the kingdom and the power and the glory forever.

HONOR IS DUE

WORD

Exalt the LORD our God!
Bow low before his feet, for he is holy!

Psalm 99:5

THOUGHT

The Lord, in all his holiness, is far greater than we could ever understand. I have often wondered what our initial response will be once the entire body of Christ finds itself gathered together for the first time in heaven and in the presence of the Lord. Of course, time as we know it will cease to exist, but I can imagine the first experience as one containing hundreds or thousands of years of elated celebration, shouts, and hand claps to the King of kings.

I can also imagine singing songs together, songs that have characteristics we cannot describe this side of heaven. We sing of the depth of his great love for us here on earth, but think of the lyrics that we will sing once we've seen him face-to-face! And what about the instruments and music to support them? I can picture heavenly choruses and orchestras of the purest sound. I'm fairly confident this new music will contain more than a couple verses and a catchy chorus and bridge.

While we do not know many details, whatever unfolds in that future first gathering before Christ in heaven, our glorified Savior and King of kings, most certainly his presence will have us in awe of his holiness. Although we long to be with him and see him face-to-face, while we are here on earth, honor is still due him—we can bow low in worship and prayer before him and stand tall and celebrate in his presence.

PRAYER

Father, I know my mind and heart scarcely understand the depth of your awe, wonder, and holiness. With my limited understanding and ability, Lord God, I attempt sincerely to worship you, exalt you, and bow low before you alone, for you alone are holy. Amen.

Our Father in heaven, may your name be kept holy.

May 22

ONE PURPOSE

WORD

*...and I will give them one heart and one purpose: to worship me forever,
for their own good and for the good of all their descendants.*

Jeremiah 32:39

THOUGHT

Today's scripture, in the context of the book of Jeremiah, displays God's intention toward Israel. Israel was to be a people after the Lord, God's people. However, God's purpose from the creation of man was to build and gather for himself a people to worship him forever. This is the story of the Bible from Genesis to Revelation.

Our number one purpose is to glorify God and worship him forever, and it's for our good! Through Christ, we are reconciled to our heavenly Father—Jews and Gentiles alike—and we become part of the magnificent story of God, who is building his beautiful community of worshipers. It is his will to build his kingdom in this way. God, from the beginning of time, has been positioning all things to glorify him!

Every heart has as its highest purpose the call to worship Yahweh God. He built that desire within us, and our hearts will never find rest apart from Christ Jesus. Living a life in worship to our Lord and Savior is for our own good because it is like coming back to our roots; it is what humans were designed for since day one. Yes, we were made to glorify God!

PRAYER

Lord, your will is for me to find myself and my purpose by living a life of worship to you. Thank you for providing all things necessary to accomplish my honoring of you. Amen.

May your kingdom come soon. May your will be done on earth, as it is in heaven.

May 23

THE LORD IS GREAT!

WORD

...but may all who search for you
be filled with joy and gladness in you.
May those who love your salvation
repeatedly shout, "The LORD is great!"

Psalm 40:16

THOUGHT

Here, the psalmist's focus is the hope for everyone who seeks the Lord to be filled with joy and gladness. Most certainly, if there is any hope to know genuine joy and gladness (and there is), it comes in seeking the Lord.

In this earth-life, we will run into trial and difficulty; we will have days that feel void of purpose, are grief-filled, or are just plain old *boring*. However, just as the Lord provides sustenance through our daily bread, he provides nourishment through the genuine joy and refreshment we are able to experience in his presence.

God has promised we will find him if we search for him with all our hearts. The sincere seeker of God has a definitive hope and promise to experience true joy and gladness in him. When our hearts are in pursuit of Christ and fully submitted to him, we are able to experience the awe and wonder of his goodness. We become full of joy and gladness of his presence; it is instinctive to shout, "The LORD is great!" Despite what our day looks or feels like, we can rejoice in his love for us—for he is great and there is none greater.

PRAYER

Holy Father, my heart is full of gratitude and praise for you this morning as I think
of your most amazing love and grace. You are my source of joy and gladness.
Great are you Lord; yes, great are you Lord! Amen.

Give us today the food we need.

THE DEPTH OF FORGIVENESS

WORD

Make allowance for each other's faults, and forgive anyone who offends you. Remember, the Lord forgave you, so you must forgive others. Above all, clothe yourselves with love, which binds us all together in perfect harmony.

Colossians 3:13–14

THOUGHT

The weight of this scripture seems to lack rationale, reason, and certainly the possibility of across-the-board application. Are we really required to forgive *anyone* who offends us? From our limited human perspective, forgiveness of any and all offenses seems impossible—there are some injustices and trespasses that seem downright inexcusable.

However, if we were to make a list of things we think are possible, most of the things God has done or calls us to do qualify for the "impossible" column, and those that are not in that column skirt awfully close to it. If you think about it, receiving our own forgiveness from God required the introduction of his supernatural intervention, and we must draw from the same supernatural source when we forgive others.

C. S. Lewis wrote, "To be a Christian means to forgive the inexcusable because God has forgiven the inexcusable in you."[17] Unforgiveness is not an option for us if we intend to experience forgiveness ourselves. And apart from Christ, forgiveness of our own sin was impossible. All praise and honor and glory to our God who accomplishes impossible things.

PRAYER

Father, as you have extended grace and mercy to me, may I walk in the same manner extending it to others. I ask the Holy Spirit to strengthen me in mercy toward all. Amen.

Forgive us our sins, as we have forgiven those who sin against us.

May 25

RADICAL CHANGE

WORD

One time Jesus entered a house, and the crowds began to gather again. Soon he and his disciples couldn't even find time to eat. When his family heard what was happening, they tried to take him away. "He's out of his mind," they said.

Mark 3:20–21

THOUGHT

What must friends, family, and neighbors have thought about Jesus when, at age thirty, the pattern of his life changed so drastically? He walked away from his career as a carpenter. He went out into the desert for a long period of time and continued a pattern of time alone in isolated places. Jesus began associating with a new group of people and devoted much of his time to them. After thirty years of little recognition, he suddenly had a growing reputation as an influential voice in the region, and he was challenging the institutionalized religious system and leaders.

On this side of history, we might read this scripture and think how ridiculous their evaluations were, but if we were there during that time, I think we might come to the same conclusion as his family.

The Bible gives numerous examples of devoted followers of God who experienced behavioral and directional changes after encounters with the Lord. Abraham, Isaac, Jacob, Joseph, David, the prophets, Ruth, the apostles, Paul—there are too many to even mention. And genuinely loving and following the leading of the Lord will potentially add your name to the list as well. When we encounter the Spirit of God and make our minds up to follow Christ wholeheartedly, our lives experience radical change.

PRAYER

Lord, may I wisely and courageously follow your lead all the days of my life, regardless of the cost of my personal reputation. I ask that you would give me the courage to do so. Amen.

Don't let us yield to temptation.

THE POWER OF PERSONAL TESTIMONY

WORD

And they have defeated him by the blood of the Lamb and by their testimony.

Revelation 12:11

THOUGHT

When we pray the Lord's Prayer, we ask the Lord to rescue us from the evil one, and one of the weapons that he's given us to combat the enemy is gathering together as believers for corporate worship. One of the most beautiful practices we enjoy when we gather together as his church is hearing the personal testimonies of our brothers and sisters in Christ. It builds our faith and encourages us in our own walk with the Lord when we get to enjoy true stories of how God has rescued or provided for his children.

I was once in a meeting of Christian brothers and sisters that seemed a bit dull, like the meeting was lacking life. Then a space was made for people who had recently experienced God's divine intervention to share testimonies. Perhaps a half dozen responded! The first story shared was one of rescue from a dark and tangled life of regret to a genuine relationship with the light and life of Christ. Then followed stories from grateful parents telling of recently returned prodigal children and a testimony of the healing of cancer.

The meeting transitioned—it came alive with hearts rejoicing together over God's continued interventions and interactions with his children. Know this: there is power in sharing your personal testimony. When we let others know how Jesus, the Lamb of God, has rescued us and intervened in our lives, it builds the faith of those around us, gives life and hope to weary hearts, and defeats the lies of the enemy.

PRAYER

Glory to God in the highest! His power and authority defeat the evil one. Thank you for the continued manifestation of your rescue and care, Lord Jesus. Holy Spirit, fill me with the courage and the words to tell others of God's goodness and what Christ has done. Amen.

But rescue us from the evil one.

GLORIOUS EVIDENCE

WORD

The disciples saw Jesus do many other miraculous signs in addition to the ones recorded in this book. But these are written so that you may continue to believe that Jesus is the Messiah, the Son of God, and that by believing in him you will have life by the power of his name.

John 20:30–31

THOUGHT

There were many, many acts of ministry administered, sermons preached, and miracles performed by Jesus while he lived and walked upon the earth as God in the flesh. These daily encounters—conversations, debates with doubters and scoffers, sermons, miracles, and even restful fellowship—caused deep and divine impressions on the human soul, liberating hearts and bringing peace to troubled minds. Lives were altered through his compassion, hope was imparted, and confidence was secured for the future.

When we read the book of John, or any of the four Gospels for that matter, we see Christ delivering life-giving instruction to the disciples as they traveled ancient roads, sat under trees to rest, and reclined at tables together over a meal. We read about the powerful, life-transforming encounters he had with unsuspecting, everyday people, such as the woman at the well, and we see multiple miracles performed with many people being healed.

Though Jesus said many more words in his lifetime than the ones recorded in the four Gospels, the writings of John contain more than enough glorious evidence to reveal Jesus Christ as the Son of God, giver of grace, lover of our souls, and Savior of the world.

PRAYER

Thank you, Lord Jesus, for all you have done to reveal to me your love, mercy, and grace. You are the Messiah—the only way to the Father—and I believe in the power of your name and embrace your will for my life. Amen.

For yours is the kingdom and the power and the glory forever.

OH, THAT THE WORLD WOULD KNOW

WORD

*I am the L*ORD*;*
there is no other God.

Isaiah 45:5

THOUGHT

Oh, that the world would not only acknowledge the truth of this statement, but would step into the freedom and beauty of its embrace. The heart of the heavenly Father has been, and remains, that all humanity will know he is the only God and his name is Yahweh. Oh, that the world would know he created them for his glory, to honor him, and he loves them deeply.

He is the Lord, and truly there is no other God. He is the Lord, and outside him there is no other hope, for his is one eternal. He is the Lord, and there is no other greater source of fulfillment to the human heart and soul. As his hope is eternal, so is his love—for he is love—and he has freely and faithfully poured it forth for all as he has given himself through Christ to all who will receive. He is the Lord, and there is no higher goal in life than to wholeheartedly serve him. In doing so, each chamber of the spiritual heart is filled to capacity.

Oh, that the world would know there is no other source of salvation or genuine life, as genuine life exists only within the Lord God—and indeed, there is no other like him.

PRAYER

Father, the heart that embraces you is the heart that is fulfilled and in peace.
You alone are worthy of worship, for you alone are God and there is no other. Amen.

Our Father in heaven, may your name be kept holy.

WHATEVER HE PLEASES

WORD

I know the greatness of the LORD—
that our Lord is greater than any other god.
The LORD does whatever pleases him
throughout all heaven and earth,
and on the seas and in their depths.
He causes the clouds to rise over the whole earth.
He sends the lightning with the rain
and releases the wind from his storehouses.

Psalm 135:5–7

THOUGHT

The days grow warmer as summer approaches. The field near my house and the surrounding woods—which were almost colorless a few weeks ago—have given way to the colors of late spring. In my area of the world, during this transition of the seasons we experience both gentle rains and fierce storms with flashes of lightning and rumbling thunder. You may be experiencing the same this time of year depending on where you live.

I almost always welcome a gentle thunderstorm. I enjoy going outside as the winds increase and cause the oaks to sway; their branches bend as they yield to the wind. Whether you're experiencing a thunderstorm, a gentle rain, or a peaceful, bright day in your corner of the world, all that occurs—every single moment and action in history—God created and set into motion. For the sons and daughters of God, there is a confidence that fills our hearts when we're reminded of the Lord's greatness, knowing God will do whatever he pleases and what he does is ultimately for his glory and our good.

Earlier in this passage of scripture, the psalmist gives us assurance by declaring the Lord is good (Ps. 135:3). Whatever the Lord does will always be what is just, what is right, and what is good. We can give thanks for his perfect and unfailing will!

PRAYER

I praise your name, oh, Most High, for you are good, and all that you do is for the glory of
your name and your kingdom. Lord, I know that you are great and your will is holy.
I'm committed to you wholeheartedly. Whatever happens in my day today,
I know it's being guided by you for your glory and your benefit. Amen.

May your kingdom come soon. May your will be done on earth, as it is in heaven.

May 30

THE ABIDING PEACE

WORD

Now may the Lord of peace himself give you his peace at all times
and in every situation. The Lord be with you all.

2 Thessalonians 3:16

THOUGHT

Paul, in the closing remarks of his letter to his friends and the believers in Thessa-lonica, hopes the peace of God is given to them in every situation. God's peace is the mysterious yet wonderful internal quality available to every recipient of his grace. This peace beyond human understanding seems elusive as we confuse it with the temporal version of peace.

Temporal peace is typically manifested in the experience of good circumstances. However, this peace quickly diminishes (or altogether flees) should struggle and chal-lenges enter our lives.

The only source capable of regulating peace with consistency is Christ, as he is the Lord of peace. When he abides in us in Spirit and we draw upon the fruit of the Spirit, his peace is present in every situation—and at all times—to calm and steady us during external pressures.

The peace Paul is hoping for his readers, and through this letter to all Christians, is the incomparable, ever-abiding internal peace of Christ. And were it not possible to abide in this peace, Paul would have never presented it to the church as he did in his letter to the Thessalonians.

PRAYER

Help me, Lord, to realize that you have placed a peace within me that circumstances cannot steal from me. Remind me by your Spirit to draw upon this peace and not be deceived into relying on any counterfeit peace of temporary value. You, Lord Jesus, are my peace. Amen.

Give us today the food we need.

THERE IS FORGIVENESS

WORD

Brothers, listen! We are here to proclaim that through this man Jesus there is forgiveness for your sins.

Acts 13:38

THOUGHT

In the 1970s, I met a gentleman who led a small church in southern Missouri. His personality and character were ones of deep, genuine graciousness, the mental image most people get when they hear the word *pastor*. Upon meeting him, you would've thought this guy had spent his entire life in church with little exposure to the darker things of the world.

Sometime later, I learned he had spent many years in prison as a young man for a serious crime. During his early prison years, this man learned of Jesus and the forgiveness of sins through a prison ministry. He understood that God's mercy and grace give us the ability to be forgiven of what we might consider the unforgivable. He was indeed forgiven by God, and later he received pardon for his sentence.

In his newfound freedom, this redeemed and restored man dedicated the rest of his life to sharing the true freedom found in Christ with others. May we all realize we have been given a great gift in Jesus and live our lives accordingly.

PRAYER

Thank you, Lord Jesus, that you provided a way for me to hear, understand, and receive your miraculous gift. May I be found sharing your story and graciousness the remainder of my days. Amen.

Forgive us our sins, as we have forgiven those who sin against us.

ALWAYS RIGHT

WORD

O LORD, I have come to you for protection;
don't let me be disgraced.
Save me, for you do what is right.

Psalm 31:1

THOUGHT

In the King James Version, the last line of this verse reads "deliver me in thy righteousness." As Christians, we embrace the validity and complete accuracy of the Bible as God's flawless and holy Word. The Bible reveals to us that God alone is wholly righteous—and as humans, we might only know and experience righteousness in our lives through the completed redemptive work of Christ.

"I trust you to make the right decision." More than a few times over the decades I have heard this phrase by someone in our church trying to make a good decision for themselves, but uncertain of what to do. Often they would entrust me to decide for them or help them make the decision. I, of course, want to encourage and assist people on their spiritual journeys if I can, but nearly always my response is usually how prone I am to mistakes, but not so with the Lord. He and his Word are always right.

Many of us have experienced the result of placing our trust in the things or people of this world and we've been met with hurt and disappointment because those things fail us. Let me assure you, there is great hope when we place our trust in God. He does not fail us. He is wholly righteous. He will *always* do what is right, he always is right, and he transforms every difficulty in our lives to work for our good and his glory.

The only sure solution to and salvation from the dilemmas we face—whether they are created by us or someone else—is God. Placing our trust in the Lord allows him to lead and care for us and will result in true peace in our hearts.

PRAYER

Lord, I can find rest and peace in knowing you always do what is right.
In those weak moments when I struggle with doubt or fear, remind me that you,
heavenly Father, do only what is right, always. Amen.

Don't let us yield to temptation.

THE OVERCOMER

WORD

I have told you all this so that you may have peace in me. Here on earth you will have many trials and sorrows. But take heart, because I have overcome the world.

John 16:33

THOUGHT

We are not promised a trouble-free life as believers in Christ, but we are encouraged by Christ that we can have peace in him when life is troublesome. In John 16:33, Jesus confirms the coming of hardships for all his followers, but tells us not to fear for he has overcome the hardships for himself and in the end so will all those entrusted to Christ. The word *overcome* means to subdue, prevail, and conquer. Although here on earth we may have many trials, as Christ acknowledges, there is nothing that our God cannot conquer.

Paul, in 2 Corinthians, encourages us that Christ is working even in our weakness and hardships. Paul had a deep-seated knowledge of the profound truth that Christ had overcome the world. Even in prison, Paul could rejoice over the work God was doing because he understood any difficulty or weakness he encountered through the lens of Christ's strength and victory.

Where in your life do you need the healing power of these precious truths? Where do you need rescue? Know this: you shall overcome because your heavenly Father himself is the Overcomer.

PRAYER

Jesus, when I'm confronted with challenges I don't understand and did not seek, may your Holy Spirit encourage me to take heart and find peace in you. For in my weakness, you are strong. Amen.

But rescue us from the evil one.

June 3

INFINITUDE

WORD

The LORD is king forever and ever!
The godless nations will vanish from the land.

Psalm 10:16

THOUGHT

There is an absence of trust in political leadership today caused by a vacuum of integrity. We hope that, where unrighteousness is rampant and unchecked, good change will come with the next emperor, king, or president. We hope for integrity and trustworthiness, along with right and good governing to return to our own country and those far away. Sadly, history is filled with countless examples of corrupted authority and abuse of position for power and self-gain.

Do not despair, for there is one who can be trusted. One who is truthful, righteous, and flawless in all his decisions and ways. He is Jehovah God, the Lord who is King forever! Yes, he is governing for all eternity. Absolute and complete reign and authority are his. Peace should flood our hearts in knowing that he governs with a love so pure, deep, and good that it is humanly unimaginable. He is seated on an eternal throne, and his rule will not end.

Even if our world is in turmoil, we can have peace knowing the Lord never ceases to be in charge. Even when concerns arise over worldly government, we know God is active. And we know he uses his devoted sons and daughters to be salt and light in a world that is often dark. Christ is the Lord, the King forever, and the people of God will shine his light in all the world's dark places.

PRAYER

Lord, you are perfect in every way, ruling over all things with justice, righteousness, and holy compassion. You are moving toward fulfilling your plan to usher in the glory of your eternal kingdom. Lord, you are the King forever; you are our King, my King. Amen.

For yours is the kingdom and the power and the glory forever.

June 4

INCOMPARABLE

WORD

Who can be compared with the LORD our God,
who is enthroned on high?

Psalm 113:5

THOUGHT

"Who is God like?"

I received this brief, honest question from a young child who was expecting a quick answer. The child's inquiry was innocent yet deeply contemplative. When I finally collected my thoughts enough to give a heartfelt, thoughtful response, it was fumbled and inadequate.

Theologians have created volumes of literature over the ages in attempt to explain God's person and characteristics. While we are grateful for their efforts of insight, none of us could truly describe *who* God is like. Who could he be compared to? No one. He is unlike all others! Any of our attempts to describe or quantify him as deity—let alone describe his boundless love—are lacking.

Our earnest attempts to intellectually understand or describe God lead to silence and awe, for he is incomparable and truly like no other.

PRAYER

Adequate words do not exist to describe you, Lord. You have created humanity
for the purpose of glorifying you, and so I lift my hands in honor of you.
I worship you, Father God, the best I can. Amen.

Our Father in heaven, may your name be kept holy.

June 5

JOYFUL

WORD

Joyful are people of integrity,
who follow the instructions of the Lord.
Joyful are those who obey his laws
and search for him with all their hearts.

Psalm 119:1–2

THOUGHT

How many times have you heard or thought these two phrases: *I just want to be happy* or *I deserve to be happy*? It doesn't matter your socioeconomic background or status—from the homeless and unemployed to the wealthy and famous—we are all tempted to find happiness for ourselves in this world wherever and however we can. If you do a quick Internet search for "what will make us happy" or "the key to happiness," you're immediately presented with a plethora of thoughts, suggestions, and opinions on how to find happiness.

We are often told that happiness is the result of wealth, fame, authority, freedom, high self-esteem, low expectations, or some combination of those. There is no shortage of books to buy on the subject. But wasn't it the act of seeking out more than we were allotted in the garden of Eden that led to discontentment in the first place?

Joy originates in a life with the Lord and can be mined from there alone. Who would foolishly resist the possibility of genuine joy? Search for the Lord with all your heart, choose the Lord, decide to walk in integrity and obedience to Him, and discover joy. To know Christ is to be truly joyful.

PRAYER

Christ Jesus, it is you that I seek today as my source for joy. I trust you as my source of life. From you alone comes glorious, inexpressible joy. Amen.

May your kingdom come soon. May your will be done on earth, as it is in heaven.

INSEPARABLE

WORD

And I am convinced that nothing can ever separate us from God's love. Neither death nor life, neither angels nor demons, neither our fears for today nor our worries about tomorrow—not even the powers of hell can separate us from God's love. No power in the sky above or in the earth below—indeed, nothing in all creation will ever be able to separate us from the love of God that is revealed in Christ Jesus our Lord.

Romans 8:38–39

THOUGHT

The greatest provisional need of humanity is life for the soul; *Zoe* life, and that is the life which originates from the singular source of God. Christ's great work of grace on the cross provided a way for us to have an inseparable relationship with him. Thankfully, through the ongoing work of his Holy Spirit in our lives, he is providing all things necessary to continue the process of causing his followers to be more like Christ with each new day. No external force existing on earth or in realms unseen can separate what God has brought together. The work that Christ has done for and within us will remain permanent, regardless of the keenest of dark weapons crafted by the enemy.

Have you ever seen two trees growing so closely together that, at one point, they meet, bind themselves together, and then continue growing as one tree? Our relationship with Christ is much like this. Once we have accepted salvation in Christ by his merciful grace and love, we are grafted into the vine, adopted into the family of God, one with Christ Jesus, feeding daily on the Bread of life.

Once bound to Jesus, we are inseparable from God himself; our sin and shame are no longer part of our identity and we cannot be detached from the depths of God's love. Praise God for his ultimate provision through Christ Jesus!

PRAYER

Lord Jesus, my heart is filled with confidence and joy at knowing the love between us is forever inseparable because of your work on the cross. Thank you! Amen.

Give us today the food we need.

June 7

JEALOUSY

WORD

The following week almost the entire city turned out to hear them preach the word of the Lord. But when some of the Jews saw the crowds, they were jealous; so they slandered Paul and argued against whatever he said.

Acts 13:44–45

THOUGHT

Prior to his conversion, Paul, then known as Saul, was a Jewish scholar, a man of well-known reputation, a Roman citizen, and wholly dedicated to Judaism. In his letter to the Philippians (3:5–6) he referred to himself as once a member of the Pharisees, and as for righteousness, obeyed the law without fault, and was a Hebrew of Hebrews.

He was a ruthless persecutor of the church and zealous in his pursuit to rid Judaism of schisms and cultish counterfeits of which he thought Christianity was one. He was convinced he was justified in his attempts to bring those associated with Jesus Christ to an end (Acts 22). He was certain his motive and mission were necessary to eliminate those committed to Jesus, whom he believed was a false teacher. Saul, the high priest, the priest's associates, and the Sadducees, were so filled with jealousy that they imprisoned the disciples (Acts 5:17).

Fortunately, when confronted by Christ on the road to Damascus, Saul realized his error and sin. Saul, the persecutor of Christianity, became Paul, a herald for all things Christ. Repentance occurred, freedom was birthed, and abundant fruit was produced throughout Paul's life and ministry for the cause of Christ. Prior to conversion, Paul had been destroying the very thing Jesus loved and gave his life for. Blind to the darkness of his heart and error of his ways, he was convinced his actions were pleasing to God.

Paul himself often became a recipient of the destructiveness of the same jealousy he had once dispensed. More than once he warned those within the body of Christ to beware of the harm and hurt jealousy can inflict.

PRAYER

Lord, I am still living in this earthly shell and I ask that, by your grace and power, you would keep the self-centered and self-destructive effects of jealousy from me. Amen.

Forgive us our sins, as we have forgiven those who sin against us.

June 8

LIFE AND LIGHT

WORD

The people who have sat in darkness
have seen a great light.
And for those who lived in the land where death casts its shadow,
a light has shined.

Matthew 4:16

THOUGHT

Prayerfully reading the Word of God instills within us light and life. His Word is the lamp to lead us in right paths, as written in Psalm 119:105. It is the heart's compass, the life-mapping instrument to lead the follower of Jesus away from the devious and cleverly placed pitfalls of the evil one.

The light from the Word reveals the Lord's instruction, his will, preferences, wisdom, and promises. We once sat in darkness, but we have now seen a great light in Christ Jesus. God's Word, the Word that became flesh and dwelt among us, is a great and precious gift that brings life and light to a dark world.

There are so many gifts to be discovered as we spend time studying the scriptures. We are reminded of the Lord's will for our lives, the work that he's done in our hearts, and the things that bring his abundant peace and joy to our days. We learn about the characteristics of God and the depths of his love. And his Word assures us that, whatever assignments the day may hold, he has already provided us with what we need to accomplish his will. His Word invites and assures us God is able to overcome whatever Satan has designed to tempt or distract us.

You light a lamp for me. The Lord, my God, lights up my darkness.[18]

PRAYER

Father, your light reveals the path that I should travel. It brings clarity to your will and how I should live my life. Your Word reminds me you have brought me out of darkness, rescued me, and set me apart as your child. I am grateful and desire to live all my days in honor of you. Amen.

Don't let us yield to temptation.

THE FRUIT OF WISDOM

WORD

But the wisdom from above is first of all pure. It is also peace loving, gentle at all times, and willing to yield to others. It is full of mercy and the fruit of good deeds. It shows no favoritism and is always sincere. And those who are peacemakers will plant seeds of peace and reap a harvest of righteousness.

James 3:17–18

THOUGHT

Throughout the book of Proverbs, we see the benefit of seeking God's wisdom. And here in James, we see important qualities and characteristics of wisdom that we should live out in our Christian walk.

By studying the Word of God, we know that God's wisdom is pure—perfect and without flaw. God's wisdom will not fail. Above all, God's wisdom manifests with perfect motivations, unlike any worldly sources of wisdom. His wisdom is not manipulative, selfish, or unkind, and neither are his ways. As James reminds us, God's wisdom manifests as genuine peace, gentleness, and a willingness to yield to others. It is not harsh, demanding, or prideful.

If we are walking in the Lord's wisdom, our lives will display mercy and be marked by the fruit of good deeds. We will not show favoritism, we will be peacemakers, and the fruit produced by God through us will yield a harvest of righteousness. May we all make the choice to ground ourselves in the wisdom of the Lord and live out that wisdom in our daily lives.

PRAYER

Lord, I pray for your perfect wisdom, for it delivers me from folly and the plans of the evil one. And it will reflect the fruit and life of your kingdom. Amen.

But rescue us from the evil one.

A GLIMPSE

WORD

After this I saw a vast crowd, too great to count, from every nation and tribe and people and language, standing in front of the throne and before the Lamb. They were clothed in white robes and held palm branches in their hands. And they were shouting with a great roar,

"Salvation comes from our God who sits on the throne and from the Lamb!"

And all the angels were standing around the throne and around the elders and the four living beings. And they fell before the throne with their faces to the ground and worshiped God. They sang,

*"Amen! Blessing and glory and wisdom
and thanksgiving and honor
and power and strength belong to our God
forever and ever! Amen."*

Revelation 7:9–12

THOUGHT

What a glorious glimpse into the celebration and worship that will happen at the second coming of Christ! The scriptures in Revelation are shrouded in mystery and provoke a sense of wonder, but it is abundantly clear that we will one day gather together to extravagantly worship the Lord our God.

Take a second to recall the most intense, holy moment of worship that you have experienced, whether alone or among thousands. Even that precious, holy moment pales in comparison to what we will experience in the presence of the Lord in the future.

Try as we may, our efforts to grasp what will unfold at the divine unveiling of God's glory are insufficient. He is unimaginable, his plans are incomprehensible, and his holiness is indescribable. On this side of heaven and time and space, we only get a glimpse.

PRAYER

Lord, thank you for giving us a glimpse into your glory—and thank you for the future that we get to spend honoring and celebrating you, the only God. I'm grateful for a tiny preview of what worship will be like then, and I ask that you would help me live a life of wholehearted worship to you now. Amen.

For yours is the kingdom and the power and the glory forever.

THE CHIEF AIM

WORD

Then the leaders of the Levites—Jeshua, Kadmiel, Bani, Hashabneiah, Sherebiah, Hodiah, Shebaniah, and Pethahiah—called out to the people: "Stand up and praise the LORD your God, for he lives from everlasting to everlasting!" Then they prayed:

"May your glorious name be praised! May it be exalted above all blessing and praise!

"You alone are the LORD. You made the skies and the heavens and all the stars. You made the earth and the seas and everything in them. You preserve them all, and the angels of heaven worship you."

Nehemiah 9:5–6

THOUGHT

The story of Nehemiah inspires us to stand willingly in the face of the impossible as we follow God's will. Nehemiah dedicated himself to what appeared to be the impossible task of rebuilding and re-establishing Jerusalem from its state of deterioration to again be testament to the glory and honor of God. The story reaches a conclusion with the people of Israel again abiding in a strong, honorable Jerusalem belonging to the Lord. The ultimate purpose in Jerusalem's restoration, however, was its re-establishment as a genuine place of worship, one of reverential honor and respect. This is also the lesson we learn and apply today.

The Father's will and intention for all of humanity (and the reason for the engagement of the unstoppable plan of reconciliation through the redemptive act of Christ), was to restore worship—to end the despair of the separated, wounded, broken, defeated soul, and restore it to God in holy communion with him. Nehemiah wept, prayed, and worked to see the ultimate restoration of Jerusalem as the dwelling place of worship of the God of Israel.

PRAYER

There is one God the Father, one Son Jesus Christ, one Holy Spirit, and one purpose for life: to worship now into eternity. The chief aim of Nehemiah was to restore your honor and worship. May that be my chief aim, to honor my Father in heaven, to make you known, and to worship your holy name. May your glorious name be praised! Amen.

Our Father in heaven, may your name be kept holy.

June 12

THE CALL TO BE A VOICE

WORD

This was John's testimony when the Jewish leaders sent priests and Temple assistants from Jerusalem to ask John, "Who are you?" He came right out and said, "I am not the Messiah."

"Well then, who are you?" they asked. "Are you Elijah?"
"No," he replied.
"Are you the Prophet we are expecting?"
"No."
"Then who are you? We need an answer for those who sent us. What do you have to say about yourself?"
John replied in the words of the prophet Isaiah:
"I am a voice shouting in the wilderness,
'Clear the way for the LORD's coming!'"

John 1:19–23

THOUGHT

The assignment of God for John the Baptist was for him to be a voice to announce the coming Messiah whose mission would alter humankind forever. Every person since the resurrection of Jesus who converts to Christ, who becomes a follower of Jesus, like John, also becomes a voice.

A voice, a messenger, committed to carrying on the vision and mission of the Lord, which is to go throughout the communities of the world sharing this story of the heart's liberation from evil's captivity. The will of God for every child of God is to be a voice for this story.

God's will for our life can be discovered through reading and studying the Bible, praying, and listening to wise counsel. No matter what Christ's call on our individual lives looks like, each of us have this in common: we are all to be "a voice" to the places God sends us.

He has told us to go into every place with the message of his kingdom, his good news, and make disciples. Each voice in his kingdom is important, each voice is powerful, and, in God's hands, each voice is fruitful. Do not be silent!

PRAYER

I choose to be a voice today, Lord Jesus, for you to speak through as you lead and will! Amen.

May your kingdom come soon. May your will be done on earth, as it is in heaven.

EVERY STEP

WORD

Teach me to do your will,
for you are my God.
May your gracious Spirit lead me forward
on a firm footing.

Psalm 143:10

THOUGHT

No one has better insight to where our next steps will be than God himself. He planned our journeys even before we arrived at the place we now stand, and he has promised to lead and guide us by his wisdom and power to the next place in his will.

Because we're unable to see the future, we can often feel anxiety about what's ahead. The Lord knows in divine detail the way we are to go and will supply what is needed along the way as we trust in him. He gives us the necessary guidance and provision for each of his assigned tasks.

Therefore, we can have faith that every step we take rests on firm footing. When we understand that the Spirit is leading us into his will and that the Lord is providing for us every step of the way, our hearts can rest, setting aside anxiety and thanking God for all he has done and all he is going to do.

PRAYER

I give thanks to your name, oh Most High! You are the Lord of my life and the Lord of this day.
Your way is always the best, and you provide me exactly what I need to walk in it.
Your way gives me hope, restores my life, and brings me joy. I'm grateful that I don't need to
worry about anything, because my life rests in the hands of my loving Creator.
Lead me by your gracious Spirit, oh, Lord my God. Amen.

Give us today the food we need.

THE TRANSFORMING POWER OF FORGIVENESS

WORD

For he has rescued us from the kingdom of darkness and transferred us into the Kingdom of his dear Son, who purchased our freedom and forgave our sins.

Colossians 1:13–14

THOUGHT

In can be difficult for us to understand forgiveness—both the forgiveness of our own sins in Christ Jesus and the forgiveness of those who have sinned against us. In fact, the word *forgiveness* is one of Merriam-Webster's top 10 percent of words in search popularity.[19] At its core, *to forgive* means to stop feeling anger toward someone or something, stop blaming, or grant relief from debt.

When we receive forgiveness through Christ, it results in the escape from darkness into light, from confusion to clarity, from bitterness to peace. And when we apply that same forgiveness in our lives toward others, our relationships are transformed for his glory.

Truly, without Christ's act on the cross, we all would stand condemned by sin. Giving our lives to him and accepting his death and resurrection on our behalf results in his unearned and undeserved grace in our lives. We, in turn, are expected to forgive those who trespass against us. Where forgiveness is present, anger, blame, and condemnation are absent.

PRAYER

Jesus, thank you for forgiving me, and may I, too, walk in forgiveness of others. Amen.

Forgive us our sins, as we have forgiven those who sin against us.

THE PATH TO SUCCESS

WORD

Jesus traveled through all the towns and villages of that area, teaching in the synagogues and announcing the Good News about the Kingdom. And he healed every kind of disease and illness. When he saw the crowds, he had compassion on them because they were confused and helpless, like sheep without a shepherd. He said to his disciples, "The harvest is great, but the workers are few. So pray to the Lord who is in charge of the harvest; ask him to send more workers into his fields."

Matthew 9:35–38

THOUGHT

We often hear from motivational speakers, accomplished businesspeople, and popular celebrities about what it takes to have a successful life, but the biblical definition of a successful life looks quite different than the world's. The path of Christ always leads away from temptation and toward true blessing and success, as defined by him. God's heart of compassion and mercy for the hollow soul is boundless, and it is of the utmost importance to him that those who are lost experience the love and freedom found in the good news.

I once had a person tell me they did not feel they were responsible to share the good news of Jesus Christ, that it was the duty of gifted evangelists. While certainly the evangelist's gift is genuine, by no means do they carry exclusivity in sharing the good news. Jesus commissions all who believe and receive his gift of grace to testify to his divine generosity.

There are three reasons we should all be engaged in sharing our faith. First, as genuine followers of Christ who are grateful for true joy and abundant life, we are responsible to tell others. Second, it is the mandate of Christ; freely we have received, so freely we must give. We are all given the directive to go into the world and make disciples (Matt. 28:19). And third, if we are like Christ, we will have compassion on the wounded, wandering, and suffering. Every Christian is called into the harvest field. We must resist any temptation to dissuade us from Christ's exciting adventurous commission. We should gratefully lean into every opportunity to share the best news for the world, the good news!

PRAYER

Lord, as I enter my day and come into contact with people, please lead me in the sensitivity and discerning of your Holy Spirit. Fill my heart with Christlike compassion for the lost. Let me be a life-giving conduit of the good news today. Amen.

Don't let us yield to temptation.

UNSHAKABLE

WORD

Let all that I am wait quietly before God,
for my hope is in him.
He alone is my rock and my salvation,
my fortress where I will not be shaken.
My victory and honor come from God alone.
He is my refuge, a rock where no enemy can reach me.
O my people, trust in him at all times.
Pour out your heart to him,
for God is our refuge.

Psalm 62:5–8

THOUGHT

When we are uncertain, overwhelmed, or afraid, we are shown the place of rescue and refuge: waiting quietly before the Lord of all heaven and earth. In our stillness and submission before him, we find hope. God alone is the safe fortress and hiding place, a sheltering harbor. Victory is not found in the resources or ways of people but in the unchanging faithfulness of God.

Christ alone is our sanctuary; he is the unshakable, impenetrable citadel of refuge. With sincerity, the psalmist invites us to trust in God at all times. When our confidence and boldness wane, and when intimidation and fear attempt to slyly slink into the soul, find the quiet place before God and pour out your heart to him, for our heavenly Father is our willing and only true refuge.

PRAYER

Lord, my Rock and my Redeemer, as I wait in quiet stillness before you, fill me with your peace and confidence. As I learn from your most life-giving and abundant Word, increase my truth and hope. I give you praise and honor this morning, for your presence is my refuge and rescue. Amen.

But rescue us from the evil one.

June 17

THE ONE AND ONLY GOD

WORD

"But you are my witnesses, O Israel!" says the LORD.
"You are my servant.
You have chosen to know me, believe in me,
and understand that I alone am God.
There is no other God—
there never has been, and there never will be."

Isaiah 43:10

THOUGHT

One very warm afternoon during a mission trip to Kampala, Uganda, I was invited to make an unscheduled visit to a ministry facility that helps unwed pregnant teen girls. During the tour of the facility, I was introduced to a young lady who ministers to the girls living there. She extended her hand to greet me and with a joy-filled smile, she introduced herself. She then began to share her story.

Like the other girls, she had once been a resident of the facility and a recipient of the kindness found within its walls. Now she was serving as an aide to help and encourage others as a witness to God's infinite goodness and grace.

While standing in the courtyard of the ministry, I asked if we might pray. When she began to pray, her joy and spiritual exuberance only increased as her words declared honor, gratefulness, and acknowledgment to our heavenly Father, the one and only God and Creator of all life. She was a small person but bold in spirit and filled with conviction, sincerity, and the power of God's transforming life.

No matter where we are in the world, we can rejoice and connect with others who are a part of God's people, celebrating his faithfulness together and declaring with praise and honor that he, indeed, is the one and only God. We can give thanks together as brothers and sisters in Christ for his redemptive love and goodness that's found throughout the world. What a wonderful thing to know him and serve as his witnesses.

PRAYER

Lord, I'm filled with gratitude that you have revealed yourself to me as the one and only God. You alone are God and there is no other. You and you alone can save and bring the lifeless to life! May your name be praised! And may you put brothers and sisters in my life who are full of encouragement and love. Amen.

For yours is the kingdom and the power and the glory forever.

MADE FOR WORSHIP

WORD

But the time is coming—indeed it's here now—when true worshipers will worship the Father in spirit and in truth. The Father is looking for those who will worship him that way. For God is Spirit, so those who worship him must worship in spirit and in truth.

John 4:23–24

THOUGHT

We were created to worship God. Unfortunately, much of the Western church has limited its understanding of worship to the music portion of a typical church service. Biblical worship, however, is to be celebrated with our entire lives and is manifested in many multiple forms: communion, prayer, scripture reading, giving, sermons, and ministering to widows and orphans. Genuine worship is offered and expressed in the many forms of art, in loving our neighbor as ourselves, and, yes, by honest hard work if done as unto the Lord. Our lives are to be continual acts of worship.

The components and characteristics of worship can become lifeless religious practices if we aren't paying attention to the state of our hearts. What causes the worship of God to ignite is the heart that bursts with love and thanksgiving for the liberator of the soul, the writer of divine destiny.

His invitation to enter into wholehearted worship is not to a certain few, but to everyone who will lay aside self and step into his divine design for honoring him. The Father seeks those who are given to his ways, those who hunger to worship in spirit and in truth.

PRAYER

Father, I bow before you this morning and exalt your name. You seek those who will worship in spirit and in truth. I hunger and thirst for your presence wholeheartedly. Amen.

Our Father in heaven, may your name be kept holy.

NOTHING CAN STAND AGAINST THE LORD

WORD

No human wisdom or understanding or plan
can stand against the LORD.

Proverbs 21:30

THOUGHT

Despite the forces of evil in our world, God still stands strong and unwavering. All who refute, challenge, and deny God will one day cease, but he will continue forever. The Bible instructs us to always be ready to defend our faith, and many of us have found ourselves in this position.

During my entire Christian life, even in debates where I found myself weak and unconvincing in a retort, I have never felt or thought God was not alive or my personal relationship with him was weak. Christ has changed my life and the lens by which I see life, and I can never be persuaded differently by human wisdom, understanding, or the plots of the evil one to disprove or dishonor him. He cannot and will not be dethroned. Nothing can stand against the Lord. Nothing!

Although we may feel like we don't have the right words to express his goodness when we're met with opposition, the greatest and most reliable evidence of God's existence and his miracle of redeeming grace abides in the hearts he has redeemed. Live your life in honor of him so that others may see his infinite glory.

PRAYER

Lord, I desire to sense your presence throughout the day. I am encouraged to know your plans cannot be thwarted, and I am grateful I am included in them. I'm thankful for my security in you. Help me live a life that honors your infinite glory. Amen.

May your kingdom come soon. May your will be done on earth, as it is in heaven.

QUENCHING THE THIRSTY HEART

WORD

Jesus replied, "If you only knew the gift God has for you and who you are speaking to,
you would ask me, and I would give you living water."

John 4:10

THOUGHT

The story of Christ's encounter with the Samaritan woman in John 4 serves us with rich insight into the heart of Jesus toward all humanity.

He was God incarnate, both God and man, during his earthly ministry. During a journey from Judea to Galilee, Jesus paused at the well of Jacob for a simple respite. There he initiated a conversation with one others likely would have ignored. His mission, though, was to all mankind and purposed toward whoever would listen and receive what he offered. His was provision void of temporal limitations. His met the need of the human heart suffering from the absence of the light and life of God.

This woman, who may have thought herself out of step with hope the remainder of her days, instead discovered provision for her greatest need, which was heaven's nourishment for the thirsting soul, the living water of Jesus.

PRAYER

Lord, you have given me living water in the good news of your salvation.
I am overwhelmed by this thought and your gift, and I'm grateful for being a recipient of
what you have done. I embrace you, I worship you, and I desire to serve you this day as the
wellspring of life that you are, the only thirst-quenching water for my heart. Amen.

Give us today the food we need.

June 21

A LIFE MARKED BY PASSION

WORD

But my life is worth nothing to me unless I use it for finishing the work assigned me by the Lord Jesus—the work of telling others the Good News about the wonderful grace of God.

Acts 20:24

THOUGHT

The word *passion* is often used in songs, poetry, and sermons. Certainly, as Christians our hearts should be marked by a passion for Christ and his kingdom. But what causes a person to reach the place where a passion for God changes every fiber of their being? At what point does passion for the Lord overtake all other desires and goals to instead embrace the assignments of God?

It's when our spirits awaken to God's glory and we realize that all worldly things that we believed to be profitable and fruitful are lacking compared to the will of the Lord. In the light of Christ and his love for us, all worldly desires and goals fall to the wayside as we embrace his will.

Jesus, in all his mercy, gave us life and eternal riches in exchange for our worthlessness. Once our hearts are transformed by Christ, we become passionate about helping others know the same freedom and love. Much like Paul here in Acts 20, after encountering the fullness of God's grace and forgiveness, we can't help but tell others about the wonderful mercy of the Lord. May we be a people marked by a passionate love of God, so much so that all our earthly desires and goals pale in comparison to what he offers.

When the captive heart realizes it is liberated from its imprisonment of the putrid dungeons of sin, and also forgiven, what emerges from a truly grateful heart is an unrestrained holy passion to love and serve wholeheartedly its liberator, Jesus Christ. This is the miracle, the power of forgiveness, and the message to share with those thinking forgiveness is not a possibility for them.

PRAYER

Father, because you have forgiven me, grace now leads and empowers me to tell others about your wonderful good news. By the power of your Spirit, help me place nothing above loving you and living out your will. Amen.

Forgive us our sins, as we have forgiven those who sin against us.

FRIENDSHIP

WORD

Timothy, I thank God for you—the God I serve with a clear conscience, just as my ancestors did. Night and day I constantly remember you in my prayers. I long to see you again, for I remember your tears as we parted. And I will be filled with joy when we are together again.

2 Timothy 1:3–4

THOUGHT

Timothy was Paul's friend, spiritual son, and co-laborer in Christ. There existed between them a pure friendship of mutual respect, and Paul's words reflect it. As brothers and sisters in Christ, we often find ourselves connecting strongly with other believers, which gives us strength, encouragement, and accountability—and these relationships are necessary in God's eyes.

Our friendships that enjoy a shared love of Christ result in a richer spiritual life and help equip us to better reflect the love of our Savior. These friendships also bolster us and lead us away from temptation.

Tell your friends today you are grateful to God for the bond you share and the encouragement they provide as you live in honor of the King, Christ the Messiah.

PRAYER

Lord, I pray today for my friends and for your blessing upon them as they seek first your kingdom and glory in all they do. I pray that my unbelieving friends would come to know your love, and I ask that you would give me the words to share of your goodness. Amen.

Don't let us yield to temptation.

A SECURED FUTURE

WORD

But I am trusting you, O Lord,
saying, "You are my God!"
My future is in your hands.
Rescue me from those who hunt me down relentlessly.

Psalm 31:14–15

THOUGHT

It's true that our foe is well-skilled, well-armed, and merciless in his attempts to wound, and were it possible, utterly destroy us. He is the enemy of God and the enemy of all that God loves. His pursuit is relentless.

The good news is that our future is solidly secure as our trust is in God and all Christ accomplished on our behalf. Though Satan is relentless, he is not omnipotent; he is limited and powerless against the Lord. Thus we find continual biblical encouragement to trust in God who firmly holds our futures in his powerful hands.

First Peter 5:9 briefly but boldly states how to best deal with the evil one: *Stand firm against him and be strong in the faith.* Though he is relentless, the enemy will flee when he is resisted. We must stand fast with trust and faith in Christ's finished work that has already conquered him. Our future is secure.

PRAYER

Father, help me discern your will and follow you through my day by the leading of your Holy Spirit. Help me rest knowing I have a secured future in you, no matter what this day or week holds, no matter what the scheme of the evil one. You are greater than any and all of his strategies. Thank you for your redemption, and thank you for holding my future in your grasp. Amen.

But rescue us from the evil one.

ABOVE ALL

WORD

*Therefore, God elevated him to the place of highest honor
and gave him the name above all other names,
that at the name of Jesus every knee should bow,
in heaven and on earth and under the earth,
and every tongue declare that Jesus Christ is Lord,
to the glory of God the Father.*

Philippians 2:9–11

THOUGHT

The earth is filled with evidence of humanity's resourcefulness and accomplishments. From ancient eras of antiquity to present day, history is filled with stories of human feats, endurance, and competitions. From the Great Wall of China to the Pyramids of Giza, from the Panama Canal to the Channel Tunnel stretching underwater the length of the Strait of Dover from England to France, from the Industrial Revolution to the Space Race—everywhere we look we can see works of human ingenuity.

The drive to excel or exceed past human boundaries or limitations is what propels innovation forward in the global community. We feel the constant push to rise above the last benchmark in nearly every human arena: athletic competitions, corporate product development and sales, technological feats, financial institutions, and entertainment.

Man, however, is not the powerbroker nor the great innovator that he assumes, for there is one who exceeds so far above and beyond him he cannot be placed within the same league categorically. He is Jesus Christ, Ruler above all who rule, authority above all other powers.

PRAYER

*Only you are Lord. Only you are above all things.
Only you are worthy of worship, honor, power, and all glory! Amen.*

For yours is the kingdom and the power and the glory forever.

GOD ALONE

WORD

He alone has spread out the heavens
and marches on the waves of the sea.

Job 9:8

THOUGHT

The above scripture is taken from Job's discussion with one of his friends during Job's time of despair. In all of Job's difficult loss, he recognized the smallness of himself and the vast holiness of God. Job declares that God himself created the earth as we know it, and in all God's greatness, he spread out the heavens and can march on the waves of the sea. God alone owns it all, and he alone is great and holy.

Have you ever seen a thick mountain fog move to cover the base of a valley? Once fog travels from a mountaintop to the base below, it covers and conceals everything in the area. Nothing is visible through the blanket of dense fog.

God is far beyond our ability to describe and define. Much like a fog that provides full cover, he is overwhelming and all-consuming. He is God alone, and should he choose, he could quickly move over the whole earth in such a way that all would be concealed by the power of his glory. We are the created; he is the Creator. We exist to glorify him—and what an honor to do so.

PRAYER

Father God, you have covered the whole earth with your glory. You alone dominate all things at all times, and you have plans for every created thing. Praise your holy name! Amen.

Our Father in heaven, may your name be kept holy.

NO ROOM FOR ANYTHING ELSE

WORD

*Barnabas was a good man, full of the Holy Spirit and strong in faith.
And many people were brought to the Lord.*

Acts 11:24

THOUGHT

Over the years, I have often been drawn to the spiritually rich and humble character of Barnabas, a notable servant of God. In the Bible, we're not given the same volume of information about Barnabas as we are other faithful servants of Jesus, yet he made major contributions to God's kingdom through his sincere love for the Lord.

What an honor it would be for any man or woman devoted to God to have someone say that he or she was a good person, full of the Holy Spirit. If something is full of one thing, there can be no room within it for other things. If one is filled with the Holy Spirit, there is no room for things that aren't of the Lord. The Holy Spirit within Barnabas is the obvious explanation for his strength in the faith.

On top of the kind words about Barnabas's character, we see many people were brought to the Lord through him. As servants of Jesus, more people coming to know Christ would be our ultimate joy, and it was something that I'm sure Barnabas himself experienced. He was a vehicle who brought many to Christ, for Barnabas had no room for anything else except for the love of Jesus.

PRAYER

Father, may I become more like you with each day. I pray goodness will be genuinely rooted in my heart by your grace. I pray to be full of your Spirit at all times, to be strong in my faith, and to trust in you fully. May I tell the world of your great deeds, everlasting love, and marvelous grace. May many come to know your mercy and freedom as I share about you with others. Amen.

May your kingdom come soon. May your will be done on earth, as it is in heaven.

AT JUST THE RIGHT TIME

WORD

There is one God and one Mediator who can reconcile God and humanity—the man Christ Jesus.
He gave his life to purchase freedom for everyone.

This is the message God gave to the world at just the right time.

1 Timothy 2:5–6

THOUGHT

Once when I was driving out West, I passed a billboard on the side of the interstate that advertised the "Messiah," who was now living in Florida, could be seen at an upcoming event. The billboard contained the dates, location, and time for the event. I remember actually laughing out loud when I saw it, but I quickly became serious as I realized that, unfortunately, many would actually think this impostor was their hope.

In Matthew 24, Jesus warned us of impostors—and many have come and gone since his warning. But we can rest assured: the Bible declares the goodness and absoluteness of Christ and his redeeming sacrifice, and it clearly declares Jesus Christ is the one true Messiah.

There is one mediator capable of genuine reconciliation with God, and he is described and identified in the Word of the Lord—both in the Old and New Testament. He gave his life so that we might have eternal life and full redemption. We need not look elsewhere, for he was given to the world at just the right time.

PRAYER

Thank you, Jesus Christ—Messiah, Savior of the world, and Lord of all!
Thank you for providing me with your love, mercy, and grace. Amen.

Give us today the food we need.

POWER OVER ANGER

WORD

Get rid of all bitterness, rage, anger, harsh words, and slander,
as well as all types of evil behavior. Instead, be kind to each other, tenderhearted, forgiving one
another, just as God through Christ has forgiven you.

Ephesians 4:31–32

THOUGHT

I have met with and ministered to many people over the past four decades who are oppressed by anger. It is easily recognized, perhaps because I was also once its prisoner. Being forgiven by Christ—and, in turn, forgiving others—strips away the power of anger and leaves it with no effect in our lives.

When the love and grace of Christ has filled the heart and soul, there is no longer room for bitterness, rage, anger, harsh words, and slander. It cannot be emphasized enough: forgiveness in and through Christ is the soul's door to freedom.

The above scripture reminds us of the power that forgiveness has in our lives and relationships. Let us set aside anger and bitterness and choose to forgive one another instead, walking in kindness and having a tender heart.

PRAYER

Father, by the power of your Holy Spirit, cause me to be found extending sincerity, tenderheartedness, kindness, and forgiveness toward all. Help me get rid of all bitterness, rage, anger, harsh words, and slander in my words, thoughts, and heart. Amen.

Forgive us our sins, just as we have forgiven those who have sinned against us.

June 29

A WIDE-OPEN DOOR

WORD

There is a wide-open door for a great work here, although many oppose me.

1 Corinthians 16:9

THOUGHT

In this simple verse, Paul gives us a wonderful example of a grateful heart devoted to trusting the leadership of Christ in all things. In the last chapter of 1 Corinthians, Paul concludes his letter to the Christians in Corinth by saying God has given him a wide-open door in the city of Ephesus to proclaim God's good news of grace.

The Lord led Paul to Ephesus, and there was much opposition and challenge for him along the way, yet Paul's writing reflects his spirit of faith and enthusiasm. He understood the best opportunities always exist within God's divine plan regardless of the challenges.

It's true that God's will may not be the "easiest" way, but it will always be the *best* way. Though challenges may arise in our journey, we are wise to resist the temptation to take the easier paths, those which may be more comfortable, less challenging, but void of God's blessing. Wherever God leads will always be the safest and most purposeful way to go. We can rest assured in this truth.

PRAYER

Lead me in your way and in your will, Lord, for your way is perfect and your will brings glory to your name. Living my life for you is my true purpose, and there is no higher call or privilege. Amen.

Don't let us yield to temptation.

THE COURSE OF CHRIST

WORD

We know that God's children do not make a practice of sinning, for God's Son holds them securely, and the evil one cannot touch them. We know that we are children of God and that the world around us is under the control of the evil one.

And we know that the Son of God has come, and he has given us understanding so that we can know the true God. And now we live in fellowship with the true God because we live in fellowship with his Son, Jesus Christ. He is the only true God, and he is eternal life.

Dear children, keep away from anything that might take God's place in your hearts.

1 John 5:18–21

THOUGHT

What is God's part in ensuring the victorious Christian life until the end, and what is our part in that? Believers in Christ have probably entertained this thread of thought throughout church history.

The passage above seems to exhibit traces of a similar tension. The Son has come, and now we know the true God. Because of Christ and his work in us, we now live in fellowship with God and *we know we are children of God*. Still, in the same passage, the exhortation is given to us to steer clear of anything that may lure us from God retaining complete prominence in our lives.

So how do we do our part in defeating sin and staying on the course the Lord has set before us? The victory is in "keeping our eyes on Jesus, the champion who initiates and perfects our faith" (Heb. 12:2). True, our foe is experienced and intentional toward our demise, but the Lord is a warrior (Ex. 15:3), invincible in battle (Ps. 24:8); the champion!

We will finish well on this course if we keep our eyes on Jesus—and at our journey's end, we will fall into the arms of the Lord, forever removed from any influence other than the love of our perfect Father.

PRAYER

Be the object of my heart, Lord, the voice who guides me and leads me victorious through the course of this life. Amen.

But rescue us from the evil one.

SACRIFICES THAT PLEASE GOD

WORD

...therefore, let us offer through Jesus a continual sacrifice of praise to God,
proclaiming our allegiance to his name. And don't forget to do good and to share with those in need.
These are the sacrifices that please God.

Hebrews 13:15–16

THOUGHT

There are many expressions of worship and praise revealed in the Bible. One way we express our love for the Lord is by a continual sacrifice of praise. We were created to worship the Lord by praising his name, and it is the one thing we will continue to do as we pass through the threshold of this earth-life into eternal life in heaven.

These verses from Hebrews also remind us that, in addition to offering sacrifices of praise and worship, we should not forget to "do good and share with those in need." This kind of sacrifice is pleasing to Christ, brings him glory, and honors his name.

Let us not forget to do either one: worship God with sacrifices of praise and do good by sharing with those in need. Both forms of sacrifice are holy and beautiful, and God is honored by both.

PRAYER

Lord, doing good and sharing with those in need is one way I might worship you. In addition to singing and proclaiming your goodness with my words, may I be vigilant to worship you by loving and giving to those in need. Please direct me to those you would have me to serve. Amen.

For yours is the kingdom and the power and the glory forever.

HE DOES WONDERFUL THINGS

WORD

Praise the LORD God, the God of Israel,
who alone does such wonderful things.
Praise his glorious name forever!
Let the whole earth be filled with his glory.
Amen and amen!

Psalm 72:18–19

THOUGHT

The Bible tells us Jesus will one day return to earth, the event referred to as his second coming. He will appear in all his majesty, culminating the end of this present age and eventually ushering in the new heavens and new earth.

Everything will be filled with the Lord's glory, and we will forever abide in the majestic beauty of his perfection—truly a wonderful thing. However, the most wonderful thing will be the privilege that the redeemed people of God have to worship him in all of his splendor, no longer interrupted or distracted by any worldly thing.

We will abide in the presence and wonder of the Father, Son, and Holy Spirit, praising God's glorious name forever.

PRAYER

I praise your name on this morning, Lord! You and your handiwork are marvelous beyond words. You have made all things for your glory. May the whole earth be filled with your glory. Amen.

Our Father in heaven may your name be honored.

PEACE IN EVERY SITUATION

WORD

...now may the Lord of peace himself give you his peace at all times and in every situation.
The Lord be with you all...May the grace of our Lord Jesus Christ be with you all.

2 Thessalonians 3:16, 18

THOUGHT

When I was seventeen, I was driving home late one night and fell asleep at the wheel. I drifted across two opposite lanes of traffic, struck a tree at an angle that flipped the car over, and then slid head-on into a second tree. I was unconscious when the police arrived and was later told their first assessment was that the operator of the car did not survive. All I remember was gaining momentary consciousness, calling for help, and hearing a voice say, "We're going to get you out." My next recollection was having multiple wounds stitched in the emergency room.

My parents were called, but my father was so emotionally shaken that he could not immediately accompany my mother to the hospital; instead, he stayed home and prayed for my survival. Answered prayer soon came in the form of God's peace. A phone call followed shortly after from my mother telling him I was going to be OK, and he arrived at the hospital a short time later. My dad later told me my mother's news on the phone was confirmation of answered prayer, but the peace of God arrived in his heart even before the phone call.

Paul writes that God is the Lord of peace. He is its source. It is not a temporary peace. He abides within his children, so we have the possibility of peace at all times and in every circumstance. May we be aware that throughout our day, no matter our circumstances, we have peace in every situation through Christ Jesus.

PRAYER

Lord Jesus, may my heart and my eyes be set upon you; you are my source for all things.
May I walk in your grace and your peace throughout this day and always. Amen.

May your kingdom come soon. May your will be done on earth, as it is in heaven.

TRUST

WORD

Give all your worries and cares to God, for he cares about you.

1 Peter 5:7

THOUGHT

There are times when simple commands like this one appear distant and difficult to execute. When I feel this way, I usually discover it is a problem of what I like to simply call *lack*: lack of faith, lack of trust, lack of listening, or lack of obedience.

The Bible clearly tells me to give all my worries to God because he cares for me, period! No excuses. No questions asked. We are called to submit fully to him, including submitting our anxieties. In fact, Jesus said emphatically that we should not worry because God knows our needs and will provide for them (Matt. 6:32–33).

During times of concern, Psalm 56:3 has been a close friend: "But when I am afraid, I will put my trust in you." Being able to see that David, a man after God's own heart, experienced times when worry and fear were real and present can be a balm to an anxious spirit. We can follow David's example of casting our cares on the Lord: David simply acknowledged his fear—simultaneously acknowledging his weakness and lack of trust—and then asked for God's intervention and the removal of his fear and worries.

PRAYER

Lord, you have said, "Seek the Kingdom of God above all else, and live righteously"
and you will provide for my needs (Matt. 6:33). You speak only truth—so, Lord, by your grace
and the power of your Holy Spirit, help me to walk in faith and in trust of you.
Lead me to seek only the kingdom and your righteousness. Amen.

Give us today the food we need.

GOD'S PROMISE OF FREEDOM

WORD

...but the Scriptures declare that we are all prisoners of sin,
so we receive God's promise of freedom only by believing in Jesus Christ.

Galatians 3:22

THOUGHT

Humanity cries out passionately for genuine liberty. We long for true freedom: freedom from worry, difficulty, strongholds, financial strain, health issues, disappointments, guilt, and shame—the list could go on.

The ultimate war for freedom is the struggle for the human soul. The enemy relentlessly works to keep individuals enslaved to darkness and despair, but God designed a flawless plan beyond evil's reach to free the human heart from the cruelest bondage. God has declared independence for any and all who would receive the liberating grace provided by Jesus Christ, the only Son of God.

In sin we're imprisoned, but in Christ we soar. Praise to the Lord for his promise of freedom. Receive Christ, receive freedom!

PRAYER

Lord, I am grateful to have many liberties, but I am most grateful for the freedom of my soul
that is made possible by the grace and forgiveness of Jesus, the greatest liberator. Amen.

Forgive us our sins, as we have forgiven those who sin against us.

HOME WITH US

WORD

Jesus replied, "All who love me will do what I say. My Father will love them,
and we will come and make our home with each of them."

John 14:23

THOUGHT

Zacchaeus had been watching Jesus from a sycamore tree when Jesus spoke to him, "Quick, come down! I must be a guest in your home today" (Luke 19:5). What excitement and joy Zacchaeus must have felt! He not only got to see Jesus, the of-the-minute famous person being talked about in the region, but he also was going to host him in his home.

In today's scripture, Jesus promises to any who will love and obey him that he will take up residence with them. Of course, Christ is referring to residence in the heart, but what if he were physically to abide in your home? How would that change your life? There would be excitement for sure, but your daily routine would probably be marked by fresh spiritual diligence and a radically Christian lifestyle if he were literally dwelling in your home.

If we knew each morning Jesus would be making his way down the hallway and into the kitchen for morning coffee with us, our lives would no doubt be lived with much higher levels of temptation avoidance and far greater intentionality.

As believers, the Holy Spirit lives within us, available to consult and lead us concerning any matter. He abides with us, so we are guided into his holiness and righteousness. Therefore, shouldn't our lives be marked by spiritual diligence and a radically Christian lifestyle? Not out of law and legalism, but out of a deep love and respect for his presence. We have the ability to be in constant relationship with him and enjoy the friendship of God, all because he chooses to make his home within us. Nothing from the world can compare or bring completeness to our lives like Christ in residence within our souls, and there is no greater privilege than to display his love and glory to the world.

PRAYER

Thank you for taking up residence within my heart, Lord Jesus.
Lead me away from all things futile and into all things fruitful.
I pray I will honor you in all the activity of this day as we walk through it together. Amen.

Don't let us yield to temptation.

CONFIDENCE IN GOD'S TRUTH

WORD

...but I will never stop loving him
nor fail to keep my promise to him.
No, I will not break my covenant;
I will not take back a single word I said.
I have sworn an oath to David,
and in my holiness I cannot lie.

Psalm 89:33–35

THOUGHT

Truth is such a valuable treasure—especially the truth of the promises of the Lord. The word *truth* is often used, but at least in modern Western culture, false or misleading statements are so often and easily used in the media and opinions are so commonly stated as facts that we scarcely know who or what to believe anymore.

However, there is still one bastion of certainty, one source of pure credibility, and one truth void of deception or wrong motivations: the Lord and his everlasting Word. When we read or hear the Bible, we know God's promises are trustworthy, accurate, and flawless. We can rest in the knowledge that whatever directives and promises God has given us through the scriptures can be relied on fully—they are what's best for us.

In today's scripture, we see God's promise to never stop loving his people. God alone is capable of making promises containing complete truth. And what a sweet, sweet truth is found in Psalm 89! He will never stop loving us, he will never break his word, and he cannot lie. What a good God indeed!

PRAYER

You, heavenly Father, are the source of truth.
Thank you for promises that are always true, always right, and always good. Amen.

But rescue us from the evil one.

July 8

HE IS OVER ALL THINGS

WORD

Yours, O LORD, is the greatness, the power, the glory, the victory, and the majesty.
Everything in the heavens and on earth is yours, O LORD, and this is your kingdom. We adore you as
the one who is over all things.

1 Chronicles 29:11

THOUGHT

Before we know Christ, we often deem ourselves or our achievements as superior and powerful, holding our successes high as treasure. We often measure power, prestige, and the accumulation of wealth and earthly accolades as valuable, and we use our status or wealth to advance ourselves upward within the human chains of command.

But then God steps on the scene, and our hearts and lives are dramatically changed. All is lost in his shadow. Once we have met Christ and experienced the love of God, nothing else compares to his glory. From greatest to least, all is God's. He is the Maker of all things, the Sustainer of all things. All things exist for his good pleasure and to glorify his kingdom. He has all the power, all the prestige, all the wealth—and he deserves all the accolades. Nothing on earth compares to him.

PRAYER

I adore you, Lord, because you are the only one glorious enough and worthy enough to adore.
I worship you this morning King of kings and God over all. Be glorified! Amen.

For yours is the kingdom and the power and the glory forever.

ONE GOD AND FATHER

WORD

*All the nations you made
will come and bow before you, LORD;
they will praise your holy name.
For you are great and perform wonderful deeds.
You alone are God.*

Psalm 86:9–10

THOUGHT

One of the most effective weapons of the enemy is confusion. He works to deceive humanity by presenting multiple religious choices and differing philosophical approaches to life. Evil attempts to disguise cleverly designed (but flawed) replicas of God's truth to confuse and frustrate people from knowing the one true God, Yahweh.

Those who choose other religions or atheism may argue with strong, passionate denials of God's truth, but in the end, the deceived will be left with regret, disappointment, and eternal separation from the Father of all life. Those given to God and his purposes will forever enjoy his eternal presence and divine communion.

There is one God, Yahweh, and he is indeed the great God of wonder. His heart is for all people to know his deep love for them as the Father of all wonder. His desire for us to know him is so great that he withheld nothing, not even his only Son, in order that we may be forgiven, granted grace, and enter into holy relationship with him and all that is good.

PRAYER

*Father, may your name be honored and praised this day.
You are great and all you do is wonderful! Amen.*

Our Father in heaven, may your name be kept holy.

July 10

SPEAK OUT

WORD

Then I said, "Look, I have come.
As is written about me in the Scriptures:
I take joy in doing your will, my God,
for your instructions are written on my heart."
I have told all your people about your justice.
I have not been afraid to speak out,
as you, O LORD, well know.
I have not kept the good news of your justice hidden in my heart;
I have talked about your faithfulness and saving power.
I have told everyone in the great assembly
of your unfailing love and faithfulness.

Psalm 40:7–10

THOUGHT

This psalm of David reflects his deep gratefulness for all things Godward, and what he felt was privilege and honor to declare the Lord and his kingdom qualities to whomever and whenever there was opportunity. He embraced it as the will of God for his life to speak out.

Jesus took joy in and was fulfilled by doing the will of the Father, not his own will—an example we should follow. We should not require a constant reminder to share the good news of Christ with others or obey God's calling on our lives. Loving and obeying God should always consume our hearts and fill our days.

When we speak out about God's goodness, our declarations should be fearless and empowered by God's spirit. We can proclaim his perfect and holy justice, the good news of his faithful, unfailing love, and his unparalleled saving grace with confidence. The message of his kingdom was not intended to be concealed from the world, but displayed as boldly as a city on a hill. That way, the world might know God has made provision for humanity's redemption through belief and obedience to his Son Jesus Christ.

PRAYER

Lord, I offer myself to you anew this morning. Use me to proclaim the life and liberty of your grace, faithfulness, and unfailing love. Please use my life as your mouthpiece to speak of you, your heart, and your flawless unfailing plans. Amen.

May your kingdom come soon. May your will be done on earth, as it is in heaven.

July 11

PRAYING EARNESTLY

WORD

*Epaphras, a member of your own fellowship and a servant of Christ Jesus,
sends you his greetings. He always prays earnestly for you, asking God to make you strong and
perfect, fully confident that you are following the whole will of God. I can assure you that he prays
hard for you and also for the believers in Laodicea and Hierapolis.*

Colossians 4:12–13

THOUGHT

Oh, that we would all have people like Epaphras in our lives! He was a genuine lover of Christ. Apparently he had given up, at least temporarily, the familiarity of his homeland to accompany Paul on his missions. He was seen by Paul as a servant of Christ and an asset to the building up of the church. He was a member of the church in Colossae, so he was acquainted with the church members' personalities, challenges, strengths, and potentials.

Paul must have often overheard Epaphras praying as he mentions those earnest and hard prayers for his spiritual family and village. And what was the content of his prayer for his brothers and sisters? That they would be strong in Christ, perfect in Christ, confident in Christ, and following the *whole* will of God.

Those like Epaphras are one of God's wonderful, beautiful, and needed provisions for expanding and sustaining our roles as we carry out the will of the Father. And may we also be like Epaphras, interceding on behalf of our spiritual family earnestly.

PRAYER

*Lord, I pray that many more people who pray earnestly and faithfully would be raised up
in the family of God. I also ask that I might be one of those people in the body of believers
who would faithfully intercede on behalf of my brothers and sisters. Amen.*

Give us today the food we need.

PRIVILEGE

WORD

*I am writing to you who are God's children
because your sins have been forgiven through Jesus.*

1 John 2:12

THOUGHT

For those receiving John's letter, I wonder how they felt as they read these words. What a joy to be counted among those whose sins have been forgiven! The letter was targeted to those who found new freedom in their decision to follow Christ; they were new recipients of God's great and marvelous grace. They were now God's children!

It's mind-boggling and awe-inspiring that God himself would forgive our sins and, in turn, provide us with spiritual freedom—all through himself! Who are we to be the recipients of such privilege? Mere worthless flesh is transformed, and we receive membership into the royal family of God.

Yes, this letter is to the specific group of believers to whom John is writing—but its contents are also for us. It's addressed to all God's children—so read, listen, and heed.

PRAYER

*Silent, grateful, and humble. Lord, this is what I'm feeling in this early morning vigil.
I'm grateful for my freedom in you. Amen.*

Forgive us our sins, as we have forgiven those who sin against us.

THE PROVISION OF SIGHT

WORD

Jesus spoke to the people once more and said, "I am the light of the world. If you follow me, you won't have to walk in darkness, because you will have the light that leads to life."

John 8:12

THOUGHT

I arrived late one evening to a small cottage located on a wooded hillside. I walked in, set my backpack down, and immediately started a fire in an old wood stove. Once the flames were steady, I decided to step out the back door for a glance. It was a cloudy night—and even though I knew there was a beautiful valley to behold, I could see nothing. In fact, I couldn't see more than about ten feet into the woods. However, the next morning the sunlight revealed one of the many striking valleys in the Ozarks.

Light causes things unseen to become visible. That seems like a simple statement, but through the lens of today's scripture, it's a powerful promise. Outside of my cottage in the woods, the light of dawn exposed a portion of a lovely southern Missouri landscape, but I would have never attempted to explore the landscape while the valley was cloaked in darkness and nothing was visible.

Jesus is the light of the world, and darkness cannot conceal him. He is our provision of sight. If we follow his bright holiness and truth, we will always be led away from temptation. He will illuminate our paths, equipping us for the journey ahead.

PRAYER

Jesus, in you we have light that leads to life. Thank you for guiding me, protecting me, and leading me away from temptation. Amen.

Don't let us yield to temptation.

THE GREATEST DELIVERANCE

WORD

Yes, Adam's one sin brings condemnation for everyone, but Christ's one act of righteousness brings a right relationship with God and new life for everyone.

Romans 5:18

THOUGHT

The death and resurrection of the Son of God changed everything—it forced Satan's death grip on the throat of humanity forever loose. Christ ended the effects of sin, which were to forever separate us from God the Father. As sons and daughters of God, we are no longer under condemnation.

Through his death and resurrection, Jesus built an indestructible bridge for all who would believe and receive him as Christ, one that gives access to a relationship with the Lord on High. Jesus is the Messiah, the only Son of God, and we rejoice in his magnificent grace-gift and the greatest form of deliverance.

Through Christ alone, we may enter into right relationship with God. As we pass through the redeeming threshold of grace, we are delivered from the evil one; we escape the darkness and enter into new life—eternal life.

PRAYER

Praise to you this morning, my Deliverer! Amen.

But rescue us from the evil one.

July 15

THE PURPOSE FOR ALL LIFE

WORD

Let everything that breathes sing praises to the LORD!
Praise the LORD!

Psalm 150:6

THOUGHT

For the heart passionately in love with the Creator of all things, singing praise to the Lord is an exciting privilege. Interestingly, praise to the Lord appears here, not as a suggestion, but as a command. Yet to the lover of God, it does not seem like a command at all, but instead an invitation to experience the ultimate of life's honors.

God designed and produced all living things to fulfill their highest of achievement in glorifying him. When we do so, we encounter human experience in its utmost beauty.

Yes, everything that has breath should worship the Lord! Praise to the Lord is to be done to him, for him. Praise to the Lord is meant to be heard, meant to be sung. Praise to the giver of life, to the one who has composed in us the ultimate song! The song of life of the redeemed.

In the age to come, we will get to see what it really looks like when everything that has breath praises the Lord. What a sight, indeed! The limitations and boundaries we experience in this earth-life will be removed in the presence of the Divine. We will break forth in an eternal song with all of creation, and we will not grow tired or weary of singing praise to the Holy One.

PRAYER

Praise you, Lord, of heaven and earth! You alone are God and your kingdom and dominion remains forever. Holy is your name! Amen.

For yours is the kingdom and the power and the glory forever.

TRUE ROYALTY

WORD

Exalt the LORD our God!
Bow low before his feet, for he is holy!

Psalm 99:5

THOUGHT

In times of old, people bowed low to pay honor and respect to authorities or those who held places of honor. The act gave visual recognition and acknowledgment to the superiority of earthly kings and queens, those in power, and people of high esteem. In some cultures, failure to display such reverence could mean imprisonment or death. Bowing displayed an attitude of adoration, courtesy, honor, and gratitude.

There exists no higher ruler than Jehovah God. Our Lord is exalted above all as he is the Creator of all. Truly, he is the only royalty worthy of worship, and one day, all will bow before him in acknowledgment of his superiority.

Because of the reconciliatory work of Christ, we worship as sons and daughters of the Most High; we are adopted heirs. The redeemed celebrate the Holy One with wholly liberated hearts. However, ahead of us awaits the most exciting and dynamic event to ever unfold; it will immeasurably exceed the current experience of worship. It is the gathering of all the redeemed together with the angelic hosts to celebrate in unhindered perfection and limitless dimensions, the Lord Most High.

PRAYER

Father, you are exalted above all things. I exalt you, honor you, and worship you. Amen.

Our Father in heaven, may your name be kept holy.

THE MASTER GARDENER

WORD

I am the true grapevine, and my Father is the gardener. He cuts off every branch of mine that doesn't produce fruit, and he prunes the branches that do bear fruit so they will produce even more.

John 15:1–2

THOUGHT

When I read this, I picture an early morning scene where the sun is slowly bringing light to a gently sloping hillside that's covered with acres of a vibrant, healthy, fruit-producing vineyard. In my mind's eye, there's an old man in the middle of the vineyard gently moving his hands methodically through the branches, carefully pushing leaves aside and inspecting the condition of each plant part, from stem and leaf to budding fruit.

He knows his vineyard well, and he understands precisely how to best care for it in order to produce the optimum harvest in quality and quantity. Occasionally, he snips what appears to be a perfectly healthy green shoot capable of bearing fruit. To the untrained eye, this action may appear counterproductive, but the old and wise vineyard master knows this is the necessary procedure for the best potential harvest.

Our Father is loving but perfect; he is holy in every way. He tends his vineyard, the body of Christ, and the individual branches within it. He is patient, intentional, nurturing, and lovingly watchful. He would never thoughtlessly, uncaringly, or prematurely snip a branch. He is purposeful in each and every one of his actions, small or large. His goal is the healthiest and most fruitful vineyard for the greatest of harvests.

PRAYER

Lord, you know me far better than I will ever know myself. I pray that you would help me know your will and do it. My desire is to produce for you the best potential harvest from my life. May you give me the courage and strength to pray as Christ did: not my will, but yours. Amen.

May your kingdom come soon. May your will be done on earth, as it is in heaven.

July 18

EVER-ENDURING, FAITHFUL LOVE

WORD

Give thanks to the LORD, for he is good!
His faithful love endures forever.

Psalm 136:1

THOUGHT

We are instructed to honor and worship God with a heart of thanksgiving. Psalm 136 includes a long list of God's accomplishments and blessings, and it begins by celebrating his goodness. The Hebrew word for "good," *tob*, means "favorable; festive; pleasing; pleasant, right, and best."[20] Emphatic, absolute, and endless is God's goodness.

During a conversation once with my young grandson he asked, "Is God ever not good?" My response was, "No, he is never not good!" While I may not have been grammatically correct, my response nevertheless contained unequivocal truth.

Twenty-six times throughout Psalm 136, the psalmist uses the phrase "his faithful love endures forever." God's goodness is manifested in his perfect love. His love is void of any deficient or flawed characteristic. His love is unfading—it never wanes, weakens, or diminishes even in the slightest—as he is love and he never lessens, weakens, or changes.

When a person who is redeemed and cared for by the love of God pauses to contemplate the divine treasure that fills their heart, thanks will flow in the form of grateful tears. The heart will sing holy melodies fit only for the ears of God whose love is everlasting, whose love is good.

PRAYER

Lord, I thank you this morning for your provision of goodness
and love, which is boundless and eternal. Amen.

Give us today the food we need.

July 19

ALIVE WITH CHRIST

WORD

You were dead because of your sins and because your sinful nature was not yet cut away. Then God made you alive with Christ, for he forgave all our sins. He canceled the record of the charges against us and took it away by nailing it to the cross. In this way, he disarmed the spiritual rulers and authorities. He shamed them publicly by his victory over them on the cross.

Colossians 2:13–15

THOUGHT

He forgave all our sins. I have been in many conversations with people over the years who found difficulty in believing God could forgive them of *all* their sins. They indicated that surely God expected them to do some sort of work to begin to inch into his good grace, but nothing is further from the truth. Our part is simply to repent by asking for forgiveness and turning from our sin, then we embrace Christ and forgiveness is granted.

Some would say it's just too simple, but the Father knew there was only one way to rescue people to himself: grace! His only Son—Jesus, the unblemished sacrificial lamb—was the offering for our sins. We cannot work our way into his good favor and grace; it's all Jesus's work of redemption. He gets all the glory for our freedom and restoration. Our part is to surrender and allow the Potter to begin forming us into the image of Jesus.

Death no longer rules in the place where Christ abides. All the charges levied against us by the evil one are dropped, cut away in the power of the cross of Christ. Now we stand alive with Christ and live as vessels of honor for our Lord and King.

PRAYER

Father, I rejoice this morning as I remember when you delivered me through the power of your resurrection life. I am forgiven and freed to be yours alone. Amen.

Forgive us our sins, as we have forgiven those who sin against us.

July 20

WONDERFUL LIGHT

WORD

...but you are not like that, for you are a chosen people. You are royal priests, a holy nation, God's very own possession. As a result, you can show others the goodness of God, for he called you out of the darkness into his wonderful light.

1 Peter 2:9

THOUGHT

Often in the early mornings as the first crack of light peaks over the horizon, I am stilled and awed by God's greatness. Light itself allows me to behold and appreciate the wonder and magnificence of creation.

In today's scripture, Peter is writing to early Christians in encouragement. In the verse just before, Peter explains that people stumble because they do not obey God's Word. However, as Christians, we are God's chosen people and his own possession. Our call is to display the goodness of the Lord and his righteous ways to all, for Christ has illuminated our once dark lives and has graciously allowed us to see his beauty and glory.

This is the wonder of wonders: Christ has invited us to follow him, he who is the light of the world. His light brings awareness of things that the darkness previously concealed.

PRAYER

Father, apart from you there is no ability to see. In the beginning, you brought physical light upon the earth, and through Christ's redemptive work, you brought spiritual light. Because of your light, there is hope. You are the light to the world. Amen.

Don't let us yield to temptation.

ALWAYS THE TRUTH

WORD

I tell you the truth, anyone who obeys my teaching will never die!

John 8:51

THOUGHT

When we search for truth in earthly sources, it's rarely found. Too often in our modern world things are presented as truth and later discovered to be false. The result has produced a culture of doubt, suspicion, and widespread despair. It's difficult to rely on those in earthly authority or trust the news—both which lead to anxiety about our world and its future.

There is, however, one voice free of flaw and falsehood. One whose words is acutely accurate, void of the slightest error, and—when heeded—bring light to the darkness, hope to the hopeless, and abundant, eternal life: Jesus.

When Jesus Christ said, "I tell you the truth," indeed it was truth, still is truth, and will forever remain truth. May we wisely seek and heed his words, for they bring life and nourishment to the hungry soul.

PRAYER

Jesus, your words are living, your words never fail, and your words are to be trusted.
May I be enveloped in the truth of your Word and obey the life-giving teachings you give. Amen.

But rescue us from the evil one.

THE GLORIOUS COMMAND

WORD

Praise the LORD!
Praise the LORD from the heavens!
Praise him from the skies!
Praise him, all his angels!
Praise him, all the armies of heaven!
Praise him, sun and moon!
Praise him, all you twinkling stars!
Praise him, skies above!
Praise him, vapors high above the clouds!
Let every created thing give praise to the LORD,
for he issued his command, and they came into being.
He set them in place forever and ever.
His decree will never be revoked.

Psalm 148:1–6

THOUGHT

For the lover of God, all creation is a wonder and display of God's magnificent and absolute creative power, a reminder that all is made by God and for God. Praise the Lord!

Although Psalm 148 isn't specifically attributed to David, it sounds an awful lot like his poetry. David could draw from his many experiences in nature as a shepherd watching over sheep during the predawn. I suppose he could easily close his eyes and imagine the quiet of pastures of sleepy sheep. He would remember what it was like to look heavenward in amazement of the stars, knowing God alone knew their number and names.

We serve an amazing, awe-inspiring, astounding Creator. He didn't have to make a natural realm filled with such beauty, but he did by his glorious command. He set all things in their place to glorify him, and he is deserving of all honor and praise.

PRAYER

I am humbled by being in your presence this morning, my Lord, King, and Savior.
Who is like you? No one! You are magnificent, and all you have made is a wonder to me.
You are worthy of all praise. Thank you for your love, your mercy, your grace,
and for giving me genuine life to worship you forever. Amen.

For yours is the kingdom and the power and the glory forever.

July 23

SHOUT!

WORD

Shout joyful praises to God, all the earth!
Sing about the glory of his name!

Psalm 66:1–2

THOUGHT

The evening was electric as about one thousand Russian Christian leaders had gathered in an auditorium in the center of Moscow. In 1991 President Boris Yeltsin had banned the Communist party and shortly after Christian leaders from the United States were invited to join their Russian counterparts to encourage, equip, and celebrate the Lord openly after so many decades of hiding and silence under the rule of Communism.

An American pastor stepped to center stage to open the conference and in English said, "Let us give praise to God!" His Russian translator repeated the sentence and suddenly the auditorium erupted with near-deafening shouts of praise to God from the Russian believers in honor and worship of the Father, Son, and Holy Spirit.

I stood in the wings of the stage with several other American pastors and leaders weeping and rejoicing in the Lord for my Russian brothers and sisters in Christ.

Our heavenly Father is worthy of all praise and honor and glory. When we find commands in scripture, like the one today, we should take them literally. God *is* due shouts of bold, confident praise, and it is a privilege to be permitted to do so openly. He *is* owed songs of praise—and much, much more. Don't be afraid to give a shout on occasion because our God is worthy of all praise.

PRAYER

Lord, you have made us for praising you. You have instructed us to sing, bow, be still, lift our hands, and, yes, shout. Praise you, Lord! Amen.

Our Father in heaven, may your name be kept holy.

EVIDENCE OF LOVE

WORD

Let me say first that I thank my God through Jesus Christ for all of you,
because your faith in him is being talked about all over the world. God knows how often
I pray for you. Day and night I bring you and your needs in prayer to God,
whom I serve with all my heart by spreading the Good News about his Son.

Romans 1:8–9

THOUGHT

Paul received encouragement and joy from hearing about the good fruit produced as a result of the growing faith in response to the sharing of the gospel. In his letter to the Roman church, he affirmed and commended their faithfulness to the gospel, which was being talked about throughout the world. He encouraged them, telling the church he prayed for them often.

The last part of this passage is our emphasis for today. Paul shares that the evidence of his love for God is found in the continued spreading of the good news of Christ. Perhaps a rephrase might read: *I serve God with all of my heart by spreading the Good News about his Son.*

How can we know that we really love God? One manifestation is our desire to share what he has done for us with others. When we're joyously full of love for someone or something, we cannot help but tell others.

PRAYER

Lord, you have given me new life, hope, and a future. I want to be found sharing the source of
my love and my life with others today in honor of you. Amen.

May your kingdom come soon. May your will be done on earth, as it is in heaven.

A WORD ABOUT HOME

WORD

Don't let your hearts be troubled. Trust in God, and trust also in me.
There is more than enough room in my Father's home. If this were not so, would I have told you that
I am going to prepare a place for you? When everything is ready, I will come and get you, so that you
will always be with me where I am. And you know the way to where I am going.

John 14:1–4

THOUGHT

When Jesus began to share the unfolding events of his mission with his disciples, including his departure and their inability to follow him, they became deeply concerned. His disciples needed information to give them peace of mind, and Jesus supplied it. He immediately addressed their insecurities and concerns and told them not to worry but to continue to trust him.

Jesus shared hope and insight into his preparations for their future and for all believers. Yes, he was going to leave them, but in doing so, he was going to prepare a place for them in his Father's house.

This planet we exist on is a work God completed in six days. But think of how many years Jesus has been gone after making the preceding statement. What awesome wonder awaits us! When we complete this life, we will enter not just another place, but the specific place of provision for which our hearts were fashioned. We will be home forever.

PRAYER

Praise your name, gracious Lord, for your love, provision, and promise. Let me serve you and your
purposes today and each day that follows until I am with you in your Father's house forever!

Give us today the food we need.

July 26

SO YOU MUST FORGIVE

WORD

Do not judge others, and you will not be judged. Do not condemn others, or it will all come back against you. Forgive others, and you will be forgiven.

Luke 6:37

THOUGHT

In walking through the themes of the Lord's Prayer each day, we encounter the theme of forgiveness weekly. Perhaps Jesus included it in the Lord's Prayer knowing we would need to be repeatedly reminded to walk in forgiveness.

In Luke 6:37, Christ again underscores the importance of giving grace to others and the life-giving principle of forgiveness. Jesus forgave every sin and every offense, regardless of the depth of its darkness. When we sincerely ask for forgiveness and repent of our transgressions, Jesus forgives us—period.

If we are to be like Jesus Christ, we must forgive in the same manner. We are to extend forgiveness to those who have offended us. Just as our salvation was born out of the grace of Christ—not of our own works and deeds—so the grace to forgive others must be drawn from the same source.

PRAYER

Thank you, Lord Jesus, for your grace to forgive me. In my sin I was not worthy to be forgiven, yet you died for me even before I was born. I pray for your grace to forgive those who offend. Amen.

Forgive us our sins, as we have forgiven those who sin against us.

CONTINUE HIS WILL

WORD

"Now my soul is deeply troubled. Should I pray, 'Father, save me from this hour'? But this is the very reason I came! Father, bring glory to your name."

Then a voice spoke from heaven, saying, "I have already brought glory to my name, and I will do so again."

John 12:27–28

THOUGHT

Several years ago, I went through a period of discouragement. I questioned whether my life and ministry work were making any real difference. I called one of my mentors for some direction. During the conversation with him, I mustered enough courage to ask him if he ever felt the urge to quit ministry; he immediately responded, "Almost every Monday!"

Even Jesus—who knew his own life story from beginning to end and knew that it would be completed in total victory—experienced internal conflict. We see this in today's scripture: "Should I pray, 'Father, save me from this hour'?"

But Jesus didn't stop praying after that question. Jesus continued by remembering his purpose on earth and commanding that he would bring glory to his Father's name. The Father's will be done, not his own. Jesus rose above this deeply troubled moment and continued the will of the Lord. He victoriously finished his course. Because Christ is leading us in the way we should go, we can finish effectively and victoriously.

PRAYER

Lord, when I am weak, troubled, and wanting to quit, may I be reminded that you are the source for everything I need to complete your will. You are leading me. Your will is my highest call, greatest privilege, and grandest adventure. Amen.

Don't let us yield to temptation.

THE ACT OF DELIVERANCE

WORD

Give justice to the poor and the orphan;
uphold the rights of the oppressed and the destitute.
Rescue the poor and helpless;
deliver them from the grasp of evil people.

Psalm 82:3–4

THOUGHT

Through the redemptive work of Christ, the Father made way for all who would follow Jesus to experience the ultimate deliverance from evil. Our Savior has also invited us to join him in the ongoing ministry of declaring and proclaiming his good news so that others would also know deliverance.

As the sons and daughters of God, we are invited to take part in relieving the fears and effects of poverty and providing security and shelter to the orphan. We are invited to declare what is right and do what is right in an unjust world. And we are invited to stand and announce that real emancipation over oppression lies within Christ and in relationship with him.

Yes, we are called to take part with Christ in the most important and enormous rescue mission in all the world: to be his voice, his hands, his feet! He has empowered us to make his cause our cause. Today is not a day to drift toward indifference and comfort, to seek our own way, or to give in to the pleasures of the world. Today, and every day following, is the day to stand in the power of his might against the wiles of the enemy, against evil. For where the spirit of the Lord is, freedom is there and evil is overcome (2 Cor. 3:17).

PRAYER

Jesus, let your name, your ways, and your fame stand gloriously strong,
towering above all the powers of darkness! Amen.

But rescue us from the evil one.

HIS SHINING GLORY

WORD

Be exalted, O God, above the highest heavens.
May your glory shine over all the earth.

Psalm 57:11

THOUGHT

This song and prayer reflect the psalmist's heart, one that's overflowing with the thoughts and exaltation of God while in the midst of God's presence. The declaration of his prayer is for God to be exalted above all things, above the highest place in the highest of heavens, and for God's glory to brilliantly shine over the entire earth, leaving no space absent of God's glorious wonder!

The sons and daughters of God are bestowed great purpose, and the fulfillment of this great purpose is accomplished in the manifestation of our highest call. And what is our highest call? To worship God with all our being.

While certainly we reflect the glory of God in our corporate church worship services, that's only part of how we exalt the Lord. Our lives lived in constant recognition and thanksgiving to the Lord are how the beauty of God's glory shine with his holy brilliance. When we live lives of worship among the poor, broken, and wounded, sharing hope and offering help, there the glory of God is reflected. When we walk in uncompromising integrity within a world comfortable with redefining truth and uprightness, then the glory of God shines bright.

PRAYER

Father, may your glory shine intensely over all the earth. May every creature, yes,
every place, be filled to overflowing with the marvel of your kingdom. Amen.

For yours is the kingdom and the power and the glory forever.

I AM THE LORD YOUR GOD

WORD

I am the LORD your God, who rescued you from the land of Egypt, the place of your slavery.

Exodus 20:2

THOUGHT

Indeed, there is no other subject or living being more complex than God. Nothing—no length of study or intense contemplation—could begin to unveil his depth and breadth. The wisest among us could not begin to understand even the tiniest of his truths without God's own help. However, as believers, it is our privilege to attempt to get to know our heavenly Father deeply. This is the greatest adventure, the believer's glorious journey and quest.

During the course of this divine exploration, we get to enjoy the Lord's true and indescribable beauty. We live our lives in awe of his glory and his love. This morning, bask in the amazing, life-giving truth that—in all his vast power, might, and knowledge—he faithfully declares, "I am the LORD your God."

PRAYER

Lord, there are times when all I can do is rejoice over the truth that I am your child and you are my God. Thank you for rescuing me out of the slavery of sin. You are the Lord my God, and I'm grateful. Amen.

Our Father in heaven, may your name be kept holy.

ALWAYS THE BEST PLAN

WORD

"For I know the plans I have for you," says the LORD.
"They are plans for good and not for disaster, to give you a future and a hope. In those days when
you pray, I will listen. If you look for me wholeheartedly, you will find me."

Jeremiah 29:11–13

THOUGHT

These verses are often used to pronounce hope and blessing upon people. Many high school and college students have been handed a graduation card with these verses tucked somewhere within. But you don't often see the verses included that come before and after these scriptures—verses that talk about Israel's seventy-year captivity in Babylon. Today's scriptures reveal the ultimate outcome for the good of Israel, but they're sandwiched within an account of great difficulty.

Perhaps that makes these words all the more valuable, though, for those willing to tarry a bit longer within the story. We are often quick to overlook the many hardships referred to in the Bible that sit right alongside beautiful promises like this one. For those who choose to serve Christ, we are protected, loved, and redeemed, but our lives will not be free of difficulties. Should we then anticipate them, fear them, deny them, or attempt to build a theology free of them? If we do, we may be setting ourselves up for disappointment.

This earth-life is challenging, and we are in need of God's grace and provision to withstand its challenges. However, we can rest knowing the Lord already has plans for us, and they are the best plans. Wholehearted seekers of God will be recipients of inexpressible good hope.

PRAYER

Oh, Lord my God, I seek you today with all my heart.
You have said those who seek you will find you. There is no one I long for like you,
for there is no one who is like you. You are my hope, my future,
my portion, and my treasure. Amen.

May your kingdom come soon. May your will be done on earth, as it is in heaven.

THE FATHER'S PROMISE

WORD

Father to the fatherless, defender of widows—
this is God, whose dwelling is holy.

Psalm 68:5

THOUGHT

While the global statistics of orphans vary, it's clear that there are millions of children under the age of eighteen across the globe who are parentless. The leading causes of this human tragedy are disease, poverty, war, natural disasters, abandonment, and accidents. Add to this children who are living in conditions where caregivers are laden with substance abuse, and the numbers rise. And if we consider the countless two-parent homes that are filled with overworked, absent, and disconnected parents who chase down extravagant materialism, then the numbers of neglected children increase worldwide.

One memory I will carry with me for the rest of my life occurred while volunteering for a children's ministry outreach to undersupported children. I will never forget a small girl, perhaps six to seven years of age, who walked up to me in a crowd of eighty to ninety such children. I said hello, and as she looked up at me with big brown eyes, she spoke these words in a sincere, heartbreaking voice: "Would you please be my daddy?"

God is the perfect Father in every way. He is perfect in character, love, motive, and care. Through the work of Christ, he has annihilated the eternal effects of the spirit of fatherlessness to all who enter into his care. He is the hope and healer for those wounded and longing for the affection of his holy fatherhood. He promises his sons and daughters never to forsake and never to abandon them. He is forever our Father.

PRAYER

Father, in you is hope the for the ultimate provision of paternal influence. Thank you for your perfect Father's heart, thank you for being the perfect Father—our Father in heaven, our Father forever.

Give us today the food we need.

THE FLAWLESS EXAMPLE

WORD

I have given you an example to follow. Do as I have done to you.

John 13:15

THOUGHT

Immediately following the washing of his disciples' feet, Jesus spoke these words. The theme of this verse, of course, is to embrace the glorious, fruitful ministry of service to God, submit ourselves to his will, and live a life in service to others. These words of Christ contain far-reaching implications.

We are to follow the example of Christ in all aspects of life. He demonstrated how to live in honor of the Father in heaven, and—upon Christ's resurrection, ascension, and sending of the Holy Spirit—Jesus provided us with the ability to do so.

When we attempt to "do as Christ has done to us," one of the hardest is in extending forgiveness in the same fashion as Jesus. Believers have no option but to forgive as Christ forgave; he made it clear that if we desire to be forgiven, we must, in turn, forgive (Matt. 6:14–15). Yes, this is a principle that seems easier said than done, but it's certainly not impossible—Christ led the way for us as our victorious example.

PRAYER

Lord, I pray for your grace, power, and wisdom to proceed forward in this day. I ask that your Holy Spirit guide me to walk as you walk, love as you love, and forgive as you forgive. Amen.

Forgive us our sins, as we have forgiven those who sin against us.

LIGHT UP THE DARKNESS

WORD

You light a lamp for me.
The LORD, my God, lights up my darkness.

Psalm 18:28

THOUGHT

One night, a storm in our area caused a power outage, and a dark evening became even darker once there was no source of light. I got out of bed, made my way through the house, and wondered if I'd left shoes or my backpack out in the floor, causing a potential tripping hazard. Another bolt of lightning flashed, providing just enough light to reveal the contents of the room and put my concerns at ease. I could walk forward with no obstacles in my path.

There are many obstacles before us in this world. Attempting to move forward in our own strength and solely by our own wisdom will cause us to stumble in the dark. God is our source of light; he is not just a momentary flash of lightning. He is a consistent light that illuminates the darkness and causes us to steer away from danger.

Is there an area in your life that needs to be lit up by the light of Christ? He is a faithful lamp unto our feet and light unto our path. Submit this area of your life to him and see him work within it.

PRAYER

In a world of darkness, Lord, you provide light. You reveal things as they are so that we might see the things in our path that cause us to stumble. You reveal them, ensure safe passage around them, or allow us to wait until you remove them. When you light up the darkness, darkness is no longer a threat to me. I seek and embrace your light, for you are the light of the world. Amen.

Don't let us yield to temptation.

HE LEADS WITH MERCY

WORD

When Lot still hesitated, the angels seized his hand and the hands of his wife and two daughters and rushed them to safety outside the city, for the LORD was merciful.

Genesis 19:16

THOUGHT

What parent or grandparent does not have a few stories to tell about how they rescued their child or grandchild from a dangerous situation? I remember our family often visiting my uncle's farm in Indiana. Those visits almost always included a long walk with my dad exploring the countryside.

During one walk, I remember my dad suddenly grabbed my shoulder and shouted, "Snake!" I hesitated, and he pulled me back to safety. Though he later identified the snake as nonpoisonous, his first response was to move me from what he perceived as potential harm.

We have no idea the number of interventions that have been supplied by our Father in heaven on our behalf. He loves us, watches over our paths, provides for us, and protects us. The Lord is our ever-present, vigilant Good Shepherd, a true source of safety. He leads us with his faithful mercy.

PRAYER

Thank you, Lord, for leading me by your skillful and merciful hand. Thank you for being my Shepherd, my guide through every moment in this life and beyond. Amen.

But rescue us from the evil one.

August 5

THE OWNER OF IT ALL

WORD

Look, the highest heavens and the earth and everything in it all belong to the LORD your God.

Deuteronomy 10:14

THOUGHT

God owns everything, everywhere, all the time! Perhaps that sounds like a child's response to the question of God's ownership, but it's certainly a sufficient one. A deep exploration of this subject is usually reserved for the brightest of theological minds and often positioned within lengthy verbiage-filled pages of Christian apologetics. However, at the end of the discussion, we can conclude that God owns everything, everywhere, all the time.

He is indeed Creator of all that has existed, does exist, and will exist. Wonder and appreciation will grow within us as we continue to discover his limitlessness as we, through new technology, come upon previously hidden gems within the Lord's making.

Space programs often discover "new" planets, galaxies, and other wonders of the universe through research, but these wonders were there the whole the time—they're only new to us. In the next decade, how many additional stars and planets already in existence will be "discovered" by humanity for the first time as technology advances?

All the while, God made it all, maintains it all, and is to be glorified by it all.

PRAYER

Lord, your kingdom is an everlasting, all-encompassing kingdom. Your power is unlimited, unrestricted, and all created things stand weak in comparison.
Your glory is omnipresent and forever, and I will worship you in all your glory. Amen.

For yours is the kingdom and the power and the glory forever.

THE MAKER AND SUSTAINER

WORD

...but the LORD made the earth by his power, and he preserves it by his wisdom.
With his own understanding he stretched out the heavens.

Jeremiah 10:12

THOUGHT

The Ottauquechee is a beautiful little river that passes through Woodstock, Vermont. On one bend of the river just at the edge of the village, the water is typically seen gently rushing through a shallow area covered with hundreds of various-sized rocks. It produces a sound so peaceful that it's capable of lulling even the most hurried of individuals to sleep given a sufficient look and listen.

A quarter of a mile downstream, a tree-covered hill awaits every photo-conscious explorer who packs a camera of some sort. And early in the morning, the sunlight unlocks a striking array of beautiful hues.

This is but one tiny place within God's unmistakable display of creative brilliance, beauty, and power—one small portion of God's created earth, displaying his radiant handiwork and his unmistakable divine imprint and signature. He is the only source capable of creating something from nothing by mere spoken word.

Who or what has the ability and power to make form from formlessness? Who or what can introduce light from darkness? Who or what can produce life from lifelessness? None but the Ancient of Days, the one named Jehovah—the Lord of the heavens and the earth, and the Sustainer and maintainer of all.

PRAYER

You alone are the God of all creation, and your name is holy. Amen.

Our Father in heaven, may your name be kept holy.

RUNNING TO WIN

WORD

Don't you realize that in a race everyone runs, but only one person gets the prize? So run to win! All athletes are disciplined in their training. They do it to win a prize that will fade away, but we do it for an eternal prize. So I run with purpose in every step. I'm not just shadowboxing.

1 Corinthians 9:24–26

THOUGHT

In these scriptures, Paul uses the runners of a race to describe the tenacity with which we, as followers of Jesus Christ, should apply ourselves in our approach to loving and serving Jesus. Jesus is our goal, and eternity with him is our prize!

Therefore we should run our race with excellence, focus, and persistence, for the award received at the finish line is not a fading award like those displayed on some shelf to gather dust. It is one that never loses value: eternity with God.

Like Paul says, we're not just shadowboxing. The enemy is real, and the work that God calls us to as his sons and daughters is vital. We are to proclaim the goodness and truth of the gospel of Jesus Christ, love the lost, care for widows and orphans, and devote ourselves to the good of our neighbors. Let's not get distracted; let's run to win.

PRAYER

Lord, it is my heart's desire to run in such a way as to win. Guide and strengthen me by your Holy Spirit, and cause my eyes to be fixed on you as my prize. Amen.

May your kingdom come soon. May your will be done on earth, as it is in heaven.

August 8

THE SHEPHERD AND GUARDIAN OF SOULS

WORD

He never sinned, nor ever deceived anyone.
He did not retaliate when he was insulted,
nor threaten revenge when he suffered.
He left his case in the hands of God, who always judges fairly.
He personally carried our sins in his body on the cross
so that we can be dead to sin and live for what is right.
By his wounds you are healed.
Once you were like sheep who wandered away.
But now you have turned to your Shepherd, the Guardian of your souls.

1 Peter 2:22–25

THOUGHT

Humble and grateful. Those are the only words to describe how I feel upon reading this passage. How could Christ, perfect and without sin, love one so imperfect, self-centered, and broken as me? And I am not alone, for without Christ, all of us find ourselves in hopeless darkness and trapped under the weight of sin.

There is only one who is truly pure, holy, and able to resurrect the listless soul. He has brought light to the darkness and life where death once reigned. He is our Shepherd, the Guardian of our souls.

Shepherding has a history of thousands of years of existence and is still practiced today. Shepherds diligently care for the welfare of their flocks in multiple ways and are committed to protecting and providing for their every need. The shepherd is the example chosen by God to illustrate his care for his people.

Christ is the Great Shepherd, and, too, the sacrificial lamb. He is the provisionary of heart and soul, the provisionary of all things pertaining to life and godliness.

By personally carrying our sins to the cross, Christ has healed our spiritual wounds, restored our relationship with our heavenly Father, and freed us from the sting of sin and death. He is worthy of all praise and honor and glory and power, today and forevermore.

PRAYER

Lord, you are my Shepherd. You faithfully and carefully watch over me.
I'm grateful for my freedom and healing that I've received through you,
and I know that you are a faithful and caring Father. Amen.

Give us today the food we need.

THE KEY TO FORGIVING

WORD

Love is patient and kind. Love is not jealous or boastful or proud or rude.
It does not demand its own way. It is not irritable, and it keeps no record of being wronged.
It does not rejoice about injustice but rejoices whenever the truth wins out. Love never gives up, never
loses faith, is always hopeful, and endures through every circumstance.

1 Corinthians 13:4–7

THOUGHT

If we search the depths of today's scripture, and by God's grace and power, apply the wisdom of the Bible's content, the result will be a God-honoring life. It can be easy to choose to volunteer in ministry, serve neighbors, and love the lost, but it's quite another thing when we are asked to lay aside our own bitterness and anger—even righteous anger—to freely forgive one another. As flawed, self-centered humans, it can be difficult for us to forgive even the smallest offenses, but it is clear that the key to forgiveness is a love for others like the one described in 1 Corinthians 13:4–7.

Although this passage is often recited at weddings, this type of love is to be displayed throughout our lives and in all relationships as Christians. Here Paul outlines how we should love as Christ-followers, and here we see that it requires a great, selfless love to successfully forgive, one that is demonstrated by Christ and empowered by his Spirit.

PRAYER

Father, the power of your love and forgiveness is often highly underestimated or ignored.
My character and actions during this earth-life are to be as yours, Lord Jesus. By your Spirit,
keep before me the qualities of your love and help me apply them in my daily walk. Amen.

Forgive us our sins, as we forgive those who sin against us.

THE GREAT INHERITANCE

WORD

...furthermore, because we are united with Christ, we have received an inheritance from God,
for he chose us in advance, and he makes everything work out according to his plan.

Ephesians 1:11

THOUGHT

The redemptive miracle of Christ eliminated our separation from the Father because of sin and paved the way to restoration and relationship with our holy God. Additionally, by his generosity and perfect love for his redeemed sons and daughters, he lavishes us with grace upon grace, promising an inheritance.

We have received an inheritance from God in Christ Jesus! Recipients of this divine inheritance will never fully comprehend the depths of this phrase; we can only marvel at the generosity of God the giver.

What is the proper response for such a gift? Even a partial realization of God's generosity generates stunning wonder and awe followed by appreciative hearts that are led to express unfettered devotion to him as he leads us in his plan. If we allow him, he can and will lead us through this earth-life in a winning fashion if we submit ourselves to his will. He is able to provide us with a vibrant spiritual life as we enjoy the unfolding discovery of his rich inheritance.

PRAYER

With a grateful and humble heart, this morning I worship you,
Lord of life and giver of the best gifts. You have established a plan and
the successful path to the destination to which you lead me. Lead me on righteous paths
and steer me away from the obstacles which would cause my stumbling. Amen.

Don't let us yield to temptation.

August 11

JESUS INTERCEDES

WORD

I'm not asking you to take them out of the world, but to keep them safe from the evil one.

John 17:15

THOUGHT

All of God's precious Word is gloriously life-giving. Sifting through its rich fields to glean truths and gather awaiting gems bring joy and hope to God's children. During the early years of my Christian experience, a wise mentor challenged me to spend an extended season reading repetitively through John 14–17. The result was an overflowing yield of spiritual treasure.

John 17:15 is one of those priceless gems. Before his prayer in John 17, Christ closed a discourse by telling his listeners that trials and sorrows would occur while they were on the earth but to be encouraged because he had overcome the world (John 16:33). Then he turned to his Father in heaven to intercede for those in his care.

He asked the Father to keep the evil one from those who are the citizens of heaven, a prayer later backed by the victory obtained as Christ was crucified, buried, and rose from the grip of death. In Christ we live, move, and overcome, and he intercedes on our behalf.

PRAYER

In my travels, you are there; in my battles, you are there; in my deliverance, you are there! Thank you that you are interceding on my behalf to keep me safe. Amen.

But rescue us from the evil one.

PERPETUAL

WORD

...so just as sin ruled over all people and brought them to death, now God's wonderful grace rules instead, giving us right standing with God and resulting in eternal life through Jesus Christ our Lord.

Romans 5:21

THOUGHT

None of history's great empires imagined their demise during their reign as a superpower. Yet each of history's great empires eventually yielded and forfeited its once strong, impenetrable position. The failures typically were attributed to famine, war, disease, internal power struggles and division, or some natural disaster. This has been the cycle, and this will continue to be the cycle.

Why? Because without exception, all of the empires or kingdoms of this world have been or are ruled by humans, and without exception, humanity is flawed and will eventually fail or cease to exist.

The Lord's kingdom, rule, and authority are from everlasting to everlasting—and his perpetual, wonderful grace now rules instead. He cannot be overpowered, and he withstands all challenges great and small. One day, a singular kingdom will rule unchallenged as no other kingdom will exist. As Revelation 11:15–16 reminds us, "The world has now become the Kingdom of our Lord and of his Christ, and he will reign forever and ever." Let us look forward with great expectancy!

PRAYER

Lord, I ask through the facilitating power of your Holy Spirit to serve you and your kingdom with diligence and affect, and I pray that I would display grace to all. Yours is the only kingdom worthy of serving, as yours is the only kingdom to reign forever. Amen

For yours is the kingdom and the power and the glory forever.

FOREVER AND EVER

WORD

Before the mountains were born,
before you gave birth to the earth and the world,
from beginning to end, you are God.

Psalm 90:2

THOUGHT

Three miles south of the small town of Paris, Arkansas, sits Subiaco Abbey, a small community established in the late 1800s. Behind the abbey lies a retreat center open to all who seek a bit of quiet contemplation and respite from the noise and complexity of the day-to-day. It is nestled on beautiful acreage with a backdrop of verdant rolling hills.

I wonder about all the events, activities, and stories that have occurred within the confines of this abbey since its establishment. Yet before the abbey was a thought in some visionary's heart, this backdrop of hills already contained an older, deeper history. And amazingly, before the hills were born—even before the earth existed—there was God. From eternity past to eternity future, there is God, and without him there is nothing.

Truly, in him all things are held together: mountains, stars, verdant hills, Subiaco Abbey, and you and me. He was here before it all, and he will be here once time as we know it is complete. From beginning to end, he is God.

PRAYER

Praise to you most gracious and eternal heavenly Father.
May your name be worshiped now and into all eternity. Amen.

Our Father in heaven, may your name be kept holy.

CLOSE FELLOWSHIP WITH GOD

WORD

Noah was a righteous man, the only blameless person living on earth at the time, and he walked in close fellowship with God.

Genesis 6:9

THOUGHT

Noah was a righteous man, one of upright character and high moral values. In today's scripture, the word *blameless* is used to describe him. This verse also tells us that Noah walked in close fellowship with God, and perhaps this is how he came to be blameless. Prior to Genesis 6:9, we learn that Noah found favor with God. From these few lines of scripture, it's safe to say Noah spent much time in communion with God and loved and respected the Lord dearly. Why else would Noah spend so much time with the Lord? And what other explanation could there be to explain his close fellowship? We seek and make time for those things we love and that are valuable to us.

As sons and daughters of God who have been brought into relationship with the Lord through Christ Jesus, we should strive to have close fellowship with our heavenly Father. It is an invaluable gift to be able to go to him freely, to be welcomed into his presence, to have our prayers heard. Let us not take this treasure of close fellowship with our Creator for granted, for it is the most precious treasure of all.

PRAYER

Father, your love, friendship, and fellowship are both dear to and needed by me. I pray for your Spirit to guard my heart and my time. May my heart be found diligently seeking you and spending time in your presence. Amen.

May your kingdom come soon. May your will be done on earth, as it is in heaven.

THE LIFE-SOURCE

WORD

For in Him we live and move and exist.
As some of your own poets have said, "We are his offspring."

Acts 17:28

THOUGHT

Compliment the industrious, admire the entrepreneur, applaud the hard worker, and congratulate the visionary. All these traits and more are healthy and commendable for individuals to pursue. However, our greatest feats, our most stunning efforts, all the accomplishments we thought were self-generated—nothing is truly self-existent. Everything and everyone finds its ability to live in God alone.

This life-source's name is Yahweh, and he is the one Creator and divine, gracious, righteous, wonderful governor of all things. He is the ultimate decision-maker, and at some future appointment of his choosing, all things formed by human hands will fail to uphold their purposes, while his will stands forever.

PRAYER

Lord, you are the life-source, our provider. You define all created order and sustain all things created.
You are holy, and you alone are worthy of honor and worship. Amen.

Give us today the food we need.

MERCY

WORD

...so it is God who decides to show mercy. We can neither choose it nor work for it.

Romans 9:16

THOUGHT

It was an early morning on a lonely two-lane country road in Arkansas. There wasn't another vehicle in sight. I just set the cruise control seven miles per hour above the posted speed limit and began to enjoy the morning sunrise when a car from the oncoming lane suddenly exhibited blue flashing lights.

I immediately pulled to the side of the road, and the police car turned and pulled in behind me. I handed the officer my license and he asked, "What's the rush, Mr. Smith?" I confessed to being in the wrong, and when he returned from his car after checking my record he said, "Just a warning. Slow down a little."

With relief and gratefulness I replied, "Thanks for the mercy." I was in the wrong and deserved to pay the penalty of my trespass. I had no choice in the officer's decision, and though he certainly didn't have to, the officer chose to extend mercy.

We all deserve judgment and sentencing for our trespasses against God. We have no argument or justification for our sin. We are in the wrong, yet God in his boundless love decided to extend mercy through his Son, Jesus Christ.

PRAYER

Thank you, Father, for extending mercy to me. Thank you for forgiving and exonerating me. Thank you for giving me new life. Amen.

Forgive us our sins, as we have forgiven those who sin against us.

August 17

UNCOMPROMISING COURAGE

WORD

Be on guard. Stand firm in the faith. Be courageous. Be strong.

1 Corinthians 16:13

THOUGHT

Jesus Christ, whom we are to imitate, taught us many valuable and life-giving qualities during his time on earth. Four are listed in this passage.

Jesus was vigilant concerning the activity and wiles of the evil one. He was uncompromising in pursuit of the will of the heavenly Father—whatever the request, wherever the leading, and whatever the odds. Jesus also had fearless courage when facing opposition, and his courage was rooted in the faithful promises of God.

We can also stand firm against temptation and the snares of the enemy, for the source of our strength is our faith in God and not in our own ability. We can humbly recognize that, in our natural strength, we are powerless, but in Christ we are strong enough, bold enough, and courageous enough to accomplish God's will.

PRAYER

Father, lead me by your Spirit. Keep my spiritual eyes and ears vigilant against attacks of the enemy, and help me stand strong and courageous by your divine wisdom and power. Amen.

Don't let us yield to temptation.

IMPENETRABLE STRENGTH

WORD

...but the Lord is faithful; he will strengthen you and guard you from the evil one.

2 Thessalonians 3:3

THOUGHT

Although invisible to our natural eyes, there are two donut-like rings of intense radiation that surround planet Earth. They're called the Van Allen radiation belts. According to NASA, these belts were "the first discovery of the space age, measured with the launch of a US satellite...in 1958."[21] It wasn't until more than fifty years later that scientists learned the belts act as an almost impenetrable, fully protective barrier that shields the Earth from high-powered electrons traveling through space.

Surely it is reassuring to know that our planet has built-in protection from highly volatile electrons roaming the universe. However, there is another invisible, impenetrable barrier of protection that is far more superior and vital to us than the Van Allen discovery: the Lord our God.

Not only is our heavenly Father the Maker and Sustainer of all things—including things such as the planet Earth and its Van Allen radiation belts—but he is also our relentlessly loving God who strengthens and guards us spiritually. The Lord in his unwavering faithfulness is able to guard us against the destructive plans of the evil one. And the same all-powerful Creator who set the universe into motion walks with you through each and every day.

PRAYER

Lord, I find the ability to withstand the plans of the enemy in your strength. I praise you for your faithfulness as my Protector and Deliverer. Amen.

But rescue us from the evil one.

August 19

THE ONLY WISE GOD

WORD

All glory to the only wise God, through Jesus Christ, forever. Amen.

Romans 16:27

THOUGHT

In Romans it appears that Paul, with his wit, wisdom, and philosophical debating abilities, decided both to exalt the Lord in his divine supremacy while simultaneously labeling all false and self-proclaimed deities as foolish and buffoonish. For there is "only one wise God," which infers that all others are not.

Indeed, there is but one Creator, one eternally reigning King, and only one wise God. Indeed, all other powerless fabrications formed by the imaginations of deceived men and women do not, in reality, exist.

Let this verse encourage you today: you serve a wise God, the *only* wise God. We can rest in his wisdom, knowing that he has already planned each of our days—and he has also planned to provide us with exactly what we need to accomplish his will, defeat temptation, serve others, and worship him fully.

PRAYER

Father, may your name be worshiped and glorified. For you, oh, Lord, are the only God!
You are alone the Maker and Sustainer of all things created.
You alone are worthy of all praise and honor. All glory to your name! Amen.

For yours is the kingdom and the power and the glory forever.

THE HIGHEST CALLING

WORD

All glory to God forever and ever! Amen.

2 Timothy 4:18

THOUGHT

Our highest call, our greatest purpose, our divine destiny, and our path to freedom are in glorifying God. Our resolve to indifference, our most successful endeavor, and the solutions to our most confusing and complex internal issues are in glorifying God. The most fulfilling journey for our hearts and the most inpactful life to live now and forever are in glorifying our Lord and Maker wholeheartedly.

The redeemed people of God have been set loose to run hard, run strong, and run well in a life wholly devoted to the Holy One. The slightest glimpse of him, revealed to the heart that is set free by him, takes one's breath away in awe and honor. May the believing, trusting heart explode with grateful praise!

PRAYER

May your name be glorified by me this day. Amen.

Our Father in heaven, may your name be kept holy.

August 21

SEEKING THE DEEPER ANSWER

WORD

As Jesus was walking along, he saw a man who had been blind from birth. "Rabbi," his disciples asked him, "why was this man born blind? Was it because of his own sins or his parents' sins?"

"It was not because of his sins or his parents' sins," Jesus answered. "This happened so the power of God could be seen in him."

John 9:1–3

THOUGHT

We can see in today's passage that the disciples, in their question to Jesus, not only limited themselves but also limited the possibilities of a limitless God. In their question, they revealed and assumed there were only two possible reasons for the man's blindness. Jesus, however, introduced a third option and also revealed it as the will of God: "This happened so the power of God could be seen in him."

When we examine his Word more deeply, this scripture passage reminds us of several important truths. First, God is not limited to the natural, the logical, or the reasonable. Second, God's will does not always appear comfortable, and it often *isn't* comfortable. Although what the Lord asks of us or allows to occur in our lives can often feel difficult and strenuous, he knows the end from the beginning, and his will is perfect in every way. Last, God's plans and purposes do not always serve a theology of natural reason and personal comfort, but even then, his plans are always good and bring glory to him.

Here's a solid truth to hold onto in times of concern, doubt, confusion, or despair: His plan is for his glory and our good. We can fully trust in Christ Jesus.

PRAYER

I pray for wisdom to ask you the right questions, Lord, so I don't attempt to limit you as to your will for me. Help me to seek your kingdom and your plans above my own. Amen.

May your kingdom come soon. May your will be done on earth, as it is in heaven.

THE MIRACLE OF GIVING AND RECEIVING

WORD

Whatever you give is acceptable if you give it eagerly. And give according to what you have, not what you don't have. Of course, I don't mean your giving should make life easy for others and hard for yourselves. I only mean that there should be some equality. Right now you have plenty and can help those who are in need. Later, they will have plenty and can share with you when you need it. In this way, things will be equal. As the Scriptures say,

"Those who gathered a lot had nothing left over,
and those who gathered only a little had enough."

2 Corinthians 8:12–15

THOUGHT

God's Word is both mystical and practical. On one hand, we are presented with unexplainable supernatural elements and realms—and on the other, we are given clear and simple daily directions for kingdom living.

This is an example of one such practical teaching. The apostle Paul was instructing a church under his care in the kingdom principle of giving and receiving. Yes, God can provide by placing a coin in the mouth of a fish (Matt. 17:24–27). However, he has also invited us to experience the blessing of working with and beside him to bring his kingdom to earth.

If there are those who are in genuine need, experiencing hardship, and unable to supply for themselves, then give freely to them as you have received freely. The tables may someday turn, and those who weren't experiencing hardships may instead find themselves in need of the help of others. If so, then freely receive as you freely gave.

Christianity is not a system intended to enable or redistribute wealth. Christianity, the church, is a living spiritual organism generated and inspired by the perfect love and righteousness of Christ. God's biblical principles, when applied through his church to meet needs, are no less a miracle than finding a coin in the mouth of a fish.

PRAYER

How, Lord, will we know the power of your living, breathing bride unless we act in accordance with your will? Lead me to be courageous in how I live my life, both in the giving and the receiving of my daily bread. Amen.

Give us today the food we need.

August 23

TENDER FORGIVENESS

WORD

*Get rid of all bitterness, rage, anger, harsh words, and slander,
as well as all types of evil behavior. Instead, be kind to each other, tenderhearted, forgiving one
another, just as God through Christ has forgiven you.*

Ephesians 4:31–32

THOUGHT

Selfishness and pride seem to be at the root of most arguments—as well as anger, jealousy, gossip, and a swarm of other similar life-draining characteristics. Paul offers solutions to these harmful stings by urging us to get rid of these hang-ups—away with them, toss them out, for they do not represent Christ or belong where Christ resides.

As the redeemed children of God, we should be known by grace and goodness. Replace bitterness, rage, anger, harsh words, and slander with kindness toward one another and display compassion and spiritual sensitivity to all.

As sons and daughters, we are to exhibit the spirit of tender forgiveness, the spirit of Jesus. Since we freely received forgiveness, so we must freely give it.

PRAYER

Father, repeatedly your Word reveals that the path of freedom is discovered in the power of forgiveness. May you give power and grace to me so that I might walk rightly in this, for this is your will, and this is your provision for the Christ-life. Amen.

Forgive us our sins, as we have forgiven those who sin against us.

August 24

WHEN MY HEART IS OVERWHELMED

WORD

*From the ends of the earth,
I cry to you for help
when my heart is overwhelmed.
Lead me to the towering rock of safety.*

Psalm 61:2

THOUGHT

I have a friend who lives in the Texas Hill Country. The region is beautiful, but it can get dangerous when sudden heavy rains cause rapidly rising water to rush through its many canyons. The local residents know well the flash-flood dangers, and they avoid crossing low-lying roads during these times.

One night, my friend miscalculated the water's depth on a flooded road and found himself quickly caught in perilous rushing water. He was able to escape from his car, but he was violently tossed downstream by the force of the floodwaters. He was desperate and praying during the event; the current suddenly pushed him into the side of a huge boulder. Amazingly, he was able to climb atop the rock and remained there until the water receded enough for him to escape. When he later shared the story, he remarked of how grateful he was to find refuge on the giant boulder.

The Lord is referred to in scripture as our rock of refuge and source of safety, a safe place to run to when we are overwhelmed. God is our perfect and powerful leader who guides us to the safe places in Christ. When your heart is overwhelmed, run to him.

PRAYER

Father, lead me to the place of refuge in you and let me abide in your peace. Amen.

Don't let us yield to temptation.

August 25

SAFE REFUGE

WORD

...for you are my safe refuge,
a fortress where my enemies cannot reach me.

Psalm 61:3

THOUGHT

God is not a temporary shelter or a momentary place of escape—we have no need for a greater, stronger, more permanent defender. In truth, God is the *only* safe refuge capable of definitive deliverance, no matter how big the enemy or how great the danger.

Jehovah is the one and only safe refuge. He is the fortress whose walls cannot be scaled. Every weapon and device used in attempt to conquer his possessions—the subjects of his kingdom (who, by the way, he views as his children and friends)—will fall broken and defeated before him as shattered, useless slivers of shard.

The enemy's intentions to harm us fall futile, failed, and fruitless when we abide within God's protection; he is the impenetrable citadel.

PRAYER

Father, you are my sole source of sure and certain deliverance from the evil one.
Thank you for your rescue and the safety of abiding within your holy power. Amen.

But rescue us from the evil one.

ALPHA AND OMEGA

WORD

*"I am the Alpha and the Omega—the beginning and the end," says the Lord God.
"I am the one who is, who always was, and who is still to come—the Almighty One."*

Revelation 1:8

THOUGHT

The Old Testament begins by disclosing God's existence prior to the creation of what we know as the world, universe, and everything contained within. He was there before it and was the one to call it into form by his power. Though humanity continues advancements and development, all things we declare as "new" are made from things existing. God, on the other hand, made something from nothing—a feat accomplished only by him.

The alpha and omega are the first and last letters of the Greek alphabet. When the Lord spoke and referred to himself as the beginning and the end, he was not referring to his beginning, for he had none. In essence, he declared everything begins and ends with him. This was also his way of saying in today's scripture that all the things in Revelation that were about to be disclosed would come to pass.

In one brief statement of clarity and precision, God delivered his unparalleled position. For those who love, trust, and serve Christ, these are words of hope and life. He is God, and there is no other!

PRAYER

Bless the Lord, my soul, and let all within me bless God's wonderful, beautiful, holy name! Amen.

For yours is the kingdom and the power and the glory forever.

THE ANCIENT ONE

WORD

*As my vision continued that night, I saw someone like a son of man
coming with the clouds of heaven. He approached the Ancient One and was led into his presence.
He was given authority, honor, and sovereignty over all the nations of the world, so that people of
every race and nation and language would obey him. His rule is eternal—
it will never end. His kingdom will never be destroyed.*

Daniel 7:13–14

THOUGHT

The Ancient One, also called the Ancient of Days, is the title for God mentioned
only three times in the Bible, and each time this title is used, it was in Daniel's vision.

In Daniel's vision, God the Father gives God the Son dominion over all the earth for
the ultimate honor and glory of God, who will be worshiped forever by all peoples. His
kingdom is solid, reliable, and true, and it will never be destroyed. We can have peace
every day knowing our Lord's sovereignty is trustworthy and true.

All things created, great and small, will one day come to an end. However, God will
always rule and reign, and the redeemed of the Lord will abide with him for eternity,
praising his name!

PRAYER

*Lord, the slightest glimpse into the future of eternity where I'll get to worship before your throne
and in your presence is overwhelming and indescribable. I will receive so much joy
from being in your presence for all my days. Amen.*

Our Father in heaven, may your name be kept holy.

THE HIGHEST GOAL

WORD

Let love be your highest goal!

1 Corinthians 14:1

THOUGHT

We plan, plot, toil, and strive to accomplish those things we define as worthwhile. We endeavor to be diligent and disciplined. These are all noble qualities. But while awards and accolades adorn walls and shelves in homes, public institutions, and museums throughout the world, what is the *truly* greatest lifetime achievement?

Our greatest and highest goal should be to love God with all our hearts and to love our neighbors as ourselves. Alongside Christ and through the love of God, we should fight to conquer what seems unconquerable, to see dark places transformed by his light, and to work with a sense of purpose and destiny to bring the gospel to the world.

No wonder today's scripture exhorts and encourages us to make love our highest goal—love that is only found in and from the purest and most powerful source: Jehovah God.

PRAYER

May I walk in your love, Lord, and bring honor to you. Amen.

May your kingdom come soon. May your will be done on earth, as it is in heaven.

WHO IS THIS MAN?

WORD

The disciples were amazed. "Who is this man?" they asked. "Even the winds and waves obey him!"

Matthew 8:27

THOUGHT

How many times had the disciples seen miracles since they first met and followed Jesus? Surely this is the Messiah, the one we've heard about and waited for, the one of whom the prophets foretold. They'd already observed him moving in the miraculous several times at this point.

However, when Christ stepped beyond the boundaries and limitations of natural order to accomplish the will of his heavenly Father and calm the storm, as seen in Matthew 8:23–27, the disciples were consumed by amazement and wonder. They observed the very forces of nature abandon their natural course to align with the commanding words of this man, Jesus Christ.

Christ continues through the facilitating force of the Holy Spirit to achieve God's plans and supply needed provision for those on mission with him. When necessary, he'll stretch past the natural order of things to meet the needs of those called to his purposes. When he does, there are still those who stand in awe and ask, *Who is this man?*

PRAYER

Lord, trusting you is still the path to peace and the accomplishment of your will.
By the power of your Holy Spirit, help me grow in trust of you. Provide me with the things
necessary to be obedient to your call and complete your will. Amen.

Give us today the food we need.

FORGIVENESS NEVER CHANGES

WORD

Whatever is good and perfect is a gift coming down to us from God our Father, who created all the lights in the heavens. He never changes or casts a shifting shadow. He chose to give birth to us by giving us his true word. And we, out of all creation, became his prized possession.

James 1:17–18

THOUGHT

While on a mission trip, I was standing one morning on a mountainside overlooking hundreds, perhaps thousands, of acres of African plains while these questions came to me: *I wonder how many human lives and life-forms have lived or passed through this region over the centuries? How will these same plains appear as the future unfolds?*

Some African plains, such as the one I observed, change into vast lakes during rainy seasons, temporarily transforming the ecosystems. Some areas change as people move in, settle, and develop the land. When severe drought occurs, entire villages of people abandon a region, relocate, and nature again reclaims ownership.

The African plains and the shifts they experience between seasons and settlements are just one example of continuous change. People, governments, and whole nations change. However, we are promised unchanging internal security, peace, freedom, and stability by God. These are good and perfect gifts that are found in God the Father who never changes. Where is the path leading to such freedom? It is found only within forgiveness, the place of mercy and grace. Much like himself, the Lord's offer of forgiveness never changes.

PRAYER

Father, from you, through you, and in you is the promised security of freedom through your forgiveness. Thank you for your mercy. Amen.

Forgive us our sins, as we have forgiven those who sin against us.

GOD'S PATH TO DESTINY

WORD

You guide me with your counsel,
leading me to a glorious destiny.

Psalm 73:24

THOUGHT

Good, accurate, effective counsel and guidance from a respected physician in a time of need is welcomed and appreciated. In fact, good counsel from good counselors in any area of our lives is highly valued, especially when the results prove effective and helpful to us.

We each have the opportunity to be led and guided by the ultimate life coach and counselor: the Holy Spirit. His instructions, directions, and formulas are individually designed for each of us to result in an optimally lived life for Christ. Following his guidance as we pursue the Lord's call on our life ultimately leads to the place the psalmist defines as a *glorious destiny*.

If we are wise, we will toss aside self-guidance and self-designed life remedies, as these will lead us to unwanted hardships. God's is the unfailing plan. His Holy Spirit is a faithful, ever-present guide.

PRAYER

I pray the same prayer as the psalmist this morning, Lord.
Please guide me with your wise counsel and lead me in your perfect way. Amen.

Don't let us yield to temptation.

THE LORD OUR HELPER

WORD

Our help is from the LORD,
who made heaven and earth.

Psalm 124:8

THOUGHT

During a heavy rain one morning, my vehicle suddenly hydroplaned on the highway and quickly spun around to face a large, rapidly approaching semitruck. Fortunately, my vehicle continued to spin out of the truck's path and over a steep embankment.

A lady passing by pulled over and asked if I were OK. I replied and thanked her for her concern. Then a gentleman in a pickup truck stopped, jumped out, and said, "I have what you need to get out!"

He grabbed a cable from his truck, hooked it onto my vehicle, and quickly pulled me to the level roadside. I thanked him; he waved, jumped back into his truck, and sped off. While I was grateful to the lady for her concern, the gentleman in the truck had everything I needed to eliminate the problem I was facing.

Our helper and deliverer is not a concerned passerby without provision to assist. He is the maker of heaven and earth, and he is able to deliver us from our challenges, battles, and problems. Our help comes from the Lord!

PRAYER

Lord Jesus, you are my helper, savior, and deliverer from the evil one.
With a grateful heart, I worship, praise, and glorify your name. Amen.

But rescue us from the evil one.

FROM EVERLASTING TO EVERLASTING

WORD

After this time had passed, I, Nebuchadnezzar, looked up to heaven. My sanity returned, and I praised and worshiped the Most High and honored the one who lives forever.

*His rule is everlasting,
and his kingdom is eternal.*

Daniel 4:34

THOUGHT

History books contain scores of chapters filled with stories of failed and fallen kings, kingdoms, emperors, empires, and nations. They are filled with countless pages containing people and places that once held broad influence, power, and prestige in the world.

These forces were once thought to be so mighty, and their words were thought to be as invincible and impenetrable as their reputations. However, new conquerors and ideals rose, engulfed the old, and ignited a new cycle of power. And so it will continue as history unfolds until the earth itself experiences its final twilight.

In today's scripture, we see Nebuchadnezzar look up to heaven to worship the Lord on high. We're reminded that only God himself holds an everlasting rule, and only his kingdom is permanent and eternal. God, Yahweh, lives, rules, abides from everlasting to everlasting. His kingdom has no twilight; there is no end!

PRAYER

Glory, honor, and praise to you, the only God—the most high God! Amen.

For yours is the kingdom and the power and the glory forever.

OUR FATHER IS HOLY

Now I am departing from the world; they are staying in this world, but I am coming to you.
Holy Father, you have given me your name; now protect them by the power
of your name so that they will be united just as we are.

John 17:11

Who is our Father in heaven? He is Yahweh, the eternal one who is always present, so we are never alone. He is the faithful one and his promises are true, so we need not fear abandonment. He is the essence of love, and his intentions are honorable and good, so we need not distrust.

In the verse for today, we see Jesus asking his followers to be united with the Holy Father just as he—the Son of God—is. We see Christ interceding on our behalf, asking the Lord to protect us while we are in this world walking the path that he set before us. Ultimately, we see reassurance of our security in Christ as he welcomes us into family with God himself as the sons and daughters of God.

He is our Father and we are his children; we need not worry, fear rejection, or feel insecure. And he is the perfect Father, our loving parent who has no faults, does not sin, does not manipulate, and gives abundant mercy and grace to his children. He is holy in all his ways.

You are my Father in heaven, and the Father of my Lord and Savior, Jesus.
You are the Father most holy. Amen.

Our Father in heaven, may your name be kept holy.

THE LIFE OF A CHRISTIAN

WORD

Dear friends, you always followed my instructions when I was with you.
And now that I am away, it is even more important. Work hard to show the results of
your salvation, obeying God with deep reverence and fear. For God is working in you, giving you the
desire and the power to do what pleases him.

Philippians 2:12–13

THOUGHT

We do not work to gain salvation or favor with God. Salvation is free to all through repentance and submission to Christ, and God's favor is lavished on us by his grace alone. However, when we enter into a genuine relationship with Christ as the result of his redeeming grace, an awakening occurs in our lives.

Mysteriously and wondrously, gratitude fills our hearts, and in turn, our lives are marked by dedication to his causes. Other ambitions and self-designed plans fall to the wayside in the awe of living a life in obedience to his call. A life changed by Christ miraculously transitions from temporal pursuits to purposes embedded with eternal qualities and benefits.

Thankfully, we don't have to go it alone. God himself guides and empowers us to fulfill his will with excellence, for his glory. We are granted the privilege and honor to live out the qualities of God's kingdom and share his love and grace with all. It's amazing that God himself—the almighty being who imagined and spoke into existence everything that exists—chooses to work in and through the life of the Christian!

PRAYER

Father, I am humbled by the sheer impact and power of this passage.
May your Holy Spirit lead and empower each moment of my life. Fill it with the display
of your salvation as you work in me. Thank you for the desire and your divine power
to do what pleases you. It is my purpose and joy in life. Amen.

May your kingdom come soon. May your will be done on earth, as it is in heaven.

ATTENTION TO DETAIL

WORD

*When the time came, we set sail for Italy. Paul and several other prisoners
were placed in the custody of a Roman officer named Julius, a captain of the Imperial Regiment.
Aristarchus, a Macedonian from Thessalonica, was also with us. We left on a ship whose home port
was Adramyttium on the northwest coast of the province of Asia; it was scheduled to make several
stops at ports along the coast of the province.*

*The next day when we docked at Sidon, Julius was very kind to Paul and let him go ashore to visit
with friends so they could provide for his needs.*

Acts 27:1–3

THOUGHT

God has a plan for our lives! Although this phrase is often used in Christian circles,
it's true—indeed, he does have a plan. Although today's scripture doesn't seem particularly inspiring or challenging at first—perhaps it even looks like a string of irrelevant
historical details—this passage shows us the attention to detail that the Lord gives to
his day-to-day plans and provisions for us.

Our lack of trust is one of the most common hinderances to following God's plan.
We usually hope to find a way to fulfill his plan while remaining in our comfort zone.
However, the Lord does not always disclose all his methods and sources along the way,
and that makes us uncomfortable. He wants us to trust him whether his method seems
reasonable or not.

For example, today's verses don't tell us if Julius was a believer, only that he was
captain of the imperial regiment. He was kind to Paul and gave him permission to go
ashore so Paul's friends could provide for his needs. Julius certainly did not have to
grant Paul permission, but he did. God used an unlikely source to make certain Paul's
needs were met in the midst of God's plan. Watch for the Julius in God's plan for you.

PRAYER

*Thank you, Lord, for all the times you have provided for me and all the times ahead
that you will provide for me. I'm grateful that when you ask me to do your will, you give attention to
all the details and supply the method and the means to accomplish it. Amen.*

Give us today the food we need.

RUNNING UNENCUMBERED

WORD

...therefore, since we are surrounded by such a huge crowd of witnesses to the life of faith, let us strip off every weight that slows us down, especially the sin that so easily trips us up. And let us run with endurance the race God has set before us. We do this by keeping our eyes on Jesus, the champion who initiates and perfects our faith. Because of the joy awaiting him, he endured the cross, disregarding its shame. Now he is seated in the place of honor beside God's throne.

Hebrews 12:1–2

THOUGHT

Olympic runners wear lightweight clothing and discard every unnecessary item to increase the odds that they will win their race. And Olympian or not, no competitive marathoner runs with a wallet in their pocket, a purse on their arm, or a backpack over their shoulders. It would be a hindrance and certainly would slow them down.

God has placed a spiritual race before us. Hindrances in this race appear as judgments, jealousy, criticisms, materialism, lusts, and much more, but unforgiveness tops the list. If unforgiveness is not stripped away from our hearts, it can cause even the strongest, brightest, and best runners to succumb to spiritual exhaustion.

How do we rid ourselves of the debilitating weight of unforgiveness? By locking our gaze on the one who provides the way for our ultimate victory. He is the champion, the pioneer of the method for the victorious run, the perfecter of our faith—he is Jesus Christ!

PRAYER

Holy Spirit, focus my eyes on Christ. May I always see him, hear him, and follow him. And by your power, wisdom, and grace, may I win the race set before me. Amen.

Forgive us our sins, as we have forgiven those who sin against us.

LIGHT THAT LEADS TO LIFE

WORD

Jesus spoke to the people once more and said, "I am the light of the world. If you follow me, you won't have to walk in darkness, because you will have the light that leads to life."

John 8:12

THOUGHT

My five-year-old grandson was visiting on one cool, cloudy autumn evening. Suddenly, with adventure-filled eyes, he said, "Grandpa, let's go ride the four-wheeler in the woods!" It was almost completely dark outside, but you know how grandpas are. A few minutes later, we were wrapped up in coats and rolling through the woods.

After about fifteen minutes on the trail, the headlights suddenly failed. In turn, I quickly braked and there we sat, surrounded by complete darkness. My grandson was a little concerned, but then I noticed I had accidentally hit the headlamp switch to the off position. One click and the light clearly revealed the way home to hot chocolate.

Jesus said if we followed him we would not walk in the darkness, for he is the light of the world. His light penetrates the darkest situations, and is the only light leading to life. Thankfully, no matter what our present circumstances are, we do not have to travel through this world without his light—a light that leads away from trappings that may ensnare and instead leads to life, safety, protection, provision, and his glorious presence.

PRAYER

Lord, I know that with you leading me by your light, I need not fear the darkness. By your guidance, I'm able to see the paths to take and the obstacles to avoid. Father, lead me into your will. Amen.

Don't let us yield to temptation.

September 8

RESCUED FROM DEATH

WORD

...for you have rescued me from death;
you have kept my feet from slipping.
So now I can walk in your presence, O God,
in your life-giving light.

Psalm 56:13

THOUGHT

Lurking in the darkness are things unknown, things unseen. The enemy of our souls strives to harm us and hinder us from doing the will of the Lord. Satan waits to see if we will blindly stumble into his trap, hoping to wound and, if possible, destroy us.

In today's scripture, death seemed imminent to the psalmist, but this passage reveals that God intervened. He prevented the psalmist from slipping to his destruction.

God's motive for the rescue was clear: so the psalmist might walk in his presence, in his life-giving light. This has been God's purpose from the beginning, to have his people in his presence—and this is the motive for God rescuing us from sin and death. God's light leads to life because it rescues us from death.

PRAYER

Lord, I am grateful and humbled for your divine intervention;
thank you for rescuing me from the evil one, from death. Amen.

But rescue us from the evil one.

THE TIMELESS SONG

WORD

...and then I heard every creature in heaven and on earth
and under the earth and in the sea. They sang:
"Blessing and honor and glory and power
belong to the one sitting on the throne
and to the Lamb forever and ever."
And the four living beings said, "Amen!"
And the twenty-four elders fell down and worshiped the Lamb.

Revelation 5:13–14

THOUGHT

My dad collected music from the era when he and my mother were first married. Sometimes he would play the recordings at family gatherings and tell us they were the timeless classics, though my grandfather disagreed. My grandfather felt the songs from *his* youth were the classics. Each generation has its classics, and I now have a selection from my own youthful years. In truth, at some point all songs and lyrics—old and new, classic or otherwise—will fade to distant memory or be forgotten altogether.

However, one song is indeed timeless; we see it in today's passage. This song and lyric is of a redeemed creation and beyond what we can imagine in this earth-life. The song is perfect, performed perfectly by every creature existing in the presence of God.

These words will forever ring and resonate through the sacred halls of God's dwelling place. They will never be uttered with insincerity. They will never vanish, grow old, or become irrelevant. They reflect truth, the only truth that will abide forever.

PRAYER

Lord, your children look forward to the day when all creation will declare this truth
before you in the most reverent way. Blessing and honor and glory
and power to the one sitting on the throne and to the Lamb forever. Amen.

For yours is the kingdom and the power and the glory forever.

OUR FATHER FOREVER

WORD

I will be your Father,
and you will be my sons and daughters,
says the LORD Almighty.

2 Corinthians 6:18

THOUGHT

Good, godly fathering is a necessity for the healthy mental and emotional development of individuals and for the well-being of entire cultures. A lack or absence of a good father can result in multiple long-term effects.

There is, however, hope—a great hope indeed! A genuine, intimate relationship with the heavenly Father awaits all those who desire it. He wants to father us with the best fatherhood there is to offer. He is always faithful, always perfect in his love toward his children, and always accurate in his guidance.

If we allow God the Father to parent us through the redemptive work of Christ, we would see a vibrant ripple effect: hearts would be healed, spirits would be freed, hurts would be resolved. For that is what God our Father does.

PRAYER

My Father in heaven, holy is your name. I am grateful for your fathering and
desire to honor you as you lead and guide me by your Holy Spirit.
I long to become more like Jesus every day, bringing honor to my heavenly Father. Amen.

Our Father in heaven, may your name be kept holy.

SHINE!

WORD

You are the light of the world—like a city on a hilltop that cannot be hidden.
No one lights a lamp and then puts it under a basket. Instead, a lamp is placed on a stand, where
it gives light to everyone in the house. In the same way, let your good deeds shine out for all to see, so
that everyone will praise your heavenly Father.

Matthew 5:14–16

THOUGHT

A brief scan of news headlines could alarm most anyone. The welfare of the future, at least from the secular vantage point, appears volatile as authorities lacking in integrity continue plotting to undermine the things that are righteous, fair, truly just, and morally sound.

In these times, feelings of worry and despair can grow. Darkness seems to advance and overpower the light. However, this is when hope in Christ shines brightest, for in him indeed abides the only hope, the only prospect of overcoming the darkness. Certainly and undoubtedly, in Christ we truly overcome.

The church, the family of God, has a great opportunity to advance the gospel during difficult times in our world. We can and should choose to live and share genuine life-giving Christianity before a world that is confused, deceived, betrayed, disillusioned, and hopeless. We are the dispensers of hope, for in Christ—the Son of God, the Messiah, the Redeemer—hope thrives in abundance! We are here to shine his light.

PRAYER

Lord, you are the God of hope, you reign forever, and your desire is for all humankind
to come to the place of experiencing your grace and the hope of your kingdom.
Keep me focused on the goals and mandates of your heart. Let me use the opportunities you place
before me today to share the love of Christ, for his is the only sure and certain hope. Amen.

May your kingdom come soon. May your will be done on earth, as it is in heaven.

September 12

OUR DAILY BREAD

WORD

Give us today the food we need.

Matthew 6:11

THOUGHT

A sobering walk through the slums of Kampala, Uganda, adjusted my definition of provision. There were multiple dusty, red-earthen lanes strewn with rubbish where scantily clothed children were standing, many with fluid draining from their eyes and noses. Their hands extended in hope to receive some small morsel of food, a piece of candy, or a coin.

A turn down one of the dusty lanes led me to a small cluster of tiny masonry huts. A woman with a baby on her hip and several toddlers about her feet smiled and invited our group of four into her humble home. There wasn't enough room for everyone, so two of our group waited outside. She didn't have sufficient food for herself and her children, yet she offered us a beverage in a gesture of generous hospitality.

When we meditate on today's scripture—especially this portion of Lord's Prayer we've been walking through repeatedly this year—we find our own *perception* of what we need daily versus what we *actually* need to fulfill God's will on a daily basis is often very different. In reality, we are able to function on far less than what we're accustomed to in the West.

The woman who offered a beverage that day in Uganda gave out of her poverty to welcome strangers; I was later told she saw this as a privilege and honor to bless others. She saw her gesture as her way of helping someone in need, a thirsty passerby. Perhaps today is the day to rethink, reevaluate, realign, readjust, and redefine the target of our Lord's words. Perhaps our actual need for the day is far different, far less, than what we perceive is needed for ourselves.

PRAYER

I pray for what is genuinely the needed provision for today.
And I pray you would teach me to be grateful for what I have, to see it is provision to do your will.
You, Lord, are a giver—may I be also. Amen.

Give us today the food we need.

FATHER, FORGIVE THEM

WORD

Jesus said, "Father, forgive them, for they don't know what they are doing."
And the soldiers gambled for his clothes by throwing dice.

Luke 23:34

THOUGHT

Jesus knew he was innocent of every accusation and charge against him. He knew lies, deception, and manipulation were used to place him upon the beams of the cross, where he would physically suffer and die. He knew the thoughts of those watching as he experienced injustice, mocking, and ridicule. He knew there were those gathered in the area of his crucifixion who were overcome with sorrow, grief, and disbelief as they watched their hero, their conqueror, and friend seemingly meet his death.

He was also aware of others filled with bitterness and jealousy, thinking they would soon be rid of this man who was stirring up controversy, causing people to question their lofty religious positions and worldly authority.

In all of this, Jesus also knew a legion of angels could be summoned for his immediate rescue should he beckon, yet he understood the only possible hope for humanity's release from the captivity of hell was dependent upon his choice to accomplish his mission. To become the Savior of the world, he must give his life as the ransom for humankind. In the midst of the injustice of the cross, he also knew he must pray a most powerful prayer for his accusers, captors, and killers—but also for every single one of us: "Father, forgive them."

PRAYER

Thank you for your mercy, Lord Jesus, and for your redeeming gift of grace, which brings
a life of abundance. Thank you for your forgiveness. Amen.

Forgive us our sins, as we have forgiven those who sin against us.

DIVINE DETAIL

WORD

The LORD directs the steps of the godly.
He delights in every detail of their lives.

Psalm 37:23

THOUGHT

Is God bothered when we come to him with things we might consider insignificant? No! God actually finds pleasure when we involve him in the details of our lives, as we see in today's verse. The Lord was meticulous in the creation of the earth, and he is meticulous in the unfolding of each of our days when we invite him into them.

God is unlimited in his creative imagination and abilities. He loves detail; reread the Pentateuch and the instruction for the Tabernacle for proof. He desires to be involved with us in the details of our relationship with him and the unfolding of his will. When we involve him, we are steered around pitfalls and into open fields where we can run with him. We are wise to invite the one who delights in details to guide our steps. He will lead us with his divine precision in the directions which will cause us success in following and forming us into Christ's likeness.

PRAYER

Father, lead me through the details of this day and each day of my life ahead. Your paths lead away from the hazards which would cause my demise. Thank you for your divine direction. Amen.

Don't let us yield to temptation.

September 15

HE WILL HELP US

WORD

Do not be afraid, for I am with you.
Do not be discouraged, for I am your God.
I will strengthen you and help you.
I will hold you up with my victorious hand.

Isaiah 41:10

THOUGHT

My grandson was still very young when I took him on his first walk into the field in front of our home. He was having a great time until he stepped into a briar patch. The thorns pierced through his jeans to his legs, and the more he attempted to pull away, the more it hurt him. He cried out for my help, and I quickly turned, saw his eyes looking to me for help, and immediately came to his aid to free him from the thorny villain. Liberating him from his dilemma was effortless on my part, but he saw it as a much larger accomplishment.

The problems we encounter as Christians may exceed our abilities to solve them, but they are never beyond the Lord's help. He is not some limited storybook personality confined to the pages of a child's bedtime reader; he is the Lord of all heaven and earth! He is our Creator God whose authority and position exceed the greatest powers and accomplishments of people, nations, and empires.

When we let out a genuine, humble cry for help to our heavenly Father, he hears us and rescues us from the cleverest of snares, darkest of nights, and fiercest of enemies. Yes, the Lord God Jehovah, Creator of heaven and earth, will strengthen us in our time of need!

PRAYER

Lord, I pray for your help and protection when trouble mounts its efforts of opposition.
I will trust in you, my deliver and my hope. Amen.

But rescue us from the evil one.

GOD IS FOREVER GLORIOUS

WORD

All glory to God forever and ever! Amen.

Galatians 1:5

THOUGHT

The American flag is referred to as "Old Glory," and one's younger years are sometimes called "the glory days." In fact, the word *glory* is used in reference to many things. If it were within my power, I would declare the word *glory* to be sacred, reserved for one purpose only: to reference God the Father in his divine, singular uniqueness.

He alone is in need of nothing—no other person and no other thing. He existed in eternity past and will into eternity future. Only he can create something from nothing. Only he is the source of eternal light, pure love, pure hope, and everlasting life. There is no other like him.

Yahweh, the only God, is worthy of all honor. He alone has a reputation of genuine and perfect character, perfect holiness. He is the Lord of all glory, worthy of all glory.

PRAYER

Father, your name is exalted; your name is praised and worshiped.
Your name, oh, Lord, is glorified forever and forever. Amen.

For yours is the kingdom and the power and the glory forever.

September 17

THE FATHER'S GIFT

WORD

*Grace, mercy, and peace, which come from God the Father and from Jesus Christ—
the Son of the Father—will continue to be with us who live in truth and love.*

2 John 3

THOUGHT

As Christians, the gifts available to us through Christ have a tendency to transform the gray and lifeless tones of this life into brilliant color, depth, and beauty. If it weren't for Christ, true, lasting love, joy, and hope would be regularly out of reach of the human heart, but a gift from the Father changed it all.

When we submit our lives to Christ, we have access to treasures that money cannot buy and time cannot steal from us—treasures like those mentioned in today's verse: grace, mercy, and peace. And these treasures are not given to us sparingly; instead, the Father lavishes them upon us daily.

Through Christ, God showers grace, mercy, and peace on all who would receive him. This does not mean we will not experience trouble in this life; however, the Father's redemptive plan made a way for humanity to forever have shelter within his holy household and an abundant life filled with immeasurable, lasting goodness.

PRAYER

*Father, you give gifts of grace, mercy, and peace. You gave the gift of Christ and eternal life.
You give us life, love, and all things good and righteous. You are our heavenly Father,
always present, always good, always holy. Amen.*

Our Father in heaven, may your name be kept holy.

September 18

PURSUING GOD'S WILL WHOLEHEARTEDLY

WORD

As slaves of Christ, do the will of God with all your heart.

Ephesians 6:6

THOUGHT

We often hear the phrase "the will of God" in Christian conversation and prayer. There are instances where the Lord's will is simple to understand—and then times when it seems so complex. What causes this paradox?

Complexity can appear when we attempt to sort and clarify our individual lives, and during these seasons when we attempt to decipher his will for us, there are two critical questions to ask ourselves: First, will the direction we pursue result in our growth of love for God? And second, will our choice reduce and eliminate self-centered goals and desires so that we are in a better position to serve him and share the hope of his good news with the world?

When we honestly answer these two questions, we can more clearly see our true decision-making motives. May our hearts always be directed toward Christ's will and the goals of his kingdom, and may we pursue his will wholeheartedly, doing the will of God with all our hearts.

PRAYER

Lord, I pray for your will to be accomplished in all matters before me today. Please help me seek your kingdom above all else. Amen.

May your kingdom come soon. May your will be done on earth, as it is in heaven.

GOD'S MIRACULOUS PROVISION

WORD

...then he told the people to sit down on the grass. Jesus took the five loaves and two fish, looked up toward heaven, and blessed them. Then, breaking the loaves into pieces, he gave the bread to the disciples, who distributed it to the people. They all ate as much as they wanted, and afterward, the disciples picked up twelve baskets of leftovers. About 5,000 men were fed that day, in addition to all the women and children!

Matthew 14:19–21

THOUGHT

In this passage, the disciples were deeply challenged when Jesus told them they needn't send the people away for food—instead, they should feed the crowd. It seemed an impossible mission, and in the limited means of the disciples, it was.

However, Jesus saw the mission through God's provision. When the disciples obeyed Jesus and surrendered to him what was available, he took the little they had to offer— five loaves and two fish—blessed it, and performed a miracle. The result was an abundant feast beyond what they could have imagined. They were astounded—and God, not man, was credited and glorified!

God's mission exceeds our natural abilities and requires us to surrender what we have for him to bless. Then, as we walk by faith on a mission for his kingdom, he steps in with his supernatural intervention and *fulfills* the mission. This is his way. That way, in the end, we will be astounded and he will be credited and glorified.

PRAYER

I pray for courage to do your work, Father. I surrender to you and your will, as it is the best path and provision. Amen.

Give us today the food we need.

HE FORGAVE OUR SINS

WORD

He is so rich in kindness and grace that he purchased our freedom with the blood of his Son and forgave our sins. He has showered his kindness on us, along with all wisdom and understanding.

Ephesians 1:7–8

THOUGHT

Our heavenly Father is wealthy in all things; after all, he owns everything (Ps. 50:9–12). But how good is it to be reminded that he is "rich in kindness and grace." What joy floods the heart as we are reminded of this truth found in today's scripture!

When the redeemed sons and daughters of God ponder the sacrifice that was made by Christ to supply freedom for our souls, overwhelming emotions appear. Christ died in our place for our sins, but he rose again so we might know forgiveness, received out of the Father's wealth of kindness and grace.

We cannot measure these gifts as he showers them upon us, for they are truly abundant. We can only experience the hope and joy contained within them and praise him with grateful hearts.

PRAYER

You have showered me with your kindness. You have overwhelmed me with your love, your mercy, and your grace, Lord. I thank you for your forgiveness, for choosing to give me life when death was what I deserved. Thank you, Father, for your rescue. Amen.

And forgive us our sins, as we have forgiven those who sin against us.

THE PROVISION OF LIGHT

WORD

Send out your light and your truth;
let them guide me.
Let them lead me to your holy mountain,
to the place where you live.
There I will go to the altar of God,
to God—the source of all my joy.
I will praise you with my harp,
O God, my God!

Psalm 43:3–4

THOUGHT

Light compromises the effects of darkness. Light reveals everything hidden in the darkness, those things that might cause us to stumble. The goal of God's light and truth is to provide unmistakable visibility leading to God and his will. He has fashioned our hearts in such a way that they thrive when we are in the right relationship with him.

Within each of us is a "spiritual homing mechanism," so to speak. God created the spiritual heart to find its peace in him and not the world's offerings. Following his light, by his Spirit, guides us to genuine joy, genuine hope, genuine life. We're all searching and longing for a place of freedom and rest, a place where we can be loved fully and completely. That place is found in the presence of God!

Sadly, some choose other paths and seek other, lesser things in an attempt to reach a sense of fulfillment. However, when we surrender our lives to Christ Jesus, by the redemptive work of Christ we are able to abide in God's presence, the place the Father always intended and always desired for us to be.

PRAYER

Lead me by your light, from the world's temporal offerings of gratification and into your presence by the divine beacon of your Holy Spirit. There awaits the joy of my heart and soul. Amen.

Don't let us yield to temptation.

RISE UP AND HELP US

WORD

Rise up! Help us!
Ransom us because of your unfailing love.

Psalm 44:26

THOUGHT

There are seasons when, from our limited perspectives, conflicts and challenges appear to be senselessly thrust upon us. It can be even more concerning when evil's intrusion appears unchallenged by God. Sometimes in these seasons, God seems silent and unresponsive. When we're frustrated and spiritually exhausted by conflict and difficulty, we can be quick to doubt God and declare him as uncaring and indifferent, but is he?

Psalm 44 is a plea for God's deliverance. The song includes reflections of God's past interventions and acknowledges his unquestionable ability to produce victory over the enemy. The psalmist believes he's been faithful to God and is confused as to why God has not come to his aid.

The final words of this psalm reveal the psalmist's heart as they acknowledge God's unfailing love. There is no other place to seek genuine help or deliverance. Redeem us, Lord, because of your mercy and your faithful love!

PRAYER

Lord, when I need help and cannot understand the delay, help me remember your past deliverances
and faithfulness. Help me remember you are on course with your divine plans and have not
abandoned me. You are at work and my trust is in you. I pray, rise up!
Come to my aid because of your great mercy. Amen.

But rescue us from the evil one.

TIMELESS

WORD

...for your kingdom is an everlasting kingdom.
You rule throughout all generations.
The LORD always keeps his promises;
he is gracious in all he does.

Psalm 145:13

THOUGHT

Time is a measurement for things from beginning to ending. The thirty-minute doctor's office wait for a checkup, a two-hour plane flight, a ten-hour drive between cities. Four years to complete high school, another four to finish college, and still another three to six years for graduate programs. We understand time because it's the core marker of how we measure our lives and our limitations.

Living things are measured by the time of a lifespan. Trees live eighty to 120 years, some flowers bloom for a couple of weeks while others last only days, and people live an average of seventy to ninety years. We even measure seasons of history by their beginnings and endings: the Stone Age, the Renaissance, the Industrial Revolution, the Information Age.

Then there is God! He is not measured by a beginning or ending because he has neither. He is not measured by a term or a period of rule over a nation or nations, for he has ruled over all things measured by time and all things that are timeless, forever. Our God has ruled throughout all generations, and he always keeps his promises!

PRAYER

All glory, honor, and power are yours forever. Amen.

For yours is the kingdom and the power and the glory forever.

GOD THE FATHER

WORD

This letter is from Jude, a slave of Jesus Christ and a brother of James.

I am writing to all who have been called by God the Father, who loves you and keeps you safe in the care of Jesus Christ.

Jude 1

THOUGHT

The depth of comfort, encouragement, and hope found in this brief verse is amazing. For the abandoned, the hopeless, and the orphan, this is a message of hope: the promise of family and a home. For the abused, the ill-treated, and those imprisoned by injustice, this is the declaration of freedom and a place of refuge for heart and soul.

For those in search of genuine, lasting love, a commitment of love, or the fruit of love, this is the awaited covenant. Our God's love does not fail, manipulate, condemn, or hurt us. He is the perfect parent, full of abundant grace, mercy, and faithfulness.

The very Creator of heaven and earth offers to father any and all of us who will respond to his invitation. He will always love with perfect and holy love, and he will always keep us safe in the care of Jesus Christ.

PRAYER

Praise your name, heavenly Father! Thank you for your graciousness and care. Thank you for your divine fatherhood. Amen.

Our Father in heaven, may your name be kept holy.

TRUST IN YOUR ETERNAL WORD

WORD

Your eternal word, O LORD,
stands firm in heaven.
Your faithfulness extends to every generation,
as enduring as the earth you created.
Your regulations remain true to this day,
for everything serves your plans.

Psalm 119:89–91

THOUGHT

To find a point in history when total peace was present in the world and humanity was absent of concern and worry is quite impossible. While there were periods of far greater levels of fear that resulted from global wars, famines, and diseases, there has never been a complete worry-free season. Our current time in history is no different.

Whether we experience times of abundance or sparseness within the pantry, whether we're in times of unchallenged position and authority or are retreating to the darkness of hillside caverns, whether our days are filled with carefree lightheartedness or ridden with challenge and uncertainty, there is always the offering of certain hope and good resolve.

Where is this hope that does not disappoint and always remains stable? In God through Christ. He has promised hope for those who trust in his eternal promise, who trust in his eternal Word. Through all generations, he is the hope of the ages.

PRAYER

Lord, as you are the Creator and Maker of all things, I rest assured that your plans
and promises will unfold by your will and design. I rest assured knowing you will see
your name glorified, and my journey in your will, will succeed. Everything serves your plans,
in which I am included, and my trust in your unfailing hope is my aim. Amen.

May your kingdom come soon. May your will be done on earth, as it is in heaven.

WHAT DO YOU WANT ME TO DO FOR YOU?

WORD

As Jesus approached Jericho, a blind beggar was sitting beside the road.
When he heard the noise of a crowd going past, he asked what was happening. They told him that
Jesus the Nazarene was going by. So he began shouting, "Jesus, Son of David, have mercy on me!"
"Be quiet!" the people in front yelled at him. But he only shouted louder, "Son of David, have mercy
on me!" When Jesus heard him, he stopped and ordered that the man be brought to him. As the man
came near, Jesus asked him, "What do you want me to do for you?" "Lord," he said, "I want to
see!" And Jesus said, "All right, receive your sight! Your faith has healed you." Instantly the man
could see, and he followed Jesus, praising God. And all who saw it praised God, too.

Luke 18:35–43

THOUGHT

God, Creator and Sustainer of all matter, unlimited in every way, responded to a plea of a blind man by asking, "What do you want me to do for you?"

Christ encouraged his followers to ask, seek, and knock (Matt. 7:7) to look to God for all things pertaining to life and godliness. He said, "I tell you, you can pray for anything, and if you believe that you've received it, it will be yours."[22]; "I tell you the truth, you will ask the Father directly, and he will grant your request because you use my name."[23]

This seems the invitation of a lifetime, to be invited by the Lord to ask him for anything. While these statements are indeed true, they are also deeply embedded in the context of fulfilling the will of God, for the glory of God. The progression of the Lord's Prayer begins by honoring God. Then to pray for his kingdom to come and his will to be done. Following those points is the prayer request for God to supply the necessary provisions needed to fulfill his will.

What is the will of the Lord in a matter and what is required to see it accomplished? This question helps frame the required need when responding to the Lord should he ask, "What do you want me to do for you?"

The blind man sought a miracle for his greatest need: sight. Jesus responded with a miracle and vision was given. The man then followed Jesus, giving God the glory, and all who witnessed the miracle also praised God!

PRAYER

Father, I pray for your will and all that is needed to fulfill it.
Provide me with what will best honor you and your kingdom. Amen.

Give us today the food we need.

September 27

FREE FROM CONDEMNATION

WORD

I heard a loud voice shouting across the heavens,
"It has come at last—
salvation and power
and the Kingdom of our God,
and the authority of his Christ.
For the accuser of our brothers and sisters
has been thrown down to earth—
the one who accuses them
before our God day and night.
And they have defeated him by the blood of the Lamb
and by their testimony.
And they did not love their lives so much
that they were afraid to die."

Revelation 12:10–11

THOUGHT

Satan is relentless in his pursuit to condemn, fault-find, and criticize us. As believers, we are opposed by the darkness until our final moment on earth as the evil one attempts to persecute us for our failures and deficiencies. He opposes any and all people who have given themselves to God.

The enemy attempts to divide us from the Lord; he lies to us about our worth in Christ, the forgiveness that we've received through the work on the cross, and the freedom we have in the redemption bought for us by Jesus. If Satan had his way, we would all forget God's goodness and lavish gifts of grace, freedom, and forgiveness that have been permanently made ours by Christ's death and resurrection.

Although the evil one would remind us of our past sins and faults in an attempt to burden us with condemnation and shame, we no longer stand in our weaknesses and failures. Instead, we are now cloaked in Christ's triumph over all our sin. Though the accuser stands demanding our doom and destruction, we will stand clothed in the righteousness of Christ, blameless before God because of the redeeming blood of Christ that covers us from all accusation.

PRAYER

Thank you, Redeemer God, for the forgiveness of my sin. Thank you that you triumphed over my weaknesses and failures through your act on the cross. Amen.

Forgive us our sins, as we have forgiven those who sin against us.

September 28

THIS IS THE WAY—WALK IN IT

WORD

Your own ears will hear him.
Right behind you a voice will say,
"This is the way you should go,"
whether to the right or to the left.

Isaiah 30:21

THOUGHT

The leadership of the Holy Spirit is accurate, clear, and precise—just as this scripture describes! God is the perfect Father, and he wants to lead and care for us in all the realms of our life. He wants us to know precisely where to walk. According to Acts 10:34, God does not show favoritism, so certainly he will reveal to us his direction clearly to anyone who seeks him.

We exist in this life to fulfill God's will and glorify his name. Therefore, we can correctly assume he wants us to unmistakably see and understand where he leads because it concerns his best and ultimate interest. We can have faith and continue to seek him and his voice wholeheartedly when working to discern his will.

Thankfully, our heavenly Father wants to lead his children in the details. We are not alone in this life, and in the details of our everyday choices we build a life well lived for his glory.

PRAYER

Let my eyes and ears stay alert to the detailed and effective guidance you offer, oh, Lord.
And may your Holy Spirit in his power lead me to successfully, wholeheartedly follow him. Amen.

Don't let us yield to temptation.

STAND YOUR GROUND

WORD

*...therefore, put on every piece of God's armor so you will be able to resist
the enemy in the time of evil. Then after the battle you will still be standing firm.
Stand your ground, putting on the belt of truth and the body armor of God's righteousness.
For shoes, put on the peace that comes from the Good News so that you will be fully prepared. In
addition to all of these, hold up the shield of faith to stop the fiery arrows of the devil. Put on
salvation as your helmet, and take the sword of the Spirit, which is the word of God.*

Ephesians 6:13–17

THOUGHT

In times of pressure and conflict, the sons and daughters of God are to be the voice declaring light and hope in Christ. In times where morality and integrity are bent or disregarded, we are to stand our ground using the weapons of God's kingdom. We are to clothe ourselves in God's armor and exude the qualities of the Christ we follow, the true King who holds our allegiance. We must radiate compassion, mercy, grace, forgiveness, gentleness, self-control, and kindness. And we are to even *love* our enemies.

We are to stand in the truth, with the truth, and for the truth, and God's Word is the absolute truth! Although the Christian life is often opposite the life the world would want us to live, we are to stand in Christ's strength and for his causes. Our war is not against flesh and blood; our war is spiritual, and the weapons of our warfare are spiritual (2 Cor. 10:4).

Can you hear the voice of God? He is saying, "Stand your ground!" Stand in prayer; stand in his truth, stand by living the Christ-life before a dark, frail, and fallen hopeless world.

PRAYER

*Father, lead me to stand grounded in your wisdom and strength by your Holy Spirit.
Cause me to be like Christ, your only Son and the Savior of the world.
I long to represent his will and his desires in his way. Amen.*

But rescue us from the evil one.

OUR GOD ENDURES FOREVER

WORD

Your throne, O God, endures forever and ever.
You rule with a scepter of justice.

Psalm 45:6

THOUGHT

I was lost on a backcountry road when I spotted an older gentleman in denim overalls walking along the lane. I pulled my car beside him and asked for directions to my destination. He said, "Well, you go down this road—seems like forever—then you'll come to the end, and you'll turn right." Of course, the road did not last forever, and I eventually did arrive at my destination.

Nothing in this world, or the universe for that matter, will last forever. Everything will come to an end. The one exception is the one God, Yahweh. The psalmist declares God, his throne, his dominion, and rule, will last "forever and ever." And not only will God's rule endure eternally outside the constraints of time, but it is also a *just* rule. Our heavenly Father created justice and upholds it eternally.

Although the phrase "forever and ever" sounds redundant, the writer drives home his point: God is the only eternal one. Yes, the redeemed of God through Christ live into eternity, but only God has existed from eternity past and will continue into eternity future. He had no beginning and he will have no ending. He lives forever and ever, and he rules forever and ever.

PRAYER

Praise you, eternal one, the only God, the most high above all things!
You rule and abide forever, you are just and merciful, and your kingdom has no end. Amen.

For yours is the kingdom and the power and the glory forever.

HE NEVER CHANGES

WORD

Long ago you laid the foundation of the earth
and made the heavens with your hands.
They will perish, but you remain forever;
they will wear out like old clothing.
You will change them like a garment
and discard them.
But you are always the same;
you will live forever.
The children of your people
will live in security.
Their children's children
will thrive in your presence.

Psalm 102:25–28

THOUGHT

We live in a world and a time in history where things change in the blink of an eye. Not only do we experience this in natural elements such as the weather, seasons, and ecosystems, but we also experience it in the fast-paced changes of technology, the economy, and our societal beliefs. In this world, stability is scarce.

However, our Father in heaven is always the same. He never changes, and he is always reliable. He is the Rock of stability, the keeper of promises, and our constant place of refuge. He is our perfect Father forever. He never makes wrong decisions, never gives tentative advice, and never wavers in his love.

When it feels like the world is full of chaos, confusion, and—of course—change, we can rest assured as the sons and daughters of God. He is our faithful Father and King, and we have security in his presence.

PRAYER

I praise you this morning, Father in heaven. Holy is your name
and perfect are all of your ways. Amen.

Our Father in heaven, may your name be kept holy.

October 2

ALONE WITH GOD

WORD

Before daybreak the next morning, Jesus got up and went out to an isolated place to pray.

Mark 1:35

THOUGHT

For all of us who are recipients of God's wonderful grace, the will of the Father is that we would allow the Holy Spirit to transform us into the image of Jesus Christ. We are called Christians—Christ-followers! We are to strive to become like Jesus in every way. One of the most important spiritual practices that Jesus displayed and intends for us to follow is the deep desire and commitment to pray.

The incarnation is a mystery and challenge to the human mind, but nevertheless, Jesus Christ is Immanuel, God with us; he is fully God, yet fully human. As Christ was fully God, was there a need for him to pray during his earth-life? A puzzling question indeed. However, this we know for sure: Jesus prayed, he prayed often, and he intended for us to do the same. He established the pattern of prayer that we can emulate in order to experience healthy, productive, and effective spiritual lives while we are on this earth.

Does the practice of prayer have to include finding a place of solitude where you're alone with God early in the day? Sometimes it does. I've not met a single person who has incorporated solitude with God into their spiritual life who wouldn't consider this practice an honor, a privilege, and a sheer joy.

PRAYER

Thank you, Father God, for the opportunity and freedom to commune and worship you deeply in the quiet places. Amen.

May your kingdom come soon. May your will be done on earth, as it is in heaven.

MOTIVES COUNT

WORD

*...and even when you ask, you don't get it because your motives are all wrong—
you want only what will give you pleasure.*

James 4:3

THOUGHT

Motives count with God. Yes, he is the good Father; his love has no limits and he is always faithful. In fact, he is perfect in all of his ways. He is never deficient of any resource; he is never unavailable for inquiry or consultation.

He invites us to join him in his most fantastic plan for humankind. Those aligned with him are promised success as defined by him, not by our own definitions. He will provide everything necessary to complete his plan for us as we serve him in our part of this divine adventure.

However, when it appears he has not provided, it is because we do not always see his broader design and purposes at work. There are times we can think he has not supplied a resource, when in reality the deeper reason for what is perceived as "unanswered" prayer is a "No" because we ask with wrong motives. The truth is, he will supply us with all that is needed to fulfill his will. We can rest assured in that.

PRAYER

*Lord, please provide me with all that's required to accomplish the desires of your heart today.
And by the power of your Holy Spirit, please bring your holy conviction
into my life when I seek something with the wrong motives. Amen.*

Give us today the food we need.

SEVENTY TIMES SEVEN

WORD

...then Peter came to him and asked,
"Lord, how often should I forgive someone who sins against me? Seven times?"

"No, not seven times," Jesus replied, "but seventy times seven!"

Matthew 18:21–22

THOUGHT

In today's scripture, Peter asked Jesus how many times forgiveness should be granted to a brother or sister who had committed an offense. Before Jesus could respond, Peter supplied what he thought to be a most generous response to an offender: seven times.

When Jesus replied, he overstated his response; that way, Peter would know the point of forgiveness is to forgive genuinely and generously. Our response to offering forgiveness to those who have wronged us is to give it in abundance and with a merciful heart—just like Jesus.

This can be difficult, especially if we have been severely wronged. However, even if we need to remove ourselves from the person or the relationship, our required response is still to forgive. Thankfully, we do not have to conjure up those feelings of forgiveness by our own might. By his Holy Spirit and by submitting our hearts fully to him, Christ Jesus will lead us to a place where we can forgive with "seventy times seven" generosity.

PRAYER

Christ, forgive me when I am seeking my own definitions for forgiveness instead of yours.
Your grace and mercy exceed human limits, and the power of
your Holy Spirit will lead me to forgive genuinely. Amen.

Forgive us our sins, as we have forgiven those who sin against us.

THE LEADER OF OUR DESTINY

WORD

...so he will do to me whatever he has planned.
He controls my destiny.

Job 23:14

THOUGHT

Job shared these words during his season of intense trial, and these words reveal God's resoluteness to lead and accomplish his purposes in Job's life. God was working to help Job fulfill his highest calling and purpose: to glorify God! This was Job's story, and this is our story as well.

The Holy Spirit leads God's children on a predetermined path. This path is created by God, marked by God, and protected by God. We walk upon the path under the Lord's leadership. Even if, like Job, we experience times of despair and trial, we can rest assured that God's glory for our good is waiting on the other side of difficult seasons. He is ever-faithful to his children, and his love is merciful and just.

The Lord is the leader of our destiny. We are created by God for his purposes. As his sons and daughters, we are marked by and protected by God. Living a life of honor to him is our highest purpose, a plan and destiny that he controls, as we are wonderfully made for his glory.

PRAYER

Father, you lead me on the path of your choosing. My life is designed by you for the purpose of glorifying you and your kingdom. Thank you for leading me and controlling my destiny. Amen.

Don't let us yield to temptation.

UNFAILING LIGHT

WORD

...then Jesus asked them, "Would anyone light a lamp and then put it under a basket or under a bed? Of course not! A lamp is placed on a stand, where its light will shine."

Mark 4:21

THOUGHT

One cool fall evening, not long after we had just moved into our home in rural Arkansas, I stepped outside and saw that most of the colorful leaves had fallen from the trees, exposing more of the wooded hillside behind our house. I noticed what appeared to be a light at the top of the hill. Curious, I began a slow and careful walk up the hill through the woods toward the light.

After covering about two hundred yards, I discovered the light source was a small incandescent lightbulb on the back porch of a house an additional fifty yards away. We had lived in our Arkansas home for a few weeks by then, but that was the first time I knew another house was located beyond the woods. Typically I wouldn't walk into the woods at night, but that dim light gave me a sense of security and direction.

In John 8:12, Jesus said he was the light of the world and if we follow him, we won't have to walk in the darkness. He will lead us through this world's challenging terrains. But in following him, we should also reflect the beauty and brilliance of his unfailing mercy and grace to a fallen and needy world, acting as that small lightbulb at the top of the hill by showing others the way.

PRAYER

Lord, thank you for your illuminating brightness of life. I'm grateful that your heart desires to draw us out of the darkness and into your marvelous light. I thank you today for your provision of grace, and I pray, by the enablement of your Holy Spirit, I might be used today as a vessel to reflect your life to those living in darkness. Amen.

But rescue us from the evil one.

BRING AN OFFERING INTO HIS PRESENCE

WORD

Give to the LORD the glory he deserves!
Bring your offering and come into his presence.
Worship the LORD in all his holy splendor.

1 Chronicles 16:29

THOUGHT

God is the Creator of all things. He is in need of nothing. He is self-contained and self-sustained. If he lacks nothing and owns everything, what impressive gift might we offer him to give him thanks for his goodness? *Ourselves!*

Our free will is the one thing the Lord created that becomes our best offering. He made us for the purpose of worship, but he does not make us worship him. Instead, he gifts us with choice. He has allowed us to decide how we will live and whom we will serve.

Through Christ, we *choose* to offer ourselves to worship the one God of all glory, to receive repentance and his merciful gift of grace, and to love him with all our being and serve him wholeheartedly. We are able to bring our offering—ourselves—and come into his presence with joy and thanksgiving.

PRAYER

I worship you, Lord, God of all majesty. You are forever the all-powerful God,
the one who is worthy of all glory and worship. Amen.

For yours is the kingdom and the power and the glory forever.

PATERNAL PROMISE

WORD

Now all glory to God our Father forever and ever! Amen.

Philippians 4:20

THOUGHT

Today's scripture is a statement of brevity, but oh, what depth, breadth, and majesty lie solidly within it! The heart and soul of the reader is left to respond in reverence and awe, wholly lost in wonderment of God's certain promise and rich prospect.

What are we rejoicing over in today's short verse? The truth that God is our Father! As amazing and humbling as it is, it is true: the Father of all life is *our* Father! He is the Father who never wrongfully or unjustifiably forsakes or ignores those in his care. He has promised his ongoing paternal presence, and we will never experience the pain of absence or neglect in his perfect love.

Because we are sons and daughters of God, not only does he promise us his presence throughout our lives here on earth, but also that we will be with him for eternity as well.

PRAYER

All glory to you, God! I worship you and exalt your name. You are holy, and you are magnificent in all your ways. I praise you; my heart is overwhelmed with awe and gratitude. You are the Father of glory, the Father of life. Amen.

Our Father in heaven, may your name be kept holy.

COMPASSION

WORD

Moved with compassion, Jesus reached out and touched him. "I am willing," he said. "Be healed!"

Mark 1:41

THOUGHT

Jesus was traveling through Galilee and was approached by a man with leprosy who, on his knees, begged him for healing. Jesus, moved with compassion because he was and is "the God of compassion" (Ex. 34:6), healed the man. Jesus was God incarnate—fully man, yet still God. While living his life on earth, Jesus was the physical manifestation of compassion, and the example, then and now, for his disciples to follow.

The compassion of Jesus contains qualities we are to adopt and utilize toward others in our daily lives. Compassion was not something he needed to work at having, build up to, or remember to extend. It was embedded within his being. Compassion was his heart, intertwined with his other characteristics of love, mercy, grace, selflessness, and holiness. They were inseparable, for he was and is the well from which these qualities are drawn.

Because of his close relationship with his Father, Jesus's discernment was sharp and fine-tuned. He was determined to do what he saw the Father doing and to be about the Father's good will. He walked on earth spiritually aware, alert, and guided by the good graces of God's kingdom. He knew how and when to respond to each situation he came upon.

We are commissioned by Christ to continue his mission, and he has given his Holy Spirit to guide and enable us. As we walk in close relationship with God, guided by God's Word, he will lead us to know when and how to respond to each situation with his compassion.

PRAYER

Holy Spirit, cause my eyes and heart to be directed by your compassion as I go about my day. When I see a need and can offer aid, may I follow your leading and reach out to those before me. Amen.

May your kingdom come soon. May your will be done on earth, as it is in heaven.

October 10

GOD'S PROVISION OF COMMUNITY

WORD

All the believers devoted themselves to the apostles' teaching, and to fellowship, and to sharing in meals (including the Lord's Supper), and to prayer.

Acts 2:42

THOUGHT

In each of our hearts we have the need and desire for community. The Trinity—God in three persons as God the Father, God the Son, and God the Holy Spirit—lives in community. Yes, the Trinity is a mystery, but nevertheless, humanity is created in God's image and one of his characteristics is living in the highest possible degree of community.

My wife and I became Christians in the same service at a small church in Louisville. The pastor and a few folks immediately invited us to meals, coffee, and small group gatherings. Each was an opportunity to provide us with different dynamics of the Christian experience. God's design of community is a necessary provision to every follower of Jesus. Certainly it was the very important link to our personal spiritual growth.

The church is God's design for those belonging to him to have community. In this community, we are supported as we grow in our love for Christ and go out into all the world and make disciples. Spiritual health, wholeness, and fulfillment are provided for us in this divinely fashioned group.

Within the community of the church, we practice devotion, commitment, and consecration to the principles and teachings of God's Word. We also practice deep, Christ-centered communion together, both through sharing meals of fellowship as well as the Lord's Supper, where we celebrate and acknowledge Christ's work on the cross. We also gather together to pray for one another and those outside of our local church body.

These are some of the ways we can support and uphold one another as we go about the world doing God's work. The church is God's provision to fill our need for community.

PRAYER

Father, thank you for providing genuine community for my spiritual welfare and the ongoing success of your mission and call. May I wisely participate in this holy organism, not forsaking its gatherings and giving thanks for its benefits. Amen.

Give us today the food we need.

FORGIVING THE UNTHINKABLE

WORD

As they stoned him, Stephen prayed, "Lord Jesus, receive my spirit." He fell to his knees, shouting, "Lord, don't charge them with this sin!" And with that, he died.

Acts 7:59–60

THOUGHT

We can forgive a person in the supermarket who rushes before us in the checkout line. We can forgive inaccurate and harmful statements against our character. We can forgive criticism and gossip. We can forgive theft, harsh words, and heated anger. But can we forgive everything?

We encounter difficulty offering forgiveness when cruel and heinous injustices are forced upon the innocent. There are consequences for those who transgress the laws of the land and for the unrepentant heart, but when genuine repentance is extended by an offender, we are to forgive.

As Christians, we are not given the option to withhold forgiveness when repentance is sought—no matter the depth or horror of the infraction. We do not overlook injustices, and we do not withhold rescue for those in harm's way when it is within our power to do so. And we are to forgive those who sin against us. There is no biblical evidence to withhold forgiveness for sins we consider deplorable and unthinkable when forgiveness is sought by the offender. Let us be free in offering forgiveness to others who are repentant, just as Christ offered it to us.

PRAYER

Father, forgive me of my sins as I forgive others who have sinned against me. Help me to be more like you—abundant in mercy and forgiveness—so I can better display your love to all. Amen.

Forgive us our sins, as we have forgiven those who sin against us.

THE KEY TO LIFE

WORD

My child, listen to me and do as I say,
and you will have a long, good life.
I will teach you wisdom's ways
and lead you in straight paths.
When you walk, you won't be held back;
when you run, you won't stumble.
Take hold of my instructions; don't let them go.
Guard them, for they are the key to life.

Proverbs 4:10–13

THOUGHT

We are encouraged in Proverbs 4:5 to get wisdom and develop good judgment or understanding. We are told God's wisdom contains far greater wealth than the gold, silver, and gems found in the world.

Then, here in Proverbs 4:10–13, we see the wisdom of God offers principles and directives to guide us toward his successful and favored paths. These principles and directives are tried, true, unfailing, and they produce good fruit for us. More importantly, they honor and glorify God.

Much has been written about finding the keys to an abundant, prosperous, and successful life in the world. The self-help section in a bookstore is loaded with advice on how to win and succeed in our time on earth. However, the *true* key to life is found in following the wisdom of the Lord. All advice outside of God's leadership will lead to disappointment in the end. The richest treasure for the soul is found in pursuing and living the Christ-life.

PRAYER

I pray for your guidance, Lord, and I pray that I would follow your wisdom and walk along your straight paths. Your wisdom and leadership are the keys to life. Amen.

Don't let us yield to temptation.

REMAIN FAITHFUL

WORD

...therefore, my dear brothers and sisters, stay true to the Lord. I love you and long to see you, dear friends, for you are my joy and the crown I receive for my work.

Philippians 4:1

THOUGHT

The ultimate defense and escape from temptation and evil remain faithfully strong as we abide within the redemptive work of our Savior and Redeemer, Jesus Christ. The writer of Hebrews strongly exhorts us to fasten our gaze on Jesus, the perfector of our faith (Heb. 12:2), for he will never cease to protect what he purchased with his own life.

Here in Philippians 4:1, Paul urges his friends in Christ to stay true to the Lord. Christ will remain faithful as our Savior and Redeemer, and in turn, we are to strive to remain faithful to him as sons and daughters of God.

God's grace spiritually transforms us upon our repentance and confession of faith in Christ, and it positions us in the impenetrable place of God's rescue and refuge. This is, indeed, the good news of the kingdom of God! There is no power or plan capable of removing us from the protection of the Lord. Let us faithfully remain true to the Lord and his work on the cross, and let us boldly spread the good news of the gospel of Christ without fear so that all may come to know his faithfulness.

PRAYER

Great are you, Lord, to deliver us from the darkest of schemes. Thank you for your unwavering care, divine protection, and flawless guidance. Amen.

But rescue us from the evil one.

October 14

GOD OF ALL LIFE

WORD

God, the LORD, created the heavens and stretched them out.
He created the earth and everything in it.
He gives breath to everyone,
life to everyone who walks the earth.

Isaiah 42:5

THOUGHT

Once while I was in New Mexico, I had the opportunity to watch a small group of antelope suddenly burst into a run through a large grassy plain. They made their way along the broad edge of a ravine and disappeared behind a hill. All this was against the backdrop of the snowcapped Rocky Mountains.

I am almost always deeply appreciative of moments in nature, such as the one in New Mexico, that visually reflect God's vast creative imagination and majesty. However, the common squirrels within the trees outside my writing nook are equally stunning to me. These agile little creatures quickly scamper across stones and effortlessly run straight up the trunks of trees; their talents amaze me!

None of these awe-provoking natural moments would exist if it wasn't for the God of all life. He imagined Creation, spoke it into being, and maintains it. Let us worship him for all the mysterious, amazing, beautiful, awe-inspiring, natural, *and* supernatural moments he has made.

PRAYER

Thank you, God of all life, for igniting the sense of appreciation within me for you and your limitless abilities to create, maintain, and give life. Worthy are you, Lord, to receive all praise. Amen.

For yours is the kingdom and the power and the glory forever.

THE ROLE OF FATHERHOOD

WORD

See how very much our Father loves us, for he calls us his children,
and that is what we are! But the people who belong to this world don't recognize that we are God's
children because they don't know him.

1 John 3:1

THOUGHT

Some years ago, several friends helped me begin a ministry to assist people whom our culture has labeled as "children at risk." Whether we're working to serve children in developed countries that have modern amenities and access to clean water or children living in underdeveloped countries in villages lacking modern plumbing, I noticed that nearly *all* children share a common need: the influence of good fathering.

Believers in Christ are blessed to receive the ultimate fathering experience. God is our Father, and he is the Father of all life. He is love's ultimate source; his provision and guidance, in and through life, are second to none. His counsel is perfect, his choices are perfect, and his wisdom is perfect. He always desires what is right, what is pure, and what is best for everyone under his care.

There are no perfect earthly fathers; each will fail to some degree, but we have assurance in the healing and redemptive parenting of God the Father, and he is perfect in all of his ways.

PRAYER

I worship you, my Father in heaven. Amen.

Our Father in heaven, may your name be kept holy.

WE ARE ALL SOWERS

WORD

He told many stories in the form of parables, such as this one:
"Listen! A farmer went out to plant some seeds. As he scattered them across his field,
some seeds fell on a footpath, and the birds came and ate them. Other seeds fell on shallow soil with
underlying rock. The seeds sprouted quickly because the soil was shallow. But the plants soon wilted
under the hot sun, and since they didn't have deep roots, they died. Other seeds fell among thorns that
grew up and choked out the tender plants. Still other seeds fell on fertile soil, and they produced a crop
that was thirty, sixty, and even a hundred times as much as had been planted!
Anyone with ears to hear should listen and understand."

Matthew 13:3–9

THOUGHT

Sermons and writings on this familiar parable of the farmer sowing seed are in abundance. Teaching on this passage often centers on the varied results of sowing, and it's important we understand those variables. The emphasis this day, however, is not upon the varied results that the sower obtains. Instead, it's to understand we are *all* to sow this life-giving seed of God's kingdom; it is the call and mission of every believer in Jesus Christ.

The will of God for us is first to worship him and then to sow the truth of his kingdom throughout the people groups of the world. Every nation, every ethnic group, every community, and every household—yes, everyone needs to hear the good news. We are the sowers of this most important message, and we're engaged in the most critical mission for humankind.

This is the will of God. This is the mandate of our Savior Jesus Christ, that we would go out into all the world and preach the gospel. So let us go!

PRAYER

King Jesus, may your kingdom come and your will be done.
May the people of the world become the people of Christ. When you return for us,
Lord, may we be found sowing seed and working within the harvest fields. Amen.

May your kingdom come soon. May your will be done on earth, as it is in heaven.

HOPE FOR THE WORLD

WORD

...and his name will be the hope of all the world.

Matthew 12:21

THOUGHT

While doctors, therapists, and counselors are legitimate resources who can help us with ailments of the mind, body, and heart, over time our world has minimized and marginalized hope's singular unfailing source: the Son of God, Jesus Christ.

He is the world's only reliable, lasting hope. We are grateful for the medical sciences and the advances to better the human condition, but still they are sources limited in their capacities as they are unable to match the living power of God. God is the hope for the hopeless, the failed, the weak, the forgotten, the rejected, the persecuted, and the outcast.

For whoever is hopeless, and wherever there is hopelessness, the name of Jesus Christ is the way of hope. He is the hope for the world. In order to access this lasting hope, all we have to do is call on him. He never fails.

PRAYER

When I am challenged with hopelessness, you remind me of your faithfulness and unlimited ability to provide me with hope. In your power and love, my concerns and fears are dissolved. Thank you for your kindness and provision. Amen.

Give us today the food we need.

AVOIDING HAZARDS

WORD

Look after each other so that none of you fails to receive the grace of God. Watch out that no poisonous root of bitterness grows up to trouble you, corrupting many.

Hebrews 12:15

THOUGHT

Forgiveness is the escape route from the darkness of spiritual, mental, and emotional captivity. Recipients of God's forgiveness can testify to its liberating power for the heart and soul. By the power of Christ, forgiveness replaces our fears with courage, exchanges our anguish for joy, and turns our anger into peace.

The richest version of forgiveness is God's forgiveness bought by the blood of his Son, Jesus Christ. His forgiveness replaces hate and disdain with love—and his love covers a multitude of sins. Forgiveness is the heart of God, and it's his desire that all experience it.

Though the source is unknown, I once read that "bitterness is unforgiveness fermented."[24] We are warned to be vigilant against unforgiveness and its effects, for unforgiveness becomes a root of bitterness. And bitterness is poisonous to its host and others. The antidote to this poison is to forgive.

PRAYER

Father, thank you for forgiving me when I was unworthy of your grace and mercy. Please guard my heart, and by the wisdom and strength of your Holy Spirit, may I forgive others as you have forgiven me. Amen.

Forgive us our sins, as we have forgiven those who sin against us.

ABLE TO SAVE

WORD

Shadrach, Meshach, and Abednego replied, "O Nebuchadnezzar, we do not need to defend ourselves before you. If we are thrown into the blazing furnace, the God whom we serve is able to save us. He will rescue us from your power, Your Majesty. But even if he doesn't, we want to make it clear to you, Your Majesty, that we will never serve your gods or worship the gold statue you have set up."

Daniel 3:16–18

THOUGHT

In the face of fierce threat and challenge, Shadrach, Meshach, and Abednego exemplified and inspired us with their hearts of commitment, courage, faith, and deep trust in God. We're reminded by this passage that the Lord is able to deliver us from evil's darkest intentions and eliminate evil's overshadowing danger and doom. We are invited and encouraged to pray for deliverance from evil, and we should.

However, the words of these three men, in their commitment and unwavering allegiance to God, are troubling for most of us, as we wonder if we would be so brave in a similar situation. They are clear to say to their captors that God will rescue them. They specify that the Lord has the power to protect them and nothing can prevent him from stepping in, but even if he doesn't intervene, come what may, they will serve only Jehovah God.

May we trust in God's all-sufficient grace for each situation when and if it arises, regardless of intensity, and exhibit the same sort of tested-by-fire faith and trust in the Lord God and his ability to rescue, redeem, and restore us in any circumstances. He is truly able to save.

PRAYER

Father, by your grace and the power of your Holy Spirit, make me resolute in my faith for the honor of your glory and name, regardless of the cost. Amen.

Don't let us yield to temptation.

GOD'S CLEAR LEADERSHIP

WORD

You led our ancestors by a pillar of cloud during the day and a pillar of fire at night so that they could find their way.

Nehemiah 9:12

THOUGHT

In this verse, Nehemiah reflects on God's past faithfulness to clearly guide his people by pillars of cloud and fire. Nehemiah later transitions from reflecting on God's faithfulness to Israel to then appealing for God's intervention on behalf of Israel again. For forty years, the Lord guided the Israelites by a pillar of cloud during the light of day and a pillar of fire in night. Why? Because he wanted them to know his will, the direction he wanted them to go.

The Lord still leads with clarity, though maybe not with pillars of cloud and fire. He has given us the unmistakable guidance of his Holy Spirit. The more time we spend seeking to learn his characteristics, ways, and voice, the more clearly we can recognize the Holy Spirit's leading.

Our God will always lead us to those places that fulfill his will, and his will is for us to love him with all of our heart, soul, mind, and strength. His will is for us to take the good news of his grace to all corners of the world. His will is for us to be selfless, help others, and encourage others. His will is for us to value the eternal things and not the temporary things of this earth. His leadership is clear, and he will show us his way.

PRAYER

Lead me, Lord, in any way you choose. Amen.

But rescue us from the evil one.

October 21

HONOR THE LORD
WITH WORSHIP

WORD

Honor the LORD for the glory of his name.
Worship the LORD in the splendor of his holiness.

Psalm 29:2

THOUGHT

I love blustery days that cause the trees to yield to the will of the wind. On these windy days, I am reminded all creation was made by God and exists for his great glory; he has made us to honor him with a life of worship, yielded to the winds of his will, his Spirit.

We are to be ever grateful for his work of redemption. In Christ, we are moved from a position of weakness, fragility, and death to become oaks of righteousness, commissioned and committed to honoring the Lord and glorifying his holy name.

Christendom's highest call and deepest privilege is the worship of God. Worship means to attribute worth, so the worship of God is attributing him with the worth due only to the Lord, for only he is the source of holiness. Through Christ alone will we experience holiness. We are exhorted by this verse to attribute our worth to solely belonging to God and to display our gratitude in wholehearted worship.

PRAYER

May your name be praised; may your name be honored! I worship you, Lord, for you are holy. Yes, I worship and bow before my King, the Father of life. Amen.

For yours is the kingdom and the power and the glory forever.

GATHER FOR WORSHIP

WORD

They will be my people, and I will be their God. And I will give them one heart and one purpose: to worship me forever, for their own good and for the good of all their descendants.

Jeremiah 32:38–39

THOUGHT

Humankind was made by God for the purpose of glorifying and honoring him in worship. The ultimate treasure in human history is not found in a global power, a ruling, definitive philosophy, or technological advances for the betterment (or perceived betterment) of humanity.

No, the ultimate treasure to be discovered is God's love for the world and the truth that he loved the world so much that he sent his Son, Jesus Christ, to die for our sins and reconcile us into a loving relationship with our heavenly Father. This is why we gather to worship: to celebrate the ultimate treasure of Christ's death and resurrection, the ultimate display of God's love.

The greatest of stories, the purest of truths, the holiest of motivations is found in God's quest to possess a people enveloped in his love for them and who will worship him forever.

PRAYER

Father of our Lord Jesus Christ, your name is holy, your name is sacred, your name is eternally praised. Thank you for the gift of your Son. May I worship you forever and ever for your glorious love. Amen.

Our Father in heaven, may your name be kept holy.

THE PERFECT WILL OF GOD

WORD

From then on Jesus began to tell his disciples plainly that it was necessary for him to go to Jerusalem, and that he would suffer many terrible things at the hands of the elders, the leading priests, and the teachers of religious law. He would be killed, but on the third day he would be raised from the dead.

But Peter took him aside and began to reprimand him for saying such things. "Heaven forbid, Lord," he said. "This will never happen to you!"

Jesus turned to Peter and said, "Get away from me, Satan! You are a dangerous trap to me. You are seeing things merely from a human point of view, not from God's."

Matthew 16:21–23

THOUGHT

I recently received a message from a student in China who wrote, "I am convinced all Christians are crazy!" The principles of God's kingdom are, indeed, often opposite to the world's principles—and, therefore, they're difficult to accept and understand for those who embrace the world's values. For example, the Bible says to lay down our lives to gain life, and give to receive. Those commands naturally seem counterintuitive.

Even to believers, God's will often seems unreasonable and irrational. In today's scripture, Peter himself thought Jesus's foretelling of his crucifixion was unthinkable. In fact, Peter was so resistant to what he had just heard from the Lord that he was quick to challenge Jesus and thus, the very will of God. Peter didn't believe his motives were out of line. He thought he was stepping in to rescue the Messiah from an ill fate, but Peter's response was not the will of God.

The will of God is often unreasonable from our human point of view, but the will of God is perfect. It brings about God's glory and honor—and that we can rejoice in.

PRAYER

Lord, I pray for your kingdom to come and your will to be done. Help me to see your way, hear your voice, and obey your will in this day and at all times. Amen.

May your kingdom come soon. May your will be done on earth, as it is in heaven.

EVERYTHING YOU NEED

WORD

Seek the Kingdom of God above all else, and he will give you everything you need.

Luke 12:31

THOUGHT

God does not promise to care for those belonging to him and then abandon them when they encounter difficulty as they carry out his will. That is not his character. There is no difficult riddle to solve or special formula to crack in order to release his provision.

He is a good Father and a just King, so if he calls us to carry out his will, he will supply what we need to complete the task. Accompanying his graciousness and generosity is his desire to teach us the ways of his kingdom, and we are to seek God's kingdom above all else. In seeking him first, he will give us everything we need.

Perhaps his provision is already before us, but it's not to our liking. I once observed a small bird feasting from a feeder filled with a variety of seed. The bird was tossing some seed on the ground as it seemed to be seeking a particular seed out of the mix. Let us not discard any part of the Lord's provision, but let us rejoice in all of it, content in his goodness and faithfulness.

PRAYER

You are a gracious Father. You are God of the possible. As I seek your kingdom and your will above all other things, you will provide me with everything I need. I have no need to fear. Amen.

Give us today the food we need.

October 25

ELIMINATE UNFORGIVENESS

WORD

When you forgive this man, I forgive him, too.
And when I forgive whatever needs to be forgiven, I do so with Christ's authority for your benefit,
so that Satan will not outsmart us. For we are familiar with his evil schemes.

2 Corinthians 2:10–11

THOUGHT

The evil one is an expert in concealing unforgiveness in our relationships. Jesus told us to forgive others just as he forgave us. Too often, though, forgiveness is spoken and accompanied with a companion thought: *I forgive them, but I will no longer trust them.*

Although there are severe instances where we are rightly unable to trust an offender any longer, let us make sure this does not block us from extending forgiveness or eliminating bitterness. When a cancer is not fully removed and eliminated from the human body, residual cancer cells will reproduce to attack again. Harboring unforgiveness at any level will cause damage to our spiritual heath. The pattern and call of Christ is to forgive others as Jesus forgave us.

In today's scripture, Paul writes that when the recipients of his letter forgive a person, he forgives the person too. Much like eliminating cancer fully from the body, here the forgiveness offered is complete and includes multiple relationships "so that Satan will not outsmart us." This includes removing unforgiveness from the church body. Let us eliminate unforgiveness together in order to strike down our enemy: the evil one who seeks to hinder Christ's work in the world.

PRAYER

Search my heart, Holy Spirit, and reveal any unforgiveness. Then fill me with your strength
and wisdom so that I may forgive as you forgive. Amen.

Forgive us our sins, as we have forgiven those who sin against us.

LEAD ME ALONG

WORD

Teach me how to live, O Lord.
Lead me along the right path,
for my enemies are waiting for me.

Psalm 27:11

THOUGHT

When my oldest son was in the sixth grade, his school sponsored an event called the Father and Son Campout. Unfortunately, I was already scheduled to be out of town and was unable to accompany him, but one of the other fathers graciously invited my son to join him and his son.

Once they arrived at the camping area, my son and two of his friends asked if they might go for a brief hike before lunch. They took off, but they did not return for lunch and were still unaccounted for by late afternoon. With nightfall approaching and the other campers unable to locate them, the group grew concerned and a couple of search parties were readied to deploy. Finally, around dusk, the boys wandered into camp with their story of getting lost in the forest.

The boys began to explore beyond the familiar paths, became disoriented, and were unable to find their way back until much later. This story ended well and without incident, except for a few hours of worry by concerned parents.

We can easily be tempted to wander off the path God has provided for us. Curiosity strikes, and we forget the paths are marked for a reason. But thankfully, not only does the Lord show us the way, he leads us along if we wisely follow him.

PRAYER

Lord, lead me in your paths and teach me your truths. Lead me away from things tempting and distracting me from your fruitful, good, and righteous plans. Amen.

Don't let us yield to temptation.

THE ULTIMATE RESCUE

WORD

Jesus gave his life for our sins, just as God our Father planned, in order to rescue us from this evil world in which we live. All glory to God forever and ever! Amen.

Galatians 1:4–5

THOUGHT

The word *vanquish* means "to overcome in battle and subdue completely." Although the word is antiquated, it beautifully and accurately describes Christ's victorious battle on our behalf. His crucifixion, death, and resurrection exposed and canceled the enemy's strategy for the demise of humanity. In other words, Christ's victory vanquished the evil one's plan to destroy us.

The result of Christ's redemptive work was not a partial victory, not just a temporary stay of execution, not a battle won within a war, but complete victory. Every prison door for every captive was opened, detached from the prison cell, and the prison guards sent fleeing.

Each within humanity may appear conquered by the evil one's plan, but one only need say yes to Christ's offer of new life to see God vanquish the effects of Satan's strategy against us.

Through the power of the cross, we are rescued from evil and liberated to pursue the destiny and divine adventure for us as planned by the heavenly Father.

PRAYER

Thank you, Lord Jesus, for your love and free gift of grace. Thank you for your sacrifice of love. Thank you for the redemptive victory for the heart and souls of all who would repent of their sin and embrace you as Savior and Lord. Thank you for eliminating the fear of death and evil and providing life in its fullness forever. Amen.

But rescue us from the evil one.

October 28

FUTURE GLORY

WORD

*...then I heard again what sounded like the shout of a vast crowd or the roar of
mighty ocean waves or the crash of loud thunder:*

*"Praise the LORD!
For the Lord our God, the Almighty, reigns.
Let us be glad and rejoice,
and let us give honor to him.
For the time has come for the wedding feast of the Lamb,
and his bride has prepared herself.
She has been given the finest of pure white linen to wear."
For the fine linen represents the good deeds of God's holy people.*

Revelation 19:6–8

THOUGHT

This life is a vapor, a brief moment in time. A flower buds briefly and unfolds
for display, then vanishes suddenly. Overextended calendars and day-to-day concerns
cause even the redeemed people of God to forget the brevity of this earth-experience.

Ours is a destiny shaped by the creative beauty of our holy God. We are made and
purposed for his honor, glory, and worship. We are to bring him glory with the totality
of our being.

In today's scripture, John glimpses into the eternal and describes, as best he can, this
future gathering awaiting the sons and daughters of God. When this event happens, it
will mark the beginning of never-endings in the eternal adoration of Christ.

PRAYER

*Father, you rule and reign with all authority and everlasting dominion. Yours is the kingdom,
the power, and the glory forever and ever. Holy is your name. Amen.*

For yours is the kingdom and the power and the glory forever.

October 29

UNIQUELY GOD

WORD

No one is holy like the Lord!
There is no one besides you;
there is no Rock like our God.

1 Samuel 2:2

THOUGHT

Pure. Complete. Perfect. Sacred. Divine. Lovely. Hallowed. Flawless. Holy. Righteous. Just.

What human word, phrase, or sentence—no matter how carefully crafted and scripted—could ever adequately describe Yahweh God? The nature, character, and person of God are ultimately undefinable by human effort and means. We get glimpses of him in creation, we learn of his character and promises from his Word, and we see his love on display in the life, death, and resurrection of Christ, but he is still indescribable.

He is God, and there is no one like him. No one is holy like the Lord. He is uniquely God. There is no Rock like him—and with thanksgiving and honor and praise, we get to call him our Father.

PRAYER

Awesome in power and awesome in wisdom are you, Father God. I am still before you
as I sit here in awe of your goodness, oh, God. Thank you for inviting me
into relationship with you as your child. Amen.

Our Father in heaven, may your name be kept holy.

TRUE VISION

WORD

And so, King Agrippa, I obeyed that vision from heaven. I preached first to those in Damascus, then in Jerusalem and throughout all Judea, and also to the Gentiles, that all must repent of their sins and turn to God—and prove they have changed by the good things they do.

Acts 26:19–20

THOUGHT

Optasia is Greek for the English word *vision*. The word *optasia* is found four times in the New Testament (Luke 1:22, 24:23; Acts 26:19; and 2 Corinthians 12:1) and literally means "the act of seeing things coming into view."[25]

The Lord's will is the true vision of every genuine believer in Christ. We see him as the substance of life, the facilitator of life, and the purpose of life. As sons and daughters of God, we see him as the center of all things—not us. We see God as the Creator of humans, and after humanity's fall, we see him as the Redeemer of humanity, the one who restored us to our intended destiny.

His vision for us is to see no other vision beyond this and declare his kingdom's good news. His vision is of us, his children, on his mission.

PRAYER

*Fill all my heart, soul, mind, and strength with the vision of you,
your kingdom, and your purpose, Lord. Amen.*

May your kingdom come soon. May your will be done on earth as it is in heaven.

REMEMBERING GOD'S FAITHFULNESS

WORD

Come and listen, all you who fear God,
and I will tell you what he did for me.

Psalm 66:16

THOUGHT

At one time in my life, I was concerned about future provision during a big transition. As I was praying over this concern one morning, I suddenly had the impression that the Lord was asking me the following question: *Where have I not provided for you and your family over the past four decades?* Nowhere!

When I reflected on the past, the Lord quickly restored my faith in his own faithfulness. It's true—he has never failed to provide me with what I need to accomplish what he asks of me.

Life transitions—whether caused by jobs, geographical relocations, family challenges, or national and international political changes—can introduce concern and even alarm about our future provision and security. For the believer, reflecting on God's past provision will bring encouragement and trust for his future provision. Remembering God's faithfulness introduces hope, especially if we recall and understand the Lord's ultimate goal for us is eternity in his presence—and he accomplished that for us at the cross.

PRAYER

Thank you, Lord, for your past and continued provision.
Supply me today with what I need to walk in your will and help me trust in you fully. Amen.

Give us today the food we need.

WHAT SHOULD WE DO?

WORD

Peter's words pierced their hearts, and they said to him and to the other apostles, "Brothers, what should we do?"

Peter replied, "Each of you must repent of your sins and turn to God, and be baptized in the name of Jesus Christ for the forgiveness for your sins. Then you will receive the gift of the Holy Spirit. This promise is to you, to your children, and to those far away—all who have been called by the Lord our God." Then Peter continued preaching for a long time, strongly urging all his listeners, "Save yourselves from this crooked generation!"

Acts 2:37–40

THOUGHT

Many years ago, I was sharing the story of Christ with a man in his late twenties. We were seated on opposite sides of a city park picnic table. He listened very carefully, interjected the occasional question, and then shared his story of internal conflict, substance abuse, family dysfunction, and hopelessness. He concluded by asking if he might be forgiven by God too—and if so, how?

God has made the path of forgiveness clear for all. His purpose from the creation of humankind has been to have deep, genuine communion, friendship, and fellowship with us. Satan's most devious and deceptive plans failed as Christ came to seek and save all who would obey him and embrace his redemptive accomplishment.

Therefore, yes, the young man at the park picnic table—no matter his history—is welcomed into the Lord's forgiveness and freedom as he submits his life to Christ. And it's the same for you and me. What should we do to receive this gift? Repent, turn to God, and receive his goodness.

PRAYER

Father, thank you for your most gracious and beautiful gift of grace, love, and mercy. Your great love was the catalyst for humanity's rescue through the redemptive act of your Son, Jesus Christ. Amen.

Forgive us our sins, as we have forgiven those who sin against us.

HE STILL SPEAKS

WORD

Come, let us worship and bow down.
Let us kneel before the LORD our maker,
for he is our God.
We are the people he watches over,
the flock under his care.
If only you would listen to his voice today!

Psalm 95:6–7

THOUGHT

In the darkness of a cool autumn morning, I heard the unmistakable sound of a small flock of geese as it neared and then passed closely overhead. By spending a lot of time in the outdoors over the years, I've learned to identify many birds by the sounds of their call or voice. Anyone can learn; the only requirement is the willingness to set the time aside to listen.

The Lord also has unmistakable and easily identifiable characteristics to his voice. Many experience and express difficultly in hearing God's leading in life, and I have struggled with this in the past myself—and I still do at times. When I do struggle to hear from the Lord, I usually discover that either I've not taken the time to listen to him or it's not yet time for the next step.

Our Father does not withhold the sound of his voice from his children. He speaks to those willing to listen. His voice is heard as we invest time in reading the Bible, praying, and listening with a heart of openness and willingness. He still speaks.

PRAYER

Lord, you have not silenced your voice. You have never ceased to let your intentions be known. Your voice guides and leads me so I can follow you wholeheartedly. Holy Spirit, help me discern my heavenly Father's voice from all other voices as I learn to listen fully. Amen.

Don't let us yield to temptation.

INCALCULABLE LUMENS

WORD

O LORD, you are my lamp.
The LORD lights up my darkness.

2 Samuel 22:29

THOUGHT

The *Merriam-Webster Dictionary* defines *lumen* as "a unit of luminous flux equal to the light emitted in a unit solid angle by a uniform point source of one candle intensity."[27] Although that sounds like a complicated mouthful, simply put, a lumen is one of the ways we measure light.

My morning walk to the Nook—the place where I read, pray, and study—is only about thirty steps from the house; however, I've encountered a lot of different critters, both mammal and reptile, on this short predawn walk, so light comes in handy for safety reasons. In the past, when I've been unable to utilize the moonlight to guide my way through the dark, I've used a dim penlight with a few lumens until I purchased a small but very bright 350-lumen flashlight. The difference is incredible.

Although here on earth we use lumens as a marker for the strength of light, God's ability to bring light into the darkest of situations cannot be calculated or measured. His spiritual light is bright and blinding and eliminates the power of darkness. All things in our path that are poised for attack and purposed to harm are exposed by the glorious light of the Lord.

PRAYER

Light of God, flood every dark situation with your illuminating brilliance. Amen.
But rescue us from the evil one.

FOREVER GLORIOUS

WORD

All glory to him who alone is God, our Savior through Jesus Christ our Lord. All glory, majesty, power, and authority are his before all time, and in the present, and beyond all time! Amen.

Jude 25

THOUGHT

These two power-infused sentences explode the truth of the ages across our earthly landscape, declaring our Savior Jesus Christ as the paramount Ruler and Redeemer. He is the supreme authority over all things existing; he is the only God.

Because of the work of Christ, we are able to know God intimately and enter into his presence. This is an amazing, world-changing truth. The King of kings and Lord of lords, who owns all glory, majesty, power, and authority, welcomes us into not just his kingdom but into his *family* through the blood of Christ Jesus. This should cause every Christian to worship and celebrate—and not just on Sundays.

This is our God, who is seamlessly perfect in all ways. This is our God, who is majestic from past to future. He is forever glorious. All glory to his name, all glory to his kingdom—all glory, all glory to him forever!

PRAYER

I worship you, Lord, with every breath and moment I have! Amen.

For yours is the kingdom and the power and the glory forever.

SPIRITUAL ADOPTION

WORD

Pray like this:
Our Father in heaven,
may your name be kept holy.

Matthew 6:9

THOUGHT

Of the seven themes found in the Lord's Prayer, this one surely is the most generous. Here, Christ himself defines our relationship to the Most High as one of a beloved child, and Christ directs us into addressing the Lord by the sweetest and most intimate of his names, *Father.*

As Christians, we cherish the peace and security found in the truth that we are no longer orphans, paupers, or outcasts begging and fending for ourselves in this dark world. Instead, through the work of Christ, the believer in Jesus is an adopted son or daughter of God the Father. He is ever strong, ever wise, and ever competent in all ways and all things—and he holds in his grasp perfect plans for all his adopted children, whom he also names as his heirs.

Charles Spurgeon wrote the following on the opening words of the Lord's Prayer: "This prayer begins where all true prayer must commence, with the spirit of adoption, 'Our Father.' There is no acceptable prayer until we can say, 'I will arise, and go unto my Father.'"[26] He is our Father and we are his children, which is a truth to be treasured for all eternity.

PRAYER

Heavenly Father, thank you for your love, mercy, and adoption through Christ's redeeming sacrifice. Thank you that I am no longer an orphan. You are my Father, perfect in all of your ways, and you have placed me in your family to remain there forever. Amen.

Our Father in heaven, may your name be kept holy.

November 6

THE POTTER'S SHOP

WORD

The LORD gave another message to Jeremiah. He said,
"Go down to the potter's shop, and I will speak to you there."

Jeremiah 18:1–2

THOUGHT

Picture a potter, a master artisan, focused on a large clump of formless clay as it spins on the potter's wheel. The clay has no will of its own or voice in the shaping process; it is completely at the will of the master artist.

Before he even applies the first pressure to the clay, the potter sees the finished vessel and its intended purpose. He carefully removes the excess, unwanted, and unneeded material that has no need in the final design. He continues to shape and form the clay into the image of his choosing, working diligently until the vessel has reached completion.

God is the potter; we are his clay (Isa. 64:8). He shapes us for his purposes and plans. He forms us into the image best suited for his intentions and pleasure. However, he has given us the gift of free will. It is our choice to surrender ourselves to the potter and his process of forming vessels that honor and glorify his name.

PRAYER

Shape me, mold me, and use me for your glory, Lord. May your will be done. Amen.

May your kingdom come soon. May your will be done on earth, as it is in heaven.

MANNA

WORD

So the people of Israel ate manna for forty years until they arrived at the land where they would settle. They ate manna until they came to the border of the land of Canaan.

Exodus 16:35

THOUGHT

God miraculously provided for the people of Israel as they traveled forty years through a wilderness region. There were no long periods of stopping to settle, plow fields, plant seed, and harvest crops. There were no visits to established cities or towns abundant with various lodging comforts, eating establishments, or relief agencies. There were no food assistance caravans from other nations.

In the forty years the Israelites spent wandering from one desolate location to another, what or who was their source and sustenance? The Ancient of Days, Yahweh. Not once did he fail to provide for them. With each new day, the Lord provided exactly what they needed to continue their journey.

God is still the provider and promise-keeper for those who willingly follow him on the journey that he chooses for them. He still supernaturally supplies for our needs. He is still—and will always be—Jehovah Jireh, the Lord our provider.

PRAYER

Thank you, Lord, for my daily bread.
Thank you for supplying me with everything I need to continue to do your will in this life.
Help me trust that each day's needs will be fulfilled by your provision. Amen.

Give us today the food we need.

ONE PRAYER

WORD

Such a prayer offered in faith will heal the sick, and the Lord will make you well.
And if you have committed any sins, you will be forgiven.

James 5:15

THOUGHT

The weight of sin is heavier than the heart can endure. The guilt and condemnation that sin produces crushes the soul and smothers life, and our attempts to hide and ignore sin will ultimately lead to eternal death.

However, sin is not an inescapable prison; it is a cavern of darkness in which the evil one uses foolishness, fear, and deception to hold his victims captive, confused, hopeless, and petrified.

In today's scripture, we're reminded that one prayer can provide us with freedom from death and darkness. One prayer provides the way of escape. One prayer provides a life of freedom. God gave his Son as the propitiation for our sin, and when we repent and seek forgiveness from the Lord, Jesus reconciles any and all liability incurred by our sin. And this gift is available to all.

PRAYER

By your abundant grace, the prayer of confession and repentance has released your loving mercy, extended your generous forgiveness, and made your freedom available in my life.
Thank you, Lord Jesus Christ, for freeing me. Amen.

Forgive us our sins, as we have forgiven those who sin against us.

A MATTER OF TRUST

WORD

The LORD directs our steps,
why try to understand everything along the way?

Proverbs 20:24

THOUGHT

During our lives, we will be confronted by the phrase *if you will*. While this phrase often seems innocent, there are instances when it contains wrong motives. The Pharisees and scribes used it to challenge Jesus in his ministry when they said things such as, "*If you will* show us a sign," "*If you will* do a miracle," and "*If you will* answer this question." This brief phrase still works to discourage the spiritually adventurous heart. Although the question may appear reasonable at first, it may have hidden intentions.

For example, "I will follow you God, *if you will* first permit me to take care of personal business," or "I will follow you, *if you will* first supply the resources." These are not statements made from a place of trust and faith; in fact, they sound more like ultimatums.

Often, the use of this phrase originates from the fear of change, discomfort, lack of control, or because the Lord's will is outside the borders of natural reason. What if Abraham, when asked by God to leave the land of his fathers, had said, "*If you will* supply all my needs before I leave, I will go"? What if David, upon hearing he would be king of Israel, had said, "*If you will* promise there will be no challenges from Saul, I will"?

Following the steps of the Lord and experiencing the beauty of his will is a matter of trust in him. When we do follow him wholeheartedly, we will see he never fails.

PRAYER

Lord, I pray my trust will be in you today as you lead,
even in the things I do not see and understand. Amen.

Don't let us yield to temptation.

RESCUED MANY TIMES

WORD

...but as soon as they were at peace, your people again committed evil in your sight, and once more you let their enemies conquer them. Yet whenever your people turned and cried to you again for help, you listened once more from heaven. In your wonderful mercy, you rescued them many times!

Nehemiah 9:28

THOUGHT

The Old Testament contains repeated examples of God's people crying out to him for help. Their predicaments were often caused by their own wrong choices, leading them into the hands of evil, tyranny, and oppression. However, when God's people found themselves in difficult circumstances due to their own disobedience, God's willingness and ability to extend mercy and deliverance to them were never-ending.

His gracious mercy exceeds our capacity to understand, and time and again, he extends it to us. For those in need of his mercy, he clearly commands that they should set their eyes and hearts resolutely on him and not turn back to their old ways.

We should strive to be obedient to his Word and his call, and we can give thanks that—even when we fail him and even when we are unfaithful—he *never* fails and he is *always* faithful. Praise the Lord in the highest, for he has rescued us many times!

PRAYER

Thank you, Father, for your rescue from the evil one. Thank you for your continued deliverance and your mercy that is new every morning. Through your wonderful mercy and grace, convict me to pursue your heart and will with all my being. Amen.

But rescue us from the evil one.

November 11

DESERVING OF ALL HONOR

WORD

O LORD, I will honor and praise your name,
for you are my God.
You do such wonderful things!
You planned them long ago,
and now you have accomplished them.

Isaiah 25:1

THOUGHT

To honor someone is to demonstrate respect, gratefulness, and sincere value toward them. We understand from the Bible that God alone is to be worshiped and no other person, place, or thing is worthy of worship outside of him. All life, all things—without the slightest exception—exist from him and for him.

The Lord is deserving of all honor and praise for all the wonderful things he has done—the things he has planned long ago and has accomplished, and for all the wonderful things to come. He alone is worthy of our highest gratitude. He alone is worthy of our deepest respect. He alone is worthy of being treasured.

The word *honor* finds its paramount purpose in reference to honoring God in his infinite worth. He alone—Father, Son, and Holy Spirit—is worthy of honor's highest position.

PRAYER

Never, Lord, can I seem to find sufficient words to fully express the awe and wonder within my heart for you. Your magnificence exceeds my abilities to feel I've adequately esteemed you with the worship and honor you deserve. Yet, this grateful servant comes humbly this morning to honor you. I praise your name! You alone are my God. Amen.

For yours is the kingdom and the power and the glory forever.

A TENDER AND COMPASSIONATE FATHER

WORD

The Lord is like a father to his children,
tender and compassionate to those who fear him.

Psalm 103:13

THOUGHT

There is a father who understands every lonely moment we have ever experienced. There is a father who has seen our failures and still loves us, a father who encourages us with perfect words of comfort and guidance. There is a father who is aware of the injustices and rejections thrust upon us and the wounds we carry as a result. This father is aware of the insecurities and emotional scars that suppress our spirits, and he understands the very delicate, intricate chambers of our hearts. He knows when we are frightened and confused, and he gives us solace.

God, our heavenly Father, will never arrive late when he says he will meet us at an appointed time. He will always keep his promises. The Lord has a path for our lives, encourages us to follow it, and will see us through to its end.

Our relationship with our heavenly Father is quite different from our relationship with our earthly one because our heavenly Father is perfect in all his ways. He is the giver of genuine mercy, truth, and peace. He is always faithful, present, and loving. He is always tender and compassionate. We have the absolute honor and privilege to call him ours.

PRAYER

Father in heaven, you are wonderful in all of your ways. When I think of you fathering me
in your perfect character—caring for me more than I certainly deserve and
more than I will ever know or imagine on this earth—I am grateful beyond words. Amen.

Our Father in heaven, may your name be kept holy.

THE COMING GLORY

WORD

Then everyone will see the Son of Man coming on the clouds with great power and glory.
And he will send out his angels to gather his chosen ones from all over the world—
from the farthest ends of the earth and heaven.

Mark 13:26–27

THOUGHT

With all the history-making events occurring across this planet and the unbelievable progress of technology, we must not forget the most paramount and glorious event advancing toward us: the second coming of Christ. Although no one can predict when or where it will happen, this moment will move forward with unhindered precision and will arrive in the timeliest of manner. Those who are redeemed look forward to this event with great expectation and anticipation—and the heavens do as well.

There is an appointed time when Christ will come to gather all those given to him. Many believe this is an antiquated tale for those who are simple and naive. But do not be mistaken: the day approaches and for the Christian, it will be glorious.

God's kingdom is here with us, but it is also yet to arrive in its fullest glory, for the kingdom began unfolding at Christ's first coming to earth. But it is also to arrive gloriously in his second coming. Do not be deceived; Christ will return in all of his glory for the culmination of the ages. Be there in right dress: Christ's covering of righteousness.

PRAYER

Lord, may your kingdom come soon, and may I be ready for that time.
Clothe me in your righteousness. Amen.

May your kingdom come soon. May your will be done on earth, as it is in heaven.

THE STEPS OF THE GOOD

WORD

...so follow the steps of the good,
and stay on the paths of the righteous.

Proverbs 2:20

THOUGHT

Although Christ is the ultimate example we are to follow to successfully fulfill his will, the Lord also provides us with excellent examples of Christian men and women who have gone before us and lived in honor of Christ. In addition to examples from the past and the present guidance of the Holy Spirit, we are to follow those who currently walk in integrity and live with the utmost goal of honoring the Lord.

The apostle Paul, when writing to the Corinthian church, encouraged his brothers and sisters in Christ to imitate him as he imitated Christ (1 Cor. 11:1). Are you living a life so that others may see your diligence to live as Christ and which they might emulate to do the same? In other words, follow me as I follow Jesus.

Christ is the Son of God and the ultimate image by which we are being shaped for the glory of God the Father. Understand the nature and character of Christ from the pages of the Bible, identify men and women—both past and present—who are given to Jesus and his causes, and follow them as they follow God. Let us all walk in the steps of the good.

PRAYER

Thank you, Lord, for those who are trustworthy disciples of Jesus, and thank you for those godly mentors you have given to guide me into a life glorifying and honoring of you. Amen.

Give us today the food we need.

BECAUSE OF LOVE

WORD

*...but God is so rich in mercy, and he loved us so much,
that even though we were dead because of our sins, he gave us life when he raised Christ from the
dead. (It is only by God's grace that you have been saved!) For he raised us from the dead along with
Christ and seated us with him in the heavenly realms because we are united with Christ Jesus.
So God can point to us in all future ages as examples of the incredible wealth of his grace and
kindness toward us, as shown in all he has done for us who are united with Christ Jesus.*

Ephesians 2:4–7

THOUGHT

Because of a great love—the depth of which we will never completely understand during our days on this earth—we have been forgiven the debt of our sin. This sin, if had it remained unchanged, unattended, and unreconciled, would have cost us everlasting life and separation from the lover of our souls.

The God of all creation was moved so deeply by his unfathomable quality and purity of love that he subjected himself to unwarranted, unimaginable mental and physical cruelty; detestable, unsubstantiated lies; contemptuous, disdainful mockery; and the foulest of scorn from cold-hearted, uncaring, and indifferent men.

The path to our forgiveness caused the Son of Man to lay bare before the filth and darkness of a corrupt world. He was the Father's holy and most precious possession, his only Son, Jesus Christ. But because of this great love, humanity received the greatest gift: grace!

PRAYER

*Lord, I am speechless over the gift of your grace, yet my heart is filled with light,
hope, gratefulness, and life because of you, Jesus Christ. Amen.*

Forgive us our sins, as we have forgiven those who sin against us.

WE MUST FOLLOW IN HIS STEPS

WORD

...for God called you to do good, even if it means suffering, just as Christ suffered for you.
He is your example, and you must follow in his steps.

1 Peter 2:21

THOUGHT

Many years ago, I was hiking with some Aussie brothers through a dense forest region of southern Australia. The tree canopy was relatively high, and the forest floor was covered by tall, thick ferns. Before departing the ranger station for the hike, we were told to be vigilant and keep an eye on the ground because of some very poisonous snakes in the region. To avoid the snakes, the ranger's best advice was to stay on the path and follow the steps of the guide.

Christians have Christ as their leader, guide, and the perfect example of how to live. God loves and is pleased by his Son, and when we strive to live like Jesus, the Father is pleased with us.

Christ is the way, knows the way, and has shown us the way that we are to follow. His choice and location of steps are acutely accurate. He was never confused, disoriented, or lost, and he continues to guide us with the same perfection and holy precision. To avoid the hazardous traps of the enemy, we must follow the steps of the guide.

PRAYER

Lord Jesus, I know this day holds many choices, directions, and paths.
You are my example and you are the one who will lead me correctly for your glory.
Open my eyes to see your every step, and may my heart wisely follow. Amen.

Don't let us yield to temptation.

NO EVIL WILL CONQUER US

WORD

If you make the LORD your refuge,
if you make the Most High your shelter,
no evil will conquer you;
no plague will come near your home.

Psalm 91:9–10

THOUGHT

While watching wildlife footage of a mother bear defending her lone cub from aggressive wolves, I noticed she was far outnumbered by the wolf pack. When the wolves advanced to attempt to take her young cub, the mother instantly became a fierce, uncompromising force of defense.

Had the wolves collectively descended on the female bear, they could have overpowered her, but the bear boldly and unyieldingly stood her ground to protect the cub. She quickly convinced the hungry assailants this was not a battle they should attempt and successfully deterred the attackers.

Our foe is loathsome, despicable, deceitful, and deadly. He is always on the prowl with the intent to harm and, if possible, utterly destroy the innocent, unprotected, and weak. One force alone displays the strength to deter evil's most keenly devised scheme. It is the power of the one God, *Yahweh*! Like a mother bear protecting her cub, he is truly a fierce, uncompromising force of defense—and with him on our side, no evil will conquer us.

PRAYER

In you, Almighty One, is my strength, encouragement, and safety.
You are my deliverance from evil, you are my victory, you are my conqueror,
and you are my God. Amen.

But rescue us from the evil one.

SING HIS PRAISE

WORD

Let the whole world glorify the LORD;
let it sing his praise.

Isaiah 42:12

THOUGHT

God is creator of all things, and he created all things for himself. He has made all we see, hear, and feel. He has designed the depth of hue in every color and meticulously formed every shape, sight, and sound in the world to accommodate his divine preferences. He has presented the world with grand physical, mental, emotional, and spiritual experiences.

Of all the things God created for humanity and himself to enjoy, perhaps the tonal and rhythmic actions of music provide the most fulfilling offering to honor and glorify God. Martin Luther is quoted in *Luther's Works* vol. 53 as saying, "Experience confirms that next to the Word of God, music deserves the highest praise."

We are to sing songs—songs of his forgiveness, joyful songs, new songs. We are to sing of his love, his justice. Let us sing praises to his name as long as we live. Of all the ways to honor God, music is such a lively and deeply spiritual offering.

PRAYER

Lord, thank you for the ability to sing, and to join
with all creation to glorify your name for all eternity. Amen.

For yours is the kingdom and the power and the glory forever.

ONE HOPE, ONE HOME, ONE LORD

WORD

"But you are my witnesses, O Israel!" says the LORD.
"You are my servant.
You have been chosen to know me, believe in me,
and understand that I alone am God.
There is no other God—
there never has been, and there never will be.
I, yes I, am the LORD,
and there is no other Savior."

Isaiah 43:10–11

THOUGHT

These words in Isaiah that describe God's indisputable and absolute superiority are accurate, unequivocal, and emphatic. These are statements of deep hope and abiding security for the child of God.

The heart that wisely journeys beyond the self is a heart in search for truth to solace the soul. Sooner or later, this genuine search leads to the Lord. Though worldly influences may initially appear to appease, everything outside of God will prove an illusion when tested, for only Jehovah is the source of genuine life for humanity's soul. In the end, everything else will be revealed as idols of some sort.

Being created by and for God leaves us situated to only find perfect peace when in a relationship with our holy God. True rest for the heart and soul is found in one source: the one God, and his name is Jesus Christ.

PRAYER

All glory to your name, heavenly Father. You are God from eternity past to eternity future.
The heavens and earth declare your majesty and the redeemed heart
gratefully declares you as Savior and Lord. Amen.

Our Father in heaven, may your name be kept holy.

A KINGDOM UNSHAKABLE

WORD

*Since we are receiving a Kingdom that is unshakable, let us be thankful and
please God by worshiping him with holy fear and awe.*

Hebrews 12:28

THOUGHT

Throughout the history of civilization, empires and worldly powers that eventually
came to ruin had once felt as if they were invincible. Their confidence stemmed from
their ability to conquer and intimidate others with the strength of their military, depth
of their wealth, or their determination to dominate.

The Romans, for example, thought their position, power, and influence were
unstoppable at one point. They conquered countries and territories using keen diplo-
matic coercion—or simply by overpowering them by force. As great, powerful, and
famous as Rome was, its empire imploded. Its plight is read in history books, and its
ruins are visited by tourists.

Although worldly powers, leaders, and nations fall, the kingdom of God is steadfast, unchanging, and eternal. And the kingdom of God is not limited, restricted, or
conquerable. No aspect of God's authority can be manipulated or compromised. The
kingdom of God faithfully keeps its promises, repels attack, and effortlessly endures.
The Lord's reign is a kingdom unshakable!

PRAYER

*Most High King, it is with reverence, respect, and honor that I give you thanks.
You have positioned one once unworthy to be a citizen of your eternal,
unshakable kingdom through the work of Christ. Amen.*

May your kingdom come soon. May your will be done on earth, as it is in heaven.

November 21

WORD OF LIFE

WORD

We proclaim to you the one who existed from the beginning, whom we have heard and seen. We saw him with our own eyes and touched him with our own hands. He is the Word of life.

1 John 1:1

THOUGHT

The most valuable gift God has ever provided is the gift of life. We pray for many things over our lifespan. We ask for daily food, money to pay bills, good health, transportation, divine guidance, protection, godly government so we might live in peace, and assistance in helping others.

These are all good things to ask for when they are sought to fulfill the will of the Lord—to declare his glory, honor his name, and fulfill the mandate of loving him with a growing holy passion. And his mandate is to spread the good news of his redemption and love to every person throughout this planet.

Life, though, is the most cherished provision from God, for the life that God gives is *real* life. Our soul quests for abundant life, and it is found only in God the Father through Christ his Son. Outside of God there is no *real* life. A search for life in another philosophy or lifestyle apart from Christ is a journey of vanity, a pursuit of which ends in sorrow and leaves the heart an empty, lonely hunter. Christ is the only true Word of life and he gives life to the full.

PRAYER

Lord, you are the God of life, eternal life which stretches beyond time and into eternity. Praise you, Lord God, provider of life in its purest and most abundant essence. Amen.

Give us today the food we need.

FORGIVEN THROUGH HIS NAME

WORD

...and he ordered us to preach everywhere and to testify that Jesus is the one appointed by God to be the judge of all—the living and the dead. He is the one all the prophets testified about, saying that everyone who believes in him will have their sins forgiven through his name.

Acts 10:42–43

THOUGHT

For those who have mocked, doubted, or denied the truth of Christ, there is forgiveness. For those who have been selfish, overindulgent, or quarrelsome, there is forgiveness. For those who have judged wrongly, condemned others, criticized, or gossiped, there is forgiveness.

For those who have been thieves, deceivers, and liars, there is forgiveness. For those who have been vain, jealous, and prideful, there is forgiveness. For those who have hated, murdered, or committed perverse injustices, there is forgiveness.

Praise God, we all have the ability to be forgiven. Jesus has no limits to the reach of his forgiveness, for those in search of his powerful grace will receive it abundantly. He extends a mercy that's motivated by immeasurable love toward any and all who will confess and repent. All sins are forgiven through his name.

PRAYER

Thank you for the grace that covers the sins separating us from communion with you, Holy Lord. And thank you that it is available to all—including me. Amen.

Forgive us our sins, as we have forgiven those who sin against us.

November 23

THE VIRTUOUS PATH

WORD

The path of the virtuous leads away from evil;
whoever follows that path is safe.

Proverbs 16:17

THOUGHT

Once on a late fall hike on an Ozark Mountain trail, I came upon one section that contained several trail signs indicating the importance of remaining on the path for the sake of personal safety. I didn't see imminent danger, but a few steps farther, just a few feet off the path and somewhat hidden, lay a high and dangerous cliff. The signs were not to restrict the enjoyment of the mountain trail, but to ensure safety on the path.

The path that is called *safe* distances us from evil's snare and is clearly marked with signs that confirm the way. There are many markers that show the way: they read *goodness*, *righteousness*, *honor*, *integrity*, *morality*, and *honesty*.

There is no mistaking this path for any other than the path of light, the path of Christ. The folk upon this path treasure mercy, grace, and love. They know their highest privilege, their dearest pleasure, is to worship the high and Holy One in everything they do.

At trail's end, the trophy awaiting these faithful sojourners is one of deep virtue: the warm, inclusive greeting from Almighty God when he says, "Well done."

PRAYER

Father, lead me in your paths. Lead me in your truth. Lead me away from evil
that I might bestow the honor due your name, Mighty One. Amen.

Don't let us yield to temptation.

November 24

RESCUER

WORD

The LORD says, "I will rescue those who love me.
I will protect those who trust in my name."

Psalm 91:14

THOUGHT

I watched as a news video revealed the desperate moments of a person being hope-lessly swept along a flooded stream. There were several attempted rescues from the water's edge. One person took a tree limb and stretched as far as he could to reach the victim but failed. Another used a long pole to attempt to do the same but, again, without success.

However, a group of people farther downstream had thrown a rope to others on the opposite bank. With the rope stretched across the water, the victim was able to grasp the line while several people pulled him safely from the water's deadly rage. I was grateful for the person's successful rescue.

As believers, we're recipients of God's promise of rescue and protection as we trust in him. He is the only one who can keep every promise he extends. He does not have to make multiple attempts at our rescue, for his efforts are perfect and successful every time. He is the only one 100 percent engaged in our welfare, and he is the only one who has the resources and is capable of successfully countering *every* evil plan against us, defeating any and all advances of destruction.

PRAYER

Thank you, Lord, for your rescue and your continued care and watchful eye over my life.
In you I place my hope, and in you I place my trust. Amen.

But rescue us from the evil one.

OUR KING FOREVER

WORD

The LORD reigns as king forever.

Psalm 29:10

THOUGHT

A few glances at global news quickly reveal the instabilities in so many nations around the world. Additionally, the level of distrust and lack of confidence in many political leaders is currently very high, leaving many questioning who might cause some semblance of stability to return. The greater question is, who has the integrity, character, and ability in which we might commit our trust?

Be assured that no matter who your country's current ruling authority is, ultimate control remains where it has always rested: in the hands of Almighty God. He is still on the throne, even when the people in power fail us, embarrass us, or lead our country astray. He will restore, resolve, repair, and one day make all things new. We can safely put our trust in the authority of the Most High God.

When the culmination of the ages occurs, the truth will stand. And the truth is—regardless of our earthly positions and influences—all will one day bow their knee and confess that Jesus Christ is Lord. He will reign as king forever.

PRAYER

Your glory, Lord Jesus, will have no end. Amen.

For yours is the kingdom and the power and the glory forever.

November 26

YOU ALONE ARE THE LORD

WORD

You alone are the LORD. You made the skies and the heavens and all the stars. You made the earth and the seas and everything in them. You preserve them all, and the angels of heaven worship you.

Nehemiah 9:6

THOUGHT

The Lord is worthy of worship, for only he imagined light and then effortlessly introduced it by the sound of his lips. When he spoke, he released new elements, components, forms, colors, and scents. And once more, his voice appeared and fashioned near countless varieties of life, big and small, each with remarkable beauty and complexity.

He is worthy of worship, for only he could envision, create, and breathe life into ones likened to his image: humankind. He provided us with freedom of choice within his design—our free will—even though we chose disobedience. And then he graciously provided us with full redemption in Christ.

God preserves all created things, and even in the separation and fall of humanity, his provision was made through Christ Jesus; we were reconciled to him, and eternal destruction was circumvented.

PRAYER

You alone are Lord. You are worthy of all worship and honor as Creator of the universe and the preserver of all life. Amen.

Our Father in heaven, may your name be kept holy.

November 27

DISCERNMENT

WORD

Look beneath the surface so you can judge correctly.

John 7:24

THOUGHT

This scripture is from a passage in John where Jesus was accused of transgressing the law by healing on the Sabbath. His accusers were attempting to rid themselves of someone who was challenging the validity of their religious system—and their own behavior. Beneath the surface, though, was the Son of Man, motivated by authentic compassion that they themselves had overlooked. Beneath the surface was the will of the heavenly Father, manifested in flesh and assigned the singular most momentous task of all time: to overcome the sin of humankind and reconcile us to God, the Creator and lover of our souls.

Christ's agenda was not to promote breaking the law or stir rebellion—he was no rebel without a cause. His agenda was to heal, restore, and free the lonely, oppressed, and imprisoned. Christ's accusers displayed self-centered jealousy and a hunger for authority, power, and control. However, Christ displayed selflessness and the desire to free and empower others. His agenda was to heal the wounded and show them the genuine love and life that exists in the will of God.

Had his accusers discerned rightly, they would have correctly assessed Jesus as one with genuine love and service to the Father, and as one who displayed the characteristics of the Father—all for the purpose of honoring and glorifying the Father. Had they looked beneath the surface, they would have recognized the Son of God himself.

PRAYER

Father, where there is foolish blindness in my life, please bring sight.
By your Holy Spirit, please reveal criticism, narrow-mindedness, selfishness, and pride within me.
May I discern rightly and act justly. Amen.

May your kingdom come soon. May your will be done on earth, as it is in heaven.

THE POWER OF COMMUNITY

WORD

God places the lonely in families;
he sets the prisoners free and gives them joy.
But he makes the rebellious live in a sun-scorched land.

Psalm 68:6

THOUGHT

Loneliness is a formidable foe. Methodical, persistent, and stealthy, loneliness can lead us to feel empty, forgotten, unloved, unvalued, or insignificant. Many of us have even experienced loneliness within our own biological families.

Although earthly families and friends may fail us, God himself exists in perfect community as Father, Son, and Holy Spirit. This deep, holy communion exists from timeless past to endless future. We are designed for connection with the Lord and with one another, and the Lord created an antidote to loneliness: community with him and with a healthy body of believers.

God, knowing and desiring community for and with us, supplied us with family, both biological and spiritual. When we embrace Christ as Savior and Lord, not only does the relationship provide us with forgiveness and eternal hope, but it also provides us with an unparalleled friendship—friendship with God himself. He escorts us from loneliness and into a community unlike any other: the family of God.

PRAYER

Thank you, Lord, for the provision of family—your family, the family of God. Amen.

Give us today the food we need.

FREEDOM TO RUN

WORD

...but now you are free from the power of sin and have become slaves of God.
Now you do those things that lead to holiness and result in eternal life.

Romans 6:22

THOUGHT

One morning while walking outside, I noticed a very young raccoon stuck helplessly in a trap. These critters are sometimes pretty pesky and destructive, so when the population expands around our home, I sometimes relocate them to remote wooded areas. However, this little guy looked up through the wire cage at me with pitiful dark eyes and a sad whimpering sound.

OK, I thought to myself, *you're pardoned.* I opened the cage door. Once outside the cage, he glanced back and then ran as fast as he could into the woods and out of my sight. While freedom from captivity generates varying joyful responses, it usually doesn't generate the desire to reenter captivity, particularly when captivity is associated with the term *slavery*.

But when the term *slavery* is associated with God—our good Father and the source of love, mercy, kindness, and grace—we encounter a different meaning. When bound and enslaved to Christ, one abides in boundless liberty. It's a puzzling truth perhaps, but in the realm of God's kingdom of unusual opposites, to be the slave of God is also to be a child of God. This is an open invitation to run freely, unencumbered, to live a life of holiness in honor to Christ.

PRAYER

Father, you have delivered me from the dungeon of sin and purchased me by the blood of Christ.
I am forever bound to you by your love. Amen.

Forgive us our sins, as we have forgiven those who sin against us.

THE ROAD TO FOLLOW

WORD

Show me the right path, O LORD;
point out the road for me to follow.
Lead me by your truth and teach me,
for you are the God who saves me.
All day long I put my hope in you.

Psalm 25:4–5

THOUGHT

One summer's day, my wife and I traveled on one of Colorado's mountainous back roads. Prior to the exploration, we studied the map and drove to a selected region. Most of our time was spent on dirt and gravel roads, sparse of directional signage. After several hours, we were ready to return to our hotel, so we reviewed the map. We discovered that just a few miles away there was a main highway that would substantially reduce our travel time.

We followed the narrow road for about an hour, but just a couple miles before we finally intersected the main highway, we came upon a roadblock with a ranger seated in his vehicle. He informed us the road was impassable because of a landslide.

"How can we get to the main road?" I asked.

"Return the way you came," he answered—which would've been a three-hour drive. Then after a pause he smiled and said, "Or you can take a short drive to the interstate on that lane," and pointed to a tiny road we hadn't seen that was hidden by a curve.

The Lord leads on distinct paths containing his impeccable truths. His will is for us to clearly see and understand where he is leading. He does not want us to mistakenly take wrong turns, so he clarifies which road to follow. For those who seek him genuinely, he points out the path and guides with perfection those who desire to be led. Therein lies our daily and eternal hope.

PRAYER

Thank you, Lord, for saving me. Thank you for your truth, spiritual tutelage, and leadership.
You are God of my hope. Amen.

Don't let us yield to temptation.

December 1

HIS GUIDED STEPS

WORD

Guide my steps by your word,
so I will not be overcome by evil.

Psalm 119:133

THOUGHT

The Word of God is reliable. The steps of those who read, listen to, and obey it are guided by insight and foresight. Those who follow in the steps of God's leading are guided with strength, endurance, and proven principles. His way is one of purity and righteousness.

These steps are firmly planted in mercy, truth, and compassion. These steps leave imprints of love, joy, peace, patience, kindness, goodness, faithfulness, gentleness, and self-control.

Fully guided by the Word of God, these steps lead away from the intentions of evil. They are steps chosen and ordained by God and empowered by the Holy Spirit, and they overcome evil's attempt to cause stumbling and blunder.

PRAYER

Father, yours are the steps which lead to life. I long to closely follow you in everything I do. Amen.

But rescue us from the evil one.

December 2

FOREVER HONORED,
FOREVER GLORIOUS

WORD

All glory to him forever and ever! Amen.

Hebrews 13:21

THOUGHT

Glory itself, in substance and character, exists in and is best reserved for honoring God alone. The word *glory*, according to *Merriam-Webster Dictionary*, means "praise, honor, or distinction" and "worshipful praise, honor, and thanksgiving."[28] All glory is owed to God because glory's essence is praise, honor, and thanksgiving. The act of glorifying has no higher goal or more noble purpose than to honor the Divine One.

As the redeemed people of God, we can join with all of creation, worshiping and glorifying him with all of our being. Let us set aside our false idols, the celebrities of our culture, and our personal pursuits in favor of honoring him in all that we do and giving him our whole heart. We should gladly, eagerly even, give glory to God alone, as God alone is worthy enough to receive worship forever!

Glory itself is a deep, mystical, and treasured gift originating from God for those created by God to use as a vehicle to magnify and honor him all of our days.

PRAYER

All glory to God in the highest! Amen and amen!

For yours is the kingdom and the power and the glory forever.

THE FATHER'S HEART

WORD

...but when the right time came, God sent his Son, born of a woman, subject to the law. God sent him to buy freedom for us who were slaves to the law, so that he could adopt us as his very own children. And because we are his children, God has sent the Spirit of his Son into our hearts, prompting us to call out, "Abba, Father." Now you are no longer a slave but God's own child. And since you are his child, God has made you his heir.

Galatians 4:4–7

THOUGHT

An instrument to measure the love and compassion of our heavenly Father's heart does not exist. However, the evidence exists, and it's found in the work of Christ on the cross and in each of his adopted sons and daughters.

We were slaves once, condemned to the darkness of sin, but we've been liberated through the redemptive power of God's Son, Jesus Christ. We were guilty of every accusation—yet exonerated and freed by the love, mercy, and sacrifice of the faultless Lamb.

We were forgiven, and—on top of that gift—the Lord then bestowed unfathomable blessings upon us: the one we offended and betrayed adopted us into his very household, his eternal kingdom, and made us his joint heirs.

PRAYER

I worship you, Father, for you are worthy of worship.
I love you and am grateful for the gift of your mercy. Amen.

Our Father in heaven, may your name be kept holy.

December 4

CARING FOR ORPHANS AND WIDOWS

WORD

Pure and genuine religion in the sight of God the Father means caring for orphans and widows in their distress and refusing to let the world corrupt you.

James 1:27

THOUGHT

One of the evidences of genuine Christianity and living a gospel-centered life is to care for orphans and widows. In caring for them, we express our desire and commitment to love and serve God as he expects, and we reflect the character of his heart and his kingdom.

Caring for orphans and widows clearly is one of the scriptural duties and privileges of every believer in Christ. In doing so, we demonstrate Christianity in a pure and genuine form. In God's view, caring for people in need mirrors his own compassion. This is one of the ways we prove God's kingdom is at work in the world through Christians today.

The church is often confronted by popular culture to produce evidence of authentic Christianity. This is one of the evidences, for pure and genuine religion is found in the care of the marginalized, the lonely, the homeless, the widowed, the orphaned, the neglected, and the hurting in their distress.

PRAYER

May I see with your eyes, Lord, hear with your ears, and feel with your heart. Direct me by your Holy Spirit how I should care for widows, orphans, and others in need in my own community. Amen.

May your kingdom come soon. May your will be done on earth, as it is in heaven.

EVERYTHING NEEDED

WORD

Now may the God of peace—
who brought up from the dead our Lord Jesus,
the great Shepherd of the sheep,
and ratified an eternal covenant with his blood—
may he equip you with all you need
for doing his will.
May he produce in you,
through the power of Jesus Christ,
every good thing that is pleasing to him.
All glory to him forever and ever! Amen.

Hebrews 13:20–21

THOUGHT

Do not worry about tomorrow. This command was spoken by Jesus to his followers (Matt. 6:34). He had complete confidence in his Father to fully provide for those on his mission. Nothing needed to accomplish the Lord's will is withheld from us.

However, worry still continues to assault those who pledge their trust in the Lord, causing us to challenge or doubt the will of God. To some, worry is a momentary problem that is quickly dismissed when God's faithfulness is remembered. To others, however, worry is seemingly an endless battle.

God's will is that we do not worry. When we do, we lose time and energy concerned with things he fully has under his control. God has promised to care for his own. As believers in Christ, we bear the weight of seeking his will and living it, and if we seek first the kingdom of God, provision for our journey on earth will manifest.

PRAYER

Thank you for your provision, Lord. Show me your way, your will, and your paths.
May my eyes be fixed on the mission at hand and my heart on your kingdom to come.
Help me be a good steward of all the gifts you have already provided to me. Amen.

Give us today the food we need.

BEGRUDGING

WORD

Do not seek revenge or bear a grudge against a fellow Israelite, but love your neighbor as yourself. I am the LORD.

Leviticus 19:18

THOUGHT

The word *begrudging* sounds antiquated, but it aptly defines an ill and troubled heart. The fruit of unforgiveness is tragic—for unforgiveness keeps its victim from experiencing the fullness of the freedom of God. One who begrudges portrays a veneer of spiritual heath, but underneath it all is decay and captivity.

Pride often keeps us from fully releasing grudges, forgiving freely, and walking in the fullness of God. Many Christians may carry grudges, and they often remain hidden and tucked away instead of fully released.

Forgiveness is an active part of God's plan for our own internal liberty and peace. Whatever you or I may be holding on to, the voice of God continues to extend his call of wisdom: *Let it go.*

PRAYER

Through you, Lord Jesus, I am forgiven. By your Holy Spirit, reveal any places in my heart that are harboring unforgiveness. Amen.

Forgive us our sins, as we have forgiven those who sin against us.

EVERYTHING HE PLANS WILL COME TO PASS

WORD

Only I can tell you the future
before it even happens.
Everything I plan will come to pass,
for I do whatever I wish.

Isaiah 46:10

THOUGHT

The God of all wisdom and power awaits ready to guide us in each of our untaken steps. He precedes us around the next bend of our journey to expose the hidden dangers of darkness that seek to cause us failure and defeat. God waits there to steady and encourage us as we scale the next hill. Though our limbs may tire from the strain, building endurance is his goal; he will not allow us to fall.

Before an event unfolds in our lives, the Lord of mercy and compassion has already planned the way. He has charted and mapped out the future for the good of those under his care and for his great glory. We have chosen to walk the Lord's path, and he leads us on it and knows it well.

Everything he has planned to the smallest of details will indeed come to pass. As the sons and daughters of God, there is no need to fret, no need to panic, and no need to fear as we traverse the rocky trails of this world. We will not fail, for we are his and he will *never* fail.

PRAYER

Security is found in trusting you, victory is found in trusting you, and life is found in trusting you, Lord Jesus. You are the one I will follow, for you lead me on the sure and certain path. Amen.

Don't let us yield to temptation.

UNDAUNTED

WORD

Then David and all Israel went to Jerusalem (or Jebus, as it used to be called), where the Jebusites, the original inhabitants of the land, were living. The people of Jebus taunted David, saying, "You'll never get in here!" But David captured the fortress of Zion, which is now called the City of David.

1 Chronicles 11:4–5

THOUGHT

The Jebusites once controlled Jerusalem and, at the time, the city was called Jebus. One day, David and all Israel gathered and looked upon the fortress of Zion, prepared to place it in the hands of its rightful owners. The Jebusites thought they were impenetrable. In their overzealous self-confidence, they mocked David and his army and shouted, "You'll never get in here!"

Fearless, determined, and undaunted, David pursued what he knew to be the will of God. He met the Jebusites in battle and the next thing recorded is the fall of Jebus, along with the presentation of the city's new name: the City of David.

Regardless of the strength of the enemy that stands against us, regardless of his threat, intimidation, tactical advantages, or strategies used to instill fear, if the Lord has spoken his will, victory is ensured. God declares his will and conquest follows. He is the Deliverer and the Overcomer. He is the victor over all evil.

PRAYER

Father, you are all powerful and all glorious.
You are the conqueror, the Lord of All! In you I place my trust. Amen.

But rescue us from the evil one.

FOR HIS GLORY

WORD

The earth is the LORD's, and everything in it.
The world and all its people belong to him.

Psalm 24:1

THOUGHT

Today, well over seven billion people live on the planet in unique groups, dispersed throughout hundreds of countries, speaking thousands of languages—and they all belong to the Lord. The earth on which we live, the seed we plant in soil, and the food we harvest and consume—it is all the Lord's possession. From highest mountain to deepest sea, every living creature is owned by God and purposed for his good pleasure.

Humanity thinks of itself as superior. We place a high value on our abilities, we reward our accomplishments, we boast of our dominance, and we demand accolades for great feats. Advanced and noble as we may seem, we are small and insignificant in light of the Divine Proprietor. Each accomplishment we tout as our own was an idea conceived in the Creator's mind, borrowed from his creative canvas.

The earth is the Lord's and everything in it. Nothing existing is independently formed, no human is self-made, self-existent, or self-sustained. God is the Maker, God is the Owner, and God's glory is the purpose of it all.

PRAYER

Let everything that has breath praise you, Lord, including myself,
for you are God and you are glorious. Amen.

For yours is the kingdom and the power and the glory forever.

December 10

THE LORD LIVES

WORD

The LORD lives! Praise to my Rock!
May the God of my salvation be exalted!

Psalm 18:46

THOUGHT

Certainly, we could all agree that the planet we live on has more places, things, and life within it than we could possibly visit in a lifetime. Even our technology-filled world that allows instant access and seemingly unlimited information still doesn't allow us to absorb all the earth contains—it's simply beyond our ability to take it all in.

Consider, though, that our planet—with all its vast, changing, expanding, and moving elements—gains all its energy, beauty, and regenerating ability from a single source: the living God! People may attempt to control or harness the earth's resources, but the living Lord spoke the entire universe into being and continues to generate its ability to continue. He alone is in control.

The Lord is eternal: he lives, has lived, and will ever live. Before the creation of the world, he was there, every bit as strong and loving as he ever has been. He is the immovable rock, the foundation of certainty, the God who delivers everlasting life. He is the God of my salvation, the God of our salvation. Because he lives, life continues. He holds everything in his hands.

PRAYER

You live, Lord; you live and reign, forever. You are my Rock, the God of my salvation. Amen.

Our Father in heaven, may your name be kept holy.

December 11

RELATIONSHIP

WORD

"Now come and have some breakfast!" Jesus said. None of the disciples dared to ask him, "Who are you?" They knew it was the Lord. Then Jesus served them the bread and the fish. This was the third time Jesus had appeared to his disciples since he had been raised from the dead.

After breakfast Jesus asked Simon Peter, "Simon son of John, do you love me more than these?"

"Yes, Lord," Peter replied, "you know I love you."

"Then feed my lambs," Jesus told him.

John 21:12–15

THOUGHT

One morning after his resurrection, Jesus joined his disciples on a beach at dawn. He prepared breakfast and ate with them. Jesus was aware of the importance and value of each moment with his disciples, aware his ascension was close at hand. He knew each moment with them was of vital importance as it would further their knowledge and the purpose of his kingdom, for soon they would embark on the most monumental mission ever.

This story reflects how Jesus Christ valued relationships—and relationships are one of the primary goals of his kingdom. In the midst of a very limited and important time frame, Jesus paused and rested with his friends to share a simple beachside breakfast.

Relationship, friendship, family—these are all words associated with the kingdom of God. The purpose of the work of Christ was to mend the broken relationship between humanity and God and restore holy communion with the Creator himself.

PRAYER

In your kingdom, Lord, relationship thrives.
Use me to further your kingdom purposes here on earth. Amen.

May your kingdom come soon. May your will be done on earth, as it is in heaven.

THE GIFT OF OTHERS

WORD

A spiritual gift is given to each of us so we can help each other.

1 Corinthians 12:7

THOUGHT

God's grace abounds, covering and filling willing recipients who are humble and openhearted. He covers them with love, mercy beyond measure, and (of course) forgiveness. Because we're now joined with the Father through Christ the Son, we are part of his global family. We are also now part of the family mission, which is living and sharing the message of the Christ-life.

To each family member a gift is given—a divine, uniquely tooled, and crafted gift. A gift that, when used together with those received by the other sons and daughters of God, creates encouraging, edifying effects. This is God's design: for us to enjoy spiritual growth as each person utilizes their gifts to contribute to the healthy development of the church in every aspect.

This is the very reason the apostle Paul refers to Christians, the church, as the *body* of Christ. The physical body functions best with every part healthy and contributing, and so does the church, the spiritual body of Christ.

The spiritual family of God, when healthy and functioning optimally, is a multifaceted missional force dispersing the love and life of the kingdom to a very needy world. Christ's intent is for us to operate as a team dedicated to his mandates: the Great Commandment and the Great Commission. Onward, church!

PRAYER

Thank you for the provision you have given us in your gifts distributed throughout the body of Christ. May we use them wisely under the guidance of your hand. Amen.

Give us today the food we need.

December 13

AMAZING

WORD

It was also written that this message would be proclaimed in the authority of his name to all the nations, beginning in Jerusalem: "There is forgiveness of sins for all who repent."

Luke 24:47

THOUGHT

The most *amazing* of gifts is extended by God through Christ: the forgiveness of sins.

First, this gift of forgiveness is amazing because God had no need of us—yet he moved on our behalf to rescue us when we ourselves committed the offense. In our sin, we were guilty and worthy of the death sentence, but by his mercy he provided a path to freedom.

Second, this gift is amazing because forgiveness is not limited to a few favored people, a specific nationality, or a particular age range; it's available to everyone who would repent of their sin.

Finally, this gift is amazing because the Lord not only frees everyone who repents, but he invites them to become members of his own household. What a gift indeed!

PRAYER

Lord, I am amazed by and grateful for your depth of mercy and love, your act of forgiveness, and the life abiding in your marvelous grace. Amen.

Forgive us our sins, as we have forgiven those who sin against us.

GUIDANCE WITH PRECISION

WORD

He renews my strength.
He guides me along right paths,
bringing honor to his name.

Psalm 23:3

THOUGHT

Modern technology has given us, with almost flawless accuracy, easy access to directions to any geographical location. Still, technology's accuracy is not *completely* flawless. For instance, a car trip to a new restaurant in town using my GPS led me to an open, empty field a couple of miles away from my destination.

While close to accurate directional guidance is appreciated, flawless guidance is certainly preferred. As humans, not only do we desire and expect precision in most of the things we do, but precision is often vital for their success. We often have to count on precision for safety. Precision is necessary when designing a skyscraper, building a vehicle or house, or performing surgery.

While precision developed by human hands is impressive, we fall incredibly short of the accuracy and precision of God. He desires to lead and guide his children on the right paths with divine precision for our safety, our good, and to bring honor to his name.

PRAYER

Father, you guide me with your care and skill.
Lead me by your Holy Spirit to live my life bringing honor to your name. Amen.

Don't let us yield to temptation.

THE UNLIMITED JESUS

WORD

...so they brought the boy. But when the evil spirit saw Jesus, it threw the child into a violent convulsion, and he fell to the ground, writhing and foaming at the mouth.

"How long has this been happening?" Jesus asked the boy's father.

He replied, "Since he was a little boy. The spirit often throws him into the fire or into water, trying to kill him. Have mercy on us and help us, if you can."

"What do you mean, 'If I can'?" Jesus asked. "Anything is possible if a person believes."

Mark 9:20–23

THOUGHT

In desperation, a loving father who was unable to help his son turned to Jesus and begged of him, "Have mercy on us and help us, *if you can*." Jesus responded quickly, "What do you mean, 'If I can'?"

Some consider Jesus's tone here to be one of bewilderment, frustration, or rebuke. Perhaps. But I hear from him the confident, resolute, "Of course I can, and I will!" Then with compassion and overwhelming certainty in the power and authority of his Father, he ends the long suffering of the man's son—and transformation comes!

The authority of Christ is not limited. All authority in heaven and on earth is his. There are no boundaries and no limitations; there are no restraints of any type to keep Jesus from doing what he desires to do. When God determines something to be done, there is no *if*; there is only *anything is possible if a person believes*.

The same Savior who rescued a boy from the clutches of darkness and liberated him to the divine potentials of a God-led and covered life, can also deliver you from whatever evil you think stalks.

PRAYER

Father, your Word is clear: I can trust you for deliverance from the evil one.
Still, I have times when doubt creeps in. Yes I believe, but help me in my unbelief.
You are the Lord; with you all things are possible. Amen.

But rescue us from the evil one.

I WILL EXALT HIM

WORD

The LORD is my strength and my song;
he has given me victory.
This is my God, and I will praise him—
my father's God, and I will exalt him!

Exodus 15:2

THOUGHT

The Lord is many things. He is the Designer and Creator of everything. He is the Sustainer; without his upholding, his management, and his governing, life would not exist. He is Savior; he conquered and halted the destruction of humanity by the evil one. He is the Deliverer: holy, righteous, all-knowing, ever-present, and never-changing—the King of all the ages.

Not only is he all of these things, but he is also our Father who loves us and calls us his sons and daughters, his heirs. We are able to confidently and proudly call him *our* God, *our* Father. Because of who God is, and because of his great mercy, love, and grace toward us, he is deserving of all worship and honor and praise.

For all his countless wonderful characteristics, he will be glorified. He is our God, and we will exalt him forever!

PRAYER

Lord, you truly are my strength, my song, and my very source for life in all its fullness.
I praise and glorify you, Mighty God. Amen.

For yours is the kingdom and the power and the glory forever.

December 17

HIS PERFECT HOLINESS

WORD

O God, your ways are holy.
Is there any god as mighty as you?

Psalm 77:13

THOUGHT

We are invited into the presence of our Father God through the work of Christ. And he is indeed the good and perfect Father. He loves his children and desires rich, genuine, intimate communion with them. Our God loves and lives in community and allows us into his community.

Our Father exhibits all of the qualities of love listed in 1 Corinthians 13, as he is love. But our God is more than the essence of love; he is where love's essence begins. He is its fountainhead, the source that all love can be traced back to.

In the love of our Father is his perfect holiness; he is worthy of our highest respect, honor, and worship. God is holy, and we worship him because he is holy. No one is holy like the Lord and no one is as mighty as he is.

PRAYER

Lord, before I seek anything from you, before I even give thanks to you for anything,
may I first and foremost come before you to worship you in the splendor of your holiness.
You are the Holy One; you are the Lord God. Amen.

Our Father in heaven, may your name be kept holy.

THE KINGDOM COMING

WORD

...but we are looking forward to the new heavens and new earth he has promised, a world filled with God's righteousness.

2 Peter 3:13

THOUGHT

God's kingdom is forever! For those whose hope is in God, no words could rightly express the excitement of the Christian for the arrival of the new heavens and earth. We will be able to see, hear, and feel the tangible and the mystical, the natural and the supernatural, concurrently.

Although curiosity and speculation abound as to what the experience will be like in God's realm of limitlessness, we know there will be no more death, disease, or discord. We will not grow tired, we will not experience pain, we will not be tempted by the enemy. And earth's current physical laws and principles will be governed by God's infinite and unlimited power and ability.

However, none of these amazing things is the main attraction for the believer in Christ. Instead, we are filled with excitement at the promise of his eternal presence, to experience worship in his future kingdom, to eternally be where his righteousness fills every place. Lord, may your kingdom come!

PRAYER

Father, I look forward to the time when your righteousness and your presence fill the new heavens and the new earth eternally. May you use me as your vessel to bring a glimpse of that kind of peace, hope, and goodness to my community today. Amen.

May your kingdom come soon. May your will be done on earth, as it is in heaven.

December 19

WHAT IS TRUTH?

WORD

Pilate said, "So you are a king?"

Jesus responded, "You say I am a king. Actually, I was born and came into the world to testify to the truth. All who love the truth recognize that what I say is true."

"What is truth?" Pilate asked. Then he went out again to the people and told them, "He is not guilty of any crime."

John 18:37–38

THOUGHT

Truth—genuine truth—is sought globally. Truth is pursued so we might know and understand what is genuine about something, someone, or our world. Truth, however, has become a rare find these days. There is so much untruth discovered daily in political, business, educational, and, yes, unfortunately even within the church arenas. No wonder doubt and skepticism within us appears at epic proportions.

Genuine truth-seekers will ultimately discover themselves in the story of Jesus. Perhaps not every question will be answered to their liking, but a genuine truth seeker will nonetheless be drawn into the story of Jesus, truth's source. Jesus has never refused to listen to those on a sincere journey for truth.

Pilate asked questions, but only to fulfill his politically appointed duty. Missing from the narrative was Pilate's sincere desire to hear with his ears and heart. Christ's answer to Pilate revealed the truth; those who "love the truth" know Christ is the King. Had Pilate genuinely sought to know the truth, he may have had an epiphany and declared not only is Jesus innocent of the charge, but also Jesus is the truth, and the way, and the life. What is truth? Christ! He is God and we are fully and completely redeemed in him! He is the truth, he is the life, and he is the way.

PRAYER

Lord Jesus, I know you speak the truth, the very words of life.
Lead me in your truth every day. Amen.

Give us today the food we need.

December 20

THE KNOWER OF HEARTS

WORD

God would surely have known it,
for he knows the secrets of every heart.

Psalm 44:20

THOUGHT

Kardiognostes is used only twice in the New Testament. This Greek word means "knower of the hearts." The disciples addressed the Lord with this word when they were praying for a replacement for Judas, "O Lord, you know every heart" (Acts 1:24).

No one knows our hearts like God, and certainly no one cares about our hearts like God. He is aware of everything that is contained in our spiritual hearts. Even the things that may be so hidden that they are secrets kept from the entire world are not hidden from the heavenly Father.

He is not only the knower of every detail, deed, and thought, but he is also the one who gently watches over the development of the heart. Our hearts mean more to him than they do to us. His intentions are to develop the healthiest, most wholesome hearts possible—hearts free of spiritual disease, strengthened by his spiritual provision, and beating in synchronization with his.

The Holy Spirit will bring to our minds anything hidden in our hearts that may weaken, endanger, and cause damage to us or the Lord's will. Unforgiveness is one of these dangers, so he will gently let us know of the things we wrongly hold against others, as unforgiveness is an ugly and damaging spiritual disease. May our hearts be pure before him.

PRAYER

Lord, you are the knower of the heart, the knower of my heart. Search my heart continually
and please keep it free of any unhealthy thought or action. Amen.

Forgive us our sins, as we have forgiven those who sin against us.

THE PRAYER OF FRIENDS

WORD

...for I know that as you pray for me and the Spirit of Jesus Christ
helps me, this will lead to my deliverance.

Philippians 1:19

THOUGHT

A letter from Paul to friends revealed his confidence in the power of their prayers—power that would lead to his deliverance from the prison cell he was unjustly thrown into. Paul had been falsely accused of inciting a riot in Philippi and sent to prison, but his stay was short as the Lord miraculously delivered him (Acts 16:20–25). Their prayers were not in vain.

Every Christian who has faced challenges has called on faithful friends to pray for them in the midst of trial. When others intercede on our behalf, there is an unmatched confidence which arises in the heart of the believer in Christ. Our shared love, faith, and prayers will strengthen one another in times of need.

I have certainly been the glad and encouraged recipient of these prayers in times past, and will no doubt be in need of them again in the future. These corporate prayers are a strong and effective weapon given us by God to build up our faith and to lead us, for as Christ himself taught us, "If two of you agree here on earth concerning anything you ask, my Father in heaven will do it for you. For where two or three gather together as my followers, I am there among them" (Matt. 18:19–20).

PRAYER

Father, I am truly grateful for the brothers and sisters in Christ you have placed in my life.
I am grateful for their friendship, encouragement, and prayers for me.
Thank you for placing us in your family and in the bond of spiritual community.
Thank you for hearing our prayers as we pray for one another. Amen.

Don't let us yield to temptation.

December 22

THE ABSENCE OF EVIL

WORD

Nothing evil will be allowed to enter, nor anyone who practices shameful idolatry and dishonesty—but only those whose names are written in the Lamb's Book of Life.

Revelation 21:27

THOUGHT

An unstoppable force approaches us, designated to arrive at a specific moment in time, a time known only by the Ancient of Days. The powers do not exist to stop or slow this event; the effects will be irreversible, and the change will be permanent.

All time, space, and created things will pass through a threshold, and everything will change. Evil will cease to exist, as it will not pass through this threshold. Only those whose names are written in the Lamb's Book of Life will enter.

Once and for all, the Lord will end the force and influence of the evil one upon Creation. Forevermore, the redeemed daughters and sons of God will live within the presence of holiness, the presence of the Lord forever.

PRAYER

I long to be in your presence, unhindered by any influence, save yours, my King. Amen.

But rescue us from the evil one.

DOMINION

WORD

Yours, O Lord, is the greatness, the power, the glory, the victory, and the majesty.
Everything in the heavens and on earth is yours, O Lord, and this is your kingdom.
We adore you as the one who is over all things.

1 Chronicles 29:11

THOUGHT

The word *dominion* is difficult to understand, as it implies the presence of unrestrained dominance. The existence of a governor of supreme ownership, one of complete and unchangeable control, an unstoppable, unavoidable, timeless, immovable force, and beyond any human effort or combined efforts to overpower, remove, or escape. This divine being is sovereign God.

The Lord has all dominion, and were God's character tyrannical in nature, this truth would produce a horrid and frightening state within all the subjects under him. However, this is not how he rules or is known. While certainly he is holy and righteous and expects those who follow him to be of similar caliber by the help of Christ, he is known by his immeasurable love and redemptive heart.

From first breath to the newness of life in Christ, from death here on earth to our welcoming into his eternal presence, his kingdom and dominion have no end. And we get the privilege to live as God's sons and daughters in his dominion forever—amazing, simply amazing!

PRAYER

Lord, you rule and reign through all eternity and your dominion is forever.
Yours is the kingdom, the power, and the glory. Amen.

For yours is the kingdom and the power and the glory forever.

THE UTMOST

WORD

...for a child is born to us,
a son is given to us.
The government will rest on his shoulders.
And he will be called:
Wonderful Counselor, Mighty God,
Everlasting Father, Prince of Peace.
His government and its peace
will never end.
He will rule with fairness and justice from the throne of his ancestor David
for all eternity.
The passionate commitment of the LORD of Heaven's Armies
will make this happen!

Isaiah 9:6–7

THOUGHT

The greatest gift given to us from our heavenly Father is Christ Jesus, God's only Son. Without the introduction of the Messiah to the earth, all would have remained hopelessly dark. God sent his Son into the world as the light of the world.

In and through Christ, we receive the gift of righteousness and instruction on how to live a life pleasing to God. In him and through him we are given all things needed to live in God's will: full redemption and freedom from sin, strength, wisdom, and access to the Father.

In Christ, we find peace, rest, and a home. Once orphaned, we are now God's children. And as sons and daughters in the kingdom of God, we are the recipients of perfect fairness, holy justice, and divine peace forever.

PRAYER

Jesus Christ, a relationship with our heavenly Father was the greatest gift of provision.
Thank you for bringing your kingdom to earth through your victorious redemptive work.
You, Lord, are making everything new. Amen.

Our Father in heaven, may your name be kept holy.

December 25

PEACE

WORD

...now may the Lord of peace himself give you his peace at all times and in every situation.

The Lord be with you all.

2 Thessalonians 3:16

THOUGHT

The morning sky appeared as a celestial field of brilliant stars, the light had yet to come, but I was anticipating dawn to soon introduce a most beautiful day. With frost-covered grass and crisp, cool air, all was wonderfully still and hushed save for what seemed like the faint whisper of peace.

When we shed our veneers and wholly surrender to honesty, a need emerges; it is the heart's quest for peace. The beautiful morning I've described provided an atmosphere of tranquility, but still it was only a temporal offering. Peace of heart has no permanence from the world's wealth, prominence, or place. Where, then, is the source to quench the heart's thirst for peace?

Peace appears when we surrender to love's greatest desire, and love's greatest desire is reconciliation, the restoration of communion between the heart of the fallen and the heart of the architect of grace, who is our Father in heaven. He is love, and his beautiful perfect will is for the heart to abide in his peace. His peace is manifest in his only Son Jesus Christ, who is forever, the Lord of peace.

PRAYER

Because of you, Lord Jesus, my heart rests in genuine peace. Your lasting peace is something the world cannot give—it is only found in your kingdom. Make me a person of peace, someone who shines with your goodness and grace in all that I do, and who lives out your will daily. Amen.

May your kingdom come soon. May your will be done on earth, as it is in heaven.

WORSHIP

WORD

Praise the LORD, everything he has created,
everything in all his kingdom.

Psalm 103:22

THOUGHT

Worshiping God is the highest of wonders for the soul set free from evil's dark dungeon and transferred into the glorious relationship with the essence of light and life, Jesus Christ. The Christian does not view worship as labor and hollow duty—quite the opposite. The believer sees worship as the pinnacle of the heart's elations and provision to give the Lord glory.

God's aim has always been and will always be to be worshiped by his creation. The worship of God is life's greatest offering, life's greatest fulfillment. Worship is God's divine destiny for us, his gift to us, and reward for us.

Our worship of God is the reason for our existence and is required daily in our lives for our spiritual health. We come to God to honor him yet in the process our soul is also replenished. Worship fills the soul with unrestrained joy, and this privilege continues as we pass from this earth-life into eternal life.

PRAYER

Lord, you have made me to worship you. Thank you for your provision in the beautiful gift of worship. It is the highest honor, the apex use for God's gift of emotion, and the privilege of heart and soul. I glorify your name, oh, God! Amen.

Give us today the food we need.

NOT OF THIS WORLD

WORD

Jesus answered, "My Kingdom is not an earthly kingdom. If it were, my followers would fight to keep me from being handed over to the Jewish leaders. But my Kingdom is not of this world."

John 18:36

THOUGHT

Many enjoy novels and films entertaining the mysterious, abstract, and intangible, but few believe in actual supernatural realms, areas of creation outside the natural realm in which we live. Most of us believe and accept what we understand, see, touch, smell, and hear. We base our choices and philosophies on the practical, measurable, predictable, controllable, and, of course, the comfortable.

Writer A. W. Tozer, in his book *The Pursuit of God,* used the phrase "other-worldly" in reference to the set-apart uniqueness of the kingdom of God from the natural world. While the earth represents a bit of his creation, God's magnitude, authority, and ability exceed our imagination's capacity. The grandness of God's kingdom stretches immeasurably beyond our comprehension and into other-worldliness.

In this world, we are like children standing on the seashore, gazing across the water to the horizon's edge. We think we can grasp the ocean's size by what our eyes can see, when—in reality—we can only see a few miles ahead. The same is true of our limited capacity to take in the fullness of God's created kingdom and his will for our lives; for now, we are limited to only what we can see, and his kingdom is not of this world. We may not always understand his commands—especially the command to forgive others like he has forgiven us—but he is God and we are not.

PRAYER

Father, you are the King of kings and Lord of all the heavens and earth.
You are holy and majestic in all your ways. You are Creator of all things seen and unseen,
and I bow humbly before you. Help me understand your commands,
and help me fulfill them for your glory—especially forgiving others like you have forgiven me. Amen.

Forgive us our sins, as we have forgiven those who sin against us.

December 28

HIS PERFECT LEADERSHIP

WORD

He leads the humble in doing right,
teaching them his way.

Psalm 25:9

THOUGHT

We have only one life to invest. The path of Jesus is the path of righteousness, and the path of righteousness leads to beautiful, God-glorifying returns. There is rest, resolve, and comfort when we know the direction we're headed in is right and best. Surprisingly, giving up our all to Christ not only leads us to the right path, but also leads us to *right* success and life abundant.

The life of Jesus Christ is the one perfect example to follow, and he desires to lead us and teach us the way to honoring our Father's heart. His leadership is unrivaled.

By his Holy Spirit, Christ guides us with perfect insight, his heart filled with compassion toward us and what is best for us. He leads with the character of a perfect friend, perfect brother, and perfect father. May we wisely allow the most perfect leader to lead us in his perfect way upon the path of righteousness.

PRAYER

Lead me in your good and perfect way, Lord Jesus.
Lead me along your paths and in your will. Amen.

Don't let us yield to temptation.

WARRIOR

WORD

The LORD is a warrior;
Yahweh is his name!

Exodus 15:3

THOUGHT

During the holiday season, we celebrate the birth of the Christ child. Immortality took mortal form as Emmanuel, God with us, came to earth. The holidays, especially the time during Christmas, are often associated with peace, gentleness, tranquility, and the celebration of the Messiah and all he would accomplish for the kingdom of God.

Christ is gentle and humble—the Prince of Peace—but our Lord is also a warrior. He is fearless, noble, righteously justified, and unstoppable. He is the conquering King of kings, resolute in his holy mission.

Jesus stands victorious against every obstacle and weapon formed against him. And he stands to disable the weapons formed against us. His warfare and tactical plans differ from those of the rulers of the world, but his power to overcome all opposition to his kingdom is unyielding and unmatched. The Lord is a warrior—he is the Holy Conqueror and our Deliverer from the evil one.

PRAYER

Lord, you deliver me from the destruction of darkness by your mighty power.
Battles may rage, but the war is won. No weapon formed against me will stand. Amen.

But rescue us from the evil one.

TRUST

WORD

Trust in the LORD with all your heart;
do not depend on your own understanding.
Seek his will in all you do,
and he will show you which path to take.

Proverbs 3:5–6

THOUGHT

With a new year approaching, our thoughts shift from reflection on the past year to the fresh year before us. Ahead of us are a new calendar year and an unfolding future. There are new commitments to make, possibilities to explore, goals to attain, and resolutions to uphold.

In all of the commitments, possibilities, goals, and resolutions we face in the year ahead, we must keep the kingdom of God in mind. The character of God and his will for us should be at the center of our plans, and we should seek him in all we set out to do. And we must remember: the values of God's kingdom and the values of the world we live in are often opposite of one another.

Although the world may encourage us to gather treasure for ourselves for our earthly security, stability, and pleasure, God encourages us to invest in eternity and to give ourselves away for the good of others. The world says to get even, but God says to forgive. The world advises us to trust only in what we see, touch, and understand, but God commands us to trust only in Him. The world leads us to do what we want and what will make us happy, but God reminds us to search out his will in all we do. In the end, his will contains real treasure and real joy.

PRAYER

Lord, I pray that as the future unfolds I will wisely seek your heart in all matters
and trust you fully. Your will for me is perfect and good. Amen.

For yours is the kingdom and the power and the glory forever.

December 31

KING FOREVER

WORD

The LORD is king!
Let the earth rejoice!
Let the farthest coastlands be glad.

Psalm 97:1

THOUGHT

On this eve of a new year, hundreds of millions of people will gather to celebrate. In Times Square of New York City alone, over a million will gather to rejoice over the coming year with hopeful prospects.

What the future holds will remain unclear to all but one: Yahweh, the one true God. The redeemed of Christ rejoice in knowing he holds all time in his hands—we can find hope and rest knowing he is at the helm and that he is our perfect Father. We know his kingdom *will* come and his will *will* be done. All he has desired and all he has promised shall come to pass, and nothing will prevent him from accomplishing his goal.

As we prepare ourselves for the coming year, let us set our minds on the things most noble, honorable, and eternal, and pursue them. This is a good time to remember that the Lord is king and we were created by God and for God. He is all we need. He is our Father, Savior, Lord, and Friend—forever!

PRAYER

I am yours, my Lord and King. You are all I will ever need. I will rejoice in you forever! Amen.

Our Father in heaven, may your name be kept holy.

NOTES

1 "Blaise Pascal Biography," Biography.com, April 2, 2014,
https://www.biography.com/scholar/blaise-pascal#early-life&awesm=~
oBrKnXMg7DuMpK.

2 Ken Drexler, "Treaty of Paris: Primary Documents in American History," Library
of Congress, February 11, 2021, https://guides.loc.gov/treaty-of-paris.

3 John 16:27, 33

4 Martin Luther, "A Mighty Fortress," trans. Frederick H. Hedge, Psalter Hymnal
(Gray, 1987) Hymnary.org,
https://hymnary.org/text/a_mighty_fortress_is_our_god_a_bulwark.

5 Holy Bible, New Living Translation®, copyright © 1996, 2004 by Tyndale
Charitable Trust.

6 Ben Brumfield, "Moore, Oklahoma, Looks Back on Tornado that Killed 24 One
Year Ago," May 20, 2014, CNN.com, https://www.cnn.com/2014/05/20/us/
oklahoma-moore-tornado-anniversary/index.html.

7 Norman, Oklahoma, Weather Forecast Office, "The Tornado Outbreak of
May 20, 2013," May 20, 2013, National Weather Service,
https://www.weather.gov/oun/events-20130520.

8 Meredith Bennet-Smith, "Algerian Hostages Saved by iPhone Compass App,"
HuffingtonPost.com, https://www.huffpost.com/entry/algerian-hostages-saved-
iphone-compass-app-saved-lives-escape_n_2536225, January 23, 2013.

9 C. N. Truman, "The Capture of Fort Eben," The History Learning Site, April 20,
2015, https://www.historylearningsite.co.uk/world-war-two/world-war-two-
in-western-europe/the-attack-on-western-europe/the-capture-of-fort-eben/.

10 "Shorter Catechism: Text and Scripture Proofs," The Westminster Standard,
accessed August 3, 2018,
https://thewestminsterstandard.org/westminster-shorter-catechism/.

11 Diane Dew, "Never Give Up: A Lesson from the Life of Lincoln," DianeDew.com,
1998, accessed August 8, 2018, http://www.dianedew.com/lincoln.htm.

12 Abraham Lincoln, quoted in President George W. Bush, "A Proclamation: National Day of Prayer 2001," The White House Archives, April 30, 2001, https://georgewbush-whitehouse.archives.gov/news/releases/2001/04/20010430-2.html.

13 "Gold Processing," Britannica, accessed November 29, 2021, https://www.britannica.com/technology/gold-processing.

14 Helen Phillips, "Introduction: The Human Brain," New Scientist, September 4, 2006, https://www.newscientist.com/article/dn9969-introduction-the-human-brain/#.UtHWWvvODSg.

15 Historia et Memoria, Luther's Works, Vol. 53, pp321-322. https://wp.cune.edu/ matthewphillips/2014/06/01/martin-luther-on-music/.

16 Quoted in Robert Krulwich, "Which is bigger: A Human Brain or the Universe?" NPR: Krulwich Wonders, July 24, 2012, https://www.npr.org/sections/krulwich/2012/07/24/157282357/which-is-bigger-a-human-brain-or-the-universe.

17 "To Be a Christian Means to Forgive the Inexcusable," The Wisdom of C.S. Lewis (blog), August 16, 2011, https://cslewiswisdom.blogspot.com/2011/08/to-be-christian-means-to-forgive.html/

18 Psalm 18:28, Holy Bible, New Living Translation®, copyright © 1996, 2004 by Tyndale Charitable Trust. Used by permission of Tyndale House Publishers. All rights reserved.

19 "Forgive," Merriam-Webster.com, accessed October 26, 2018, https://www.merriam-webster.com/dictionary/forgive.

20 "tob," P.C. Study Bible, W.E. Vine with eds. Merrill F. Unger and William White, An Expository Dictionary of Biblical Words (Nashville: Thomas Nelson, 1985).

21 Karen C. Fox, "NASA's Van Allen Probes Spot an Impenetrable Barrier in Space," NASA.gov, November 26, 2014, https://www.nasa.gov/content/goddard/van-allen-probes-spot-impenetrable-barrier-in-space.

22 Mark 11:24, Holy Bible, New Living Translation®, copyright © 1996, 2004.

23 John 16:23, Holy Bible, New Living Translation®, copyright © 1996, 2004.

24 Dr. Gregory Popcak, https://catholicexchange.com/five-steps-to-begin-overcoming-bitterness.

25 "Optasia," The New American Standard New Testament Greek Lexicon, BibleStudyTools.com, accessed February 10, 2019, https://www.biblestudytools.com/lexicons/greek/nas/optasia.html.

[26] Charles Spurgeon's, Morning and Evening
https://www.biblegateway.com/devotionals/morning-and-evening/2020/10/29

[27] Charles Spurgeon's, Morning and Evening
https://www.biblegateway.com/devotionals/morning-and-evening/2020/10/29

[28] "Glory," Merriam-Webster's Dictionary, accessed February 10, 2019,
https://www.merriam-webster.com/dictionary/glory.

ACKNOWLEDGMENTS

Most visions and projects, regardless of nature, are made better by the shared offerings of gifted and skilled contributors who align their efforts to produce the maximum in fruitful effect. *Awake in the Dawn* may have been singularly conceived, but the offerings presented in these pages exist because of the labors of several to whom I am extremely grateful.

Amanda Johnson and Kate Etue, editors. Paul Mills, composer and producer of the companion music to *Awake in the Dawn*. Greg Lucid, networker and vision weaver. Jenn David, ideas and design. Jonathan Merkh, Jennifer Gingerich, Billie Brownell, and the entire Forefront Books team. Dianna Smith, Hannah and Manit Attakul, Brian and Megan Barr, and a much wider and beautiful community of spiritual family and friends.

COMPANION MUSIC

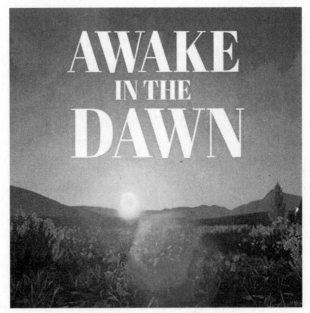

CD cover image created by Manit Attakul

Download the *Awake in the Dawn* music written and recorded specifically to accompany the *Awake in the Dawn* devotional book.

Download: Craig Smith *Awake in the Dawn* from Amazon/iTunes/Spotify and other music platforms.

Compact disc format is available upon request:

Awake in the Dawn (CD)

P.O. Box 756

Van Buren, AR 72957

$20.00 USD (includes shipping, USA and Canada only)

VILLAGE2VILLAGE MISSION

YOUR PURCHASE OF THIS BOOK WILL ASSIST OUR MISSION TO HELP CHILDREN.

The Dual Mission of *Awake in the Dawn*
Hope Village

Awake in the Dawn was produced to encourage Christians to pursue the powerful keys given by Christ to his followers in Matthew 6:9–13 to live the Lord's Prayer.

Proceeds from *Awake in the Dawn* are used to help children such as the ones pictured of Hope Village Uganda, through the nonprofit organization Village2Village.

Village2Village is committed to building cultures of hope by establishing Hope Villages, with current locations in Uganda, Thailand, and Arkansas, and the unfolding possibility of El Salvador.

For further information or to become a part of this growing community, visit www.village2village.co.